For Anarchism

History Workshop Series

General Editor: Raphael Samuel,
Ruskin College, Oxford

Metropolis: London
Histories and Representations since 1800
David Feldman and Gareth Stedman Jones (eds)

Patriotism: The Making and Unmaking of British National Identity
Volume 1: History and Politics
Volume 2: Minorities and Outsiders
Volume 3: National Fictions
Raphael Samuel

New Views of Co-operation
Stephen Yeo (ed.)

The Radical Soldier's Tale:
John Pearman 1819–1908
Carolyn Steedman

Slavery:
And Other Forms of Unfree Labour
Leonie Archer (ed.)

Socialism and the Intelligentsia 1880–1914
Carl Levy (ed.)

Disciplines of Faith:
Studies in Religion, Politics and Patriarchy
Jim Obelkevich et al. (eds)

The Enemy Within:
Pit Villages and the Miners' Strike of 1984–5
Raphael Samuel et al. (eds)

Voices of the People:
The Politics and Life of 'La Sociale' at the End of the Second Empire
Adrian Rifkin and Roger Thomas

Language, Gender and Childhood
Valerie Walkerdene et al. (eds)

The Progress of Romance:
The Politics of Popular Fiction
Jean Radford (ed.)

Theatres of the Left 1880–1935:
Workers' Theatre Movements in Britain and America
Raphael Samuel et al.

The Worst Street in North London:
Campbell Bunk, Islington, between the Wars
Jerry White

For Anarchism
History, Theory, and Practice

edited by David Goodway

Routledge
London and New York

First published 1989
by Routledge
11 New Fetter Lane, London EC4P 4EE
29 West 35th Street, New York, NY 10001

Introduction © David Goodway 1989
Chapter 4 © Peter Marshall 1989
Chapter 6 © Alan Carter 1989
All other material © Routledge 1989

Printed and bound in Great Britain by
The Guernsey Press Co. Ltd., Guernsey, Channel Islands.

British Library Cataloguing in Publication Data
For anarchism: history, theory and practice.
1. Anarchism
I. Goodway, David
335'.83

Library of Congress Cataloging in Publication Data
also available

ISBN 0 415 02954 6
ISBN 0 415 02955 4 Pbk

71912

Contents

Part III Practice

Maps and figures

WITHDRAWN

Maps

Figures

Contributors

Murray Bookchin is founder and Director Emeritus of the Institute for Social Ecology, Rochester, Vermont. A prolific writer, his books include *Post-Scarcity Anarchism* (1971), *Toward an Ecological Society* (1980), and *The Ecology of Freedom* (1982). He lives in Burlington, Vermont.

Tom Cahill is Lecturer in Politics, University of Lancaster. He is editor of the *Bulletin of Anarchist Research*.

Alan Carter is Lecturer in Philosophy, Heythrop College, University of London. He is the author of *Marx: A Radical Critique* (1988) and *The Philosophical Foundations of Property Rights* (1989).

Robert Graham is the author of several articles and reviews on the intellectual history of anarchism. He lives in Canada.

David Goodway is Lecturer in History, Department of External Studies, University of Leeds. He has published *London Chartism 1838–1848* (1982). He is convenor of the Anarchist Research Group and is currently working on a history of British Neo-Romanticism.

Daniel Guérin is a French writer whose many books cover a wide range of political, historical, social, and sexual topics. Among those to have been translated into English are *Fascism and Big Business, Anarchism: From Theory to Practice, Class Struggle in the First French Republic*, and *100 Years of Labor in the USA*. He died in April 1988, aged 83.

Carl Levy is a Research Fellow, University of Kent. He is editor of *Socialism and the Intelligentsia, 1880–1914* (1987), also in the History Workshop series, and author of several essays on Max Weber, Antonio Gramsci, and modern intellectuals.

Peter Marshall is a freelance writer who lives in North Wales. His books include *William Godwin* (1984) and *Cuba Libre*: *Breaking the Chains?* (1987). He is currently working on a history of libertarian ideas.

Geoffrey Ostergaard is Senior Lecturer in Political Science, University of Birmingham. He is the author of *Co-operative Democracy* with J. A. Banks (1955), *Power in Co-operatives* with A. H. Halsey (1965), *The Gentle Anarchists* with Melville Currell (1971), and *Nonviolent Revolution in India* (1985).

Nick Rider gained a PhD from the University of Lancaster in 1988 with his thesis, 'Anarchism, urbanization and social conflict in Barcelona, 1900–1932'. He is now working as a freelance researcher and translator.

Michael Smith is Head of Learning Resources, Kingston Polytechnic. He is the author of *The Libertarians and Education* (1983) among other works.

Introduction

David Goodway

Anarchism flourished between the 1860s and the 1930s. During these decades it attracted the adherence of mass movements of the working class, principally in Europe and the Americas. Its heyday can be more precisely located from around 1880 until the First World War. But libertarian thinkers were developing the anarchist critique of contemporary nineteenth-century society during the earlier decades, beginning indeed with William Godwin in the 1790s (although he remained unrecognized as an anarchist theorist and precursor until exactly one hundred years later).

Anarchism was especially strong in France, Italy, Spain, Russia, and the United States (but only in the immigrant communities of America, particularly among the Russian Jews and Italians). It was a powerful force in the Low Countries, on the one hand, and, on the other, in Latin America. In Britain and the Anglo-Saxon world at large anarchism remained, of course, a negligible influence.

Partly because of its protean nature, it is notoriously difficult to delineate anarchism. I consider it helpful to view anarchism as combining a socialist critique of capitalism with a liberal critique of socialism, a (*laissez-faire*) liberal rejection of the state, both as status quo and as a vehicle for social change, with a socialist insistence upon human solidarity and communitarianism.[1] In total, then, anarchism can be understood as the most extreme form of libertarian socialism, the term so frequently employed as its synonym.

However this may be, anarchism is a revolutionary doctrine. And it was in two of the revolutions of the twentieth century that anarchism achieved some kind of practical political success.

First, anarchists were active in the Russian Revolution of 1917. In particular, large areas of the Ukraine were controlled over several years by the revolutionary peasantry and the insurrectionary army of the anarchist Nestor Makhno. In 1920–1, though, the anarchists of the Ukraine were suppressed by the Bolsheviks. 1917 was in fact the climacteric for anarchists internationally. The apparent success of a proletarian revolution in Russia inspired revolutionaries everywhere and caused them to support the new Communist parties. (Pre-war syndicalism, in which anarchists had played a major role, provided the institutional mechanism and ideological tendency which greatly aided this political switch from libertarian to authoritarian socialism.) Equally illusory were the gains of advancing social democracy; but reformist socialism was less likely to attract the allegiance, at least immediately, of anarchists than Communism.

Only in the Hispanic world did anarchism retain its former hold after the First World War. In Spain the movement was vast, the anarcho-syndicalist CNT claiming a membership of approximately one million at its peak and the outbreak of the Spanish Civil War in 1936 precipitated what anarchists call the 'Spanish Revolution'. In response to the Nationalist coup, the anarchist workers and peasants, joined by socialists, throughout Republican Spain collectivized the land, factories, and public utilities. Anarchist self-management worked exceedingly well for a year or two until, first, its erosion by Stalinist counter-revolution and, ultimately, the victory of the Francoist generals.

The catastrophic defeat of Spanish anarchism by 1939, followed by the Second World War, completed anarchism's drastic decline as an international force of revolt. Despite apparent revivals in its fortunes, especially in the 1960s, above all in and after 1968, anarchism from the 1940s has had scarcely a toehold in any labour movement and has appealed instead to some students, fewer intellectuals (among whom it was Marxism which made huge advances in the 1960s and 1970s, at least in Britain and the USA), and others peripheral, *until now*, to the mainstream of events.[2] But anarchism seems currently to be in the process of removing itself from its consignment to the scrap-heap of history. It is certainly the purpose of this volume to assert that anarchist theory has been never more relevant, that anarchist practice is necessary, and that, therefore, the history of anarchism must be seriously and appropriately studied.

Anarchists have traditionally identified the major social, economic, and political problems as consisting of capitalism, inequality (including the domination of women by men), sexual repression, militarism, war, authority, and the state. They have opposed parliamentarianism – that is, liberal or bourgeois democracy, participation in representative institutions – as any kind of means for rectifying these ills. Positively, what anarchists advocate are egalitarianism, co-operation (mutual aid), workers' control (self-management), individualism, freedom, and complete decentralization (organization from the bottom up). As means, they propose direct action (spontaneity) and direct democracy (wherever possible, for they are ultra-democrats, supporting delegation against representation).

To the historian it is clear that classical anarchism was a direct response to nineteenth-century developments. Industrialization, the increase in size of the unit of production, the increasing powers of the state (even the liberal state), and the escalation of the scale on which wars were fought[3] all caused many craftsmen and peasants to become anarchists. And, given the conditions of the period, perhaps their remedies for the problems against which they reacted were not as unrealistic as they have seemed to most commentators, especially with respect to their application in the apparently changed circumstances of the twentieth century.

On the other hand, it is exactly the dominant developments – social, economic, political – of the present century that continue to render the anarchist case relevant, even compelling. The threat of nuclear war is the outcome of the actions of irresponsible states. The impending ecological catastrophe must be attributed to rampant capitalism and delinquent politicians and states (both liberal capitalist and Communist). Above all, the warnings of the nineteenth-century anarchists concerning the dangers inherent in authority (i.e. power) and the state are prescient given the twentieth-century experience of the growing size of organizations and the tyranny of all states, particularly totalitarian states, fascist or communist, naturally, but also the most liberal 'democratic' states. 'Small is beautiful' has been one relatively recent, influential response to organizational size outstripping human comprehension and control. It is also notable that the feminist onslaught on patriarchial society is largely consistent with traditional anarchist analysis and practice.

Indeed, the 'new social movements' of the 1970s and 1980s, which have been puzzling sociologists and Marxists alike, are markedly libertarian in structure, outlook, and action, but entirely unselfconscious as to the degree to which they relate to classical anarchism. I am thinking here especially of the women's movement, the peace movement, and the Greens – Murray Bookchin provides a total overview in Chapter 10 of this book, 'New social movements: the anarchic dimension'. But there are a significant number of 'smaller' movements, such as the new wave of co-ops which Tom Cahill discusses in Chapter 9.

So, despite anarchism's dramatic eclipse as a socio-political force since the Second World War, its criticisms – and its solutions, even if difficult to put into practice – remain extraordinarily, increasingly, apposite.

In addition, as we approach the end of the twentieth century, the conventional left, reformist socialist and revolutionary Marxist alike, is afflicted by a general crisis. There is, however, this historic third stream of left-wing thought and action: anarchism. Amidst the wreckage of their organizations and ideologies, other radicals would only gain by familiarizing themselves with and entering into a dialogue with the traditional libertarian critique and its positive proposals.

In his sour 'Reflections on anarchism' of 1969, E. J. Hobsbawm contends: 'With the exception of Kropotkin, it is not easy to think of an anarchist theorist who could be read with real interest by non-anarchists.'[4] This hostile judgement, in its essentials, is, regrettably, difficult to dispute. Max Stirner's great work, *The Ego and His Own*, *is* one of the most original ever written *and* it was extensively read from its rediscovery in the 1890s until after the First World War. (Similarly, it should be remembered that Godwin's *Political Justice* was a best-seller in the 1790s, though it has been undervalued ever since.) Still, Stirner is 'a man of one idea' (as Hazlitt observed of Robert Owen), and his iconoclastic individualism, his recognition that every set of beliefs, however emancipatory in principle, leads only to further self-enslavement and delusion, offers nothing positive, however salutary reading him may be, to social revolutionaries and activists.[5] As for Proudhon, his ideas have proved immensely stimulating to a remarkable range of French opinion, but they have not exported at all well.[6]

Paradoxically, it is within the last forty to fifty years – during the lowest point of anarchism's fortunes – that a new generation of distinguished anarchist thinkers, primarily American and British, has emerged. Their work does deserve to 'be read with real interest by non-anarchists', but it is still too little-known outside libertarian circles. I am referring to, particularly, Murray Bookchin, a contributor to this volume, and Colin Ward, of both of whom more later, and their forerunners Alex Comfort and Paul Goodman. Yet Comfort's inimitable contribution to anarchist theory both peaked and culminated in his classic *Authority and Delinquency in the Modern State* (1950).[7] And Paul Goodman, who died in 1972, can be cited with the greatest approval, praised for his 'level-headed, realistic humanity', in a recent *Times Literary Supplement* article, while being described as 'all but forgotten now'.[8]

Since the late 1970s there has been significant intellectual activity in North America, marked by the establishment of several theoretical – as opposed to agitational – journals, all of them good. Most impressive is the Canadian *Our Generation*, founded in 1961 as *Our Generation against Nuclear War*, which, although it had already long since become an anarchist publication in effect, reconstituted itself in 1985, changing its self-description from 'an independent radical journal' to 'a journal dealing with the theory and practice of contemporary anarchism and libertarian socialism'. *Our Generation* is closely associated with Black Rose Books of Montréal, probably the foremost anarchist publisher in the world currently. In Baltimore, *Social Anarchism* has been published since 1980, growing out of the substantial anthology of anarchist thought, *Reinventing Anarchy*.[9] The newest is *Harbinger*, an 'occasional' journal advocating Murray Bookchin's social ecology and 'affiliated' with the Institute for Social Ecology of Rochester, Vermont. Unfortunately, the unpretentiously stimulating *Black Rose* of Boston, my personal favourite amongst these periodicals, has, after publishing nine issues between 1979 and 1982, only appeared erratically (another three numbers down to the time of writing, autumn 1987).

Surveying the North American scene, it is striking – and supportive of the general argument which I am trying to develop – that *Telos*, the nearest equivalent that the USA has to the *New Left Review*, publishes articles both on the work of libertarians and by libertarians themselves: among them Paul Goodman, Murray Bookchin, Cornelius Castoriadis (Paul Cardan) and his collaborator Claude Lefort, and John Clark. Such undogmatic inclusiveness is still, I fear, unthinkable with respect to any British Marxist periodical.

In Britain things are altogether different. Although there appears to be a strong upsurge of interest in anarchism among young people, with new anarchist groups thriving, a dozen or more anarchist newspapers being printed, and a considerable volume of anarchist books and pamphlets, new as well as old titles, being sold, there is a disconcerting absence of theoretical journals. Freedom Press, which celebrated its centenary in 1986 and still remains the principal British publisher, only began to bring out *The Raven*, its first 'journal of ideas' since 1971, in 1987, and it is unclear what form this quarterly will eventually take. The *Cienfuegos Press Anarchist Review*, an extraordinary, lively ragbag, produced six issues from 1976 until its collapse in 1982. At the time of writing, the status of *Anarchy* (second series) is entirely uncertain. This really only leaves *Solidarity*, which has been appearing regularly and provocatively since 1961. Although *Solidarity* was responsible for introducing 'Paul Cardan' and *Socialisme ou barbarie* to British readers in the 1960s, by entirely shunning its Marxist past yet refusing to embrace any form of the anarchist tradition, eschewing it not only in name but also in terms of historical experience or philosophy, I personally do not find it surprising that it has failed to maintain an influentially independent libertarian position and condemned itself to a peripheral existence.[10]

It was against this background that the Anarchist Research Group was formed in 1984–5.[11] The Group's most public manifestations have been its contributions in 1985 and 1986 to History Workshops 19 and 20, both held in Leeds, and now the publication of this book. In both History Workshops there were separate workshops on anarchism, convened by myself (as convenor also of the Research Group), at which members gave papers. In both years the anarchism stream was so well supported that it was second only to women's history in popularity. A very much higher proportion of those attending the anarchism sessions have been young people – in their teens and early twenties – than at the other strands, in which, it would seem, the generation of 1968 predominated. (This is just one of the pointers to a current resurgence of anarchism in Britain.)

In 1985 we were fortunate to have Murray Bookchin, a major attraction, fresh from a tour of the West German Greens, as a speaker at the opening and the closing plenaries. Daniel Guérin was ultimately prevented, on his doctor's orders, from travelling from Paris in 1986 (but sent a written paper to the Workshop, part of which appears as Chapter 3, his intended contribution to this collection).

In each year the papers covered the fields of anarchist history, theory, and contemporary practice. Ten have been selected for publication, and this threefold differentiation has been emphasized for their presentation here. In total, I think, they provide a representative sample of the best research now being conducted on anarchism – by writers who are themselves libertarians.

Anarchist historiography is a frustrating field, traditionally tending to be hagiographic or, still worse, antiquarian in approach. When it has come to their own past – or, indeed, the past in general – anarchists have not subjected it to radical analysis or acted as the innovators they have been in other disciplines. So historical work has been untouched by the vital currents in recent Anglo-American anarchist thought.

Over the last twenty to thirty years the major advances in radical historiography – I would say in historiography *tout court* – have occurred in social history, which since the 1950s has emerged as an excitingly independent field of history (at its most ambitious straining to become *total history*). Much of its attention has been directed to popular movements, of the kind that anarchism was in its decades as a mass movement; yet anarchism has been largely overlooked by the new social historians. Most of the theory underlying this social history is derived from the Marxism of its pioneer, and still outstanding, practitioners. Do these Marxist origins and preoccupations invalidate social history for anarchists? Possibly so, but the case would have to be argued and, to my knowledge, it has not.

Alan Carter remarks in Chapter 6 on the 'ahistorical nature of much of anarchist thinking'. The task confronting a philosopher like him is to elaborate further his 'Outline of an anarchist theory of history' in conjunction with other theorists and for such a historical theory (or theories) to be applied and creatively developed by practising historians. What is, of course, required is an approach applicable not merely to the history of anarchism and other libertarian movements but to history *per se*: a way of writing history completely divorced from conventional bourgeois history, with its largely uncritical glorification of the past and the deeds of heroic individuals and, equally, with its stigmatization of the crimes of villains and traitors. Would such an anarchist history, I wonder, be fundamentally different from today's radical social history?

Meanwhile, libertarians do not object to Christopher Hill's treatment of the radicals of the 1640s and 1650s as, centrally, in *The World Turned Upside Down: Radical Ideas during the English Revolution* (1972) or to E. P. Thompson's *The Making of the English Working Class* (1963). Thompson, in fact, has in the course of his political odyssey fairly recently declared for 'libertarian Communism'.[12]

As for E. J. Hobsbawm, while he has been notoriously harsh in his treatment of anarchism,[13] no other (non-anarchist) historian has shown a greater awareness of the international importance of anarchism in the labour movements of the late nineteenth and early twentieth centuries.[14] Hobsbawm is ideologically hostile to anarchism but he has always treated it seriously as a social and political force. This, I would contend, is extremely unusual.

What is necessary, if anarchist historians are to hold their own, commanding the attention of other historians and being read by fellow radicals, is, I am sure – certainly until the day they are equipped with a specifically anarchist historical theory and practice – for them to write history informed by the methods and concerns of social history, now far from being 'new'. Carl Levy and Nick Rider provide in their chapters exemplary instances, one 'macro', the other 'micro', of how this should be done and what the benefits are. Carl Levy (Chapter 1) reviews the entire course of Italian anarchism and, among other things, accounts for its continuing importance, after its early decline into minority status, not only in Italy itself, but throughout the world as it was carried by a diaspora of exiles and emigrants. Nick Rider (Chapter 2), working within the conceptual framework of urbanization – Barcelona expanded vastly between 1915 and 1930 – is able both to savage the textbook characterization of Spanish anarchism as an inflexible, purist ideology of 'mindless revolutionism' as well as to begin to account for the rise of radical anarchism as a mass force in the early 1930s.

Another historian who has applied the perspectives of social history is the anarchist sympathizer Joaquín Romero Maura, who has, sadly, since abandoned historical research, in the masterly essay, 'The Spanish case';[15] in the article, 'Terrorism in Barcelona and its impact on Spanish politics, 1904–1909' (in which, incidentally, he contends that Francisco Ferrer, while innocent in 1909, was 'the master-mind behind the 1905 and 1906 attempts on the life of Alfonso XIII');[16] and in his published doctoral thesis.[17] Two other social-historical examples from the historiography of Spanish anarchism are *Anarchists of Andalusia, 1868–1903* by Temma Kaplan, a Marxist who severely criticizes Hobsbawm's analysis of Andalusian anarchism as millenarian, and *The Anarchists of Casas Viejas*, an outstanding book by Jerome R. Mintz, a non-anarchist anthropologist who tears to tatters Hobsbawm's account of the Casas Viejas rising.[18]

The foremost contemporary historian of anarchism is without doubt Paul Avrich. He has no rivals with respect to both the quantity and the quality of his scholarly production. Over twenty years he has published on first Russian and then American anarchism: *The Russian Anarchists* (1967); *Kronstadt, 1921* (1970); *An American Anarchist: The Life of Voltairine de Cleyre* (1978); *The Modern School Movement: Anarchism and Education in the United States* (1980); and *The Haymarket Tragedy* (1984).[19] These are all beautifully written and intensively researched volumes. In each of his American series, however, Avrich emphasizes that his approach is 'largely biographical, focusing on individual men and women in actual situations', although he is at pains to observe that he has 'not ignored the social and economic background'.[20] What this amounts to, in practice, is highly traditional history, indeed political history or, at best, unreconstructed labour history. Only *The Modern School Movement*, with its dual focus on education and a radical culture – and the extensive use of oral testimony – departs significantly towards social history. Even in his *Russian Rebels, 1600–1800*, at the beginning of which he stresses that it is only 'in recent years' that 'a number of outstanding scholars . . . have shown a proper appreciation of the role of spontaneous mass movements in shaping history', naming E. J. Hobsbawm, George Rudé, E. P. Thompson, and also Barrington Moore Jr, his own text is oddly uninfluenced by the work of these historians.[21] The pity of all this is that Avrich's labours on anarchist – and Russian – history have been marginalized so far as other radical historians of radical movements are concerned, not by his anarchist commitment but by his conventional methodology. (I am not saying that traditional political history is completely redundant, rather lamenting that the finest living anarchist historian should be working primarily in an intellectual backwater.)[22]

Anarchist thought, as I have already asserted, is in remarkably healthy shape. Political theorists and philosophers concern themselves in part with the work of the classic thinkers, but they are also extending the frontiers of libertarian theory by addressing themselves to the changing world of the late twentieth century.

In Chapter 4 Peter Marshall demonstrates that Godwin, Stirner, and Kropotkin all had very different notions of what constitutes 'human nature' (when one would have assumed that the first two would have shared a similar standpoint) and then proceeds, in the course of a discussion informed by modern issues and knowledge, to challenge its very existence as it is usually understood.

Robert Graham, examining in Chapter 5 the role of contract in anarchist theory, first engages most usefully in a lengthy discussion of Proudhon, the major anarchist who has been most neglected by Anglophone commentators – very few of his voluminous writings have been translated into English – and concludes by highlighting the stature of a recent work of libertarian political theory: *The Problem of Political Obligation: A Critique of Liberal Theory* by Carole Pateman.[23]

Daniel Guérin has a typically French admiration for Proudhon, to whom he refers frequently in 'Marxism and anarchism' (Chapter 3).* In Guérin's widely read *Anarchism: From Theory to Practice*, Kropotkin (and all the other anarchist communists) is

---

* Since this Introduction was written, Daniel Guérin has died in Paris, during the night of 13 April 1988, at the age of 83. Appreciations have appeared in *Le Monde*, 15 April 1988; *Socialist Worker Review*, June 1988; *Freedom*, June 1988.

scarcely mentioned, and Proudhon and Bakunin are presented as the central anarchist thinkers. This imbalance is only slightly redressed in his huge anthology *Ni Dieu ni maître*, and Proudhon is allocated the greatest space.[24] Guérin's long-standing engagement with Proudhon's work has concluded with *Proudhon oui et non*, a volume collecting four studies.[25]

A prolific author of political, social, and historical works, Guérin, from the 1960s, has come out in a series of autobiographical volumes revealing his bisexuality and detailing his promiscuous homosexual encounters.[26] The late Peter Sedgwick commented:

> If Daniel Guérin escapes a final definition as a homosexual, a heterosexual or a putative androgyne, that is part of his strength. His entire creative life has been spent in the effort to interpret to one another standpoints of a partial validity but with a claim to all-inclusiveness. As a mediator between libertarian socialism and 'authoritarian' Bolshevism, as a spokesperson for anarchism among Marxists and for Marxism among the *anarchisants* he has been the honest broker among ideologies as he is the rare interpreter of sexualities one to another.[27]

This comparison between his sexuality and his politics is one by which Guérin himself is 'particularly impressed'.[28]

The extent of Guérin's Marxism is probably concealed to most readers of the English translation of his *Anarchism*. Here the paper given in New York in 1973 and first published in English in 1981 by the Cienfuegos Press, as a pamphlet entitled *Anarchism and Marxism*, becomes essential complementary reading. It is a 'recasting' of this pamphlet which has been prepared for the present collection as 'Marxism and anarchism'.

If readers are unconvinced by Guérin's attempt to draw Marxism and anarchism close together, they should bear two points in mind. First, Guérin, a revolutionary since 1929 – he has been a syndicalist, *socialiste de gauche*, Trotskyist, and now a libertarian communist – extensively read, and equipped with an acute intellect, has been working on this project for decades. Second, the attempt may be doomed to failure from the outset, for it is such a synthesis of anarchism and Marxism which is so decisively criticized by Alan Carter.[29]

Sympathy with Guérin's position would be confined to only a small minority of anarchists.[30] Historically, anarchists have overwhelmingly rejected Marxism, in both its theory and its practice. But as Geoffrey Ostergaard observes in his 'Indian anarchism' (Chapter 7): 'Some forms of western anarchism, notably anarcho-syndicalism, have accepted much of the Marxian analysis of class in capitalist society.' And the majority of anarchists have identified the workers – along with the peasants – as constituting the social force which will make the anarchist revolution. In contrast, few anarchists have accepted historical materialism; and while Marxists and most anarchists have theoretically concurred in the ultimate ideal of a stateless, free, communist society, they have bitterly disagreed about the means to be employed in achieving this end.

As Alan Carter points out in Chapter 6, the disagreement between anarchists and Marxists has centred around the role of the state in revolutionary change. It is his achievement to provide a model of historical change which turns historical materialism on its head by arguing that it is not the forces of production which determine the superstructure of the state, *but the state which develops the forces of production*.

Alan Carter's mode of philosophical analysis and argument is likely to be unfamiliar to and, at times, difficult for most readers. It takes its place, though, within an influential development in Anglophone Marxist philosophy, concerned with the rationality of individual choice, heralded, a decade ago, by the seminal work whose conclusions he comprehensively rejects: G. A. Cohen's *Karl Marx's Theory of History: A Defence*.[31] Analytic theory has previously only touched upon anarchist concerns in the books of Michael Taylor, *Anarchy and Co-operation* (revised and reissued as *The Possibility of Co-operation*) and *Community*, *Anarchy and Liberty*.[32]

There can be no doubt that the foremost contemporary anarchist thinker is the American Murray Bookchin, an outstandingly original theorist, almost certainly the most innovative since Kropotkin, with whom indeed he merits comparison.[33] Here is the anarchist theorist writing today whose work *should* be read with real interest by non-anarchists.

In what does Bookchin's originality consist? What is the nature of his achievement? Given the profusion and wide-ranging character of his writings, it is difficult to provide an adequate account in summary form. Most obviously, he has conjoined modern ecological thought – he was a pioneering writer on environmental issues in the 1950s, publishing *Our Synthetic Environment* in 1962 – with traditional anarchism in propounding what he calls 'social ecology'. He contends that the technological capabilities of late twentieth-century industrialism – the actuality of 'post-scarcity' – provide the material conditions for the realization of the utopian aspirations of anarchism. He has incisively refuted not only the Leninist belief in the role of the vanguard party in bringing about a classless society but *also* the historic view shared by Marxists, socialists of all kinds, and, as I have already stressed, most anarchists that the working class will provide the social motor whereby social revolution will be achieved. Instead, he argues, the working class is in an advanced state of decomposition in the capitalist societies of the west.[34]

Bookchin attempts to be a total social thinker – like so many nineteenth-century theorists, most obviously Marx – synthesizing radical politics, modern science, anthropology, philosophy, history, in a way to which we have grown unaccustomed in the twentieth century with the rise of various specialisms. Such a project is exciting and necessary but exceptionally daring and, even more, recklessly dangerous. Can one person, should one person, be, in all reason, as ambitious as this nowadays? (Throughout Bookchin's writings I am continually reminded of his outstanding libertarian compatriot, Lewis Mumford, twenty-six years his senior – Bookchin was born in 1921 – who also exposes himself to similar criticisms but who, unlike Bookchin, has always bolstered his books with massive bibliographies.)[35] For my part, as I have said, I regard the attempt as necessary, though I am only too aware of the pitfalls, and wish to emphasize this aspect as one of Bookchin's achievements and, moreover, claims to originality.

So Bookchin advocates a new revolutionary theory and practice, which will be consciously utopian, based on a comprehension of ecology and present-day technology, a rejection of socialist delusions about the working class, and an appreciation that the potentiality of abundance at last brings the possibility of anarchism. The philosophical basis is Hegelian, the spirit insurrectionary, even Bakuninist, the vision related to Kropotkin's,[36] but the flavour thoroughly contemporary and his own. The origins are to be found, paradoxically it may seem, in Marxism – he was first a Communist, then a Trotskyist from the 1930s to the 1950s – and, in my opinion, this accounts for his theoretical strength, historical grasp, and overall punch;[37] yet the inspiration has increasingly reached back to the libertarian tradition of New England and the American Revolution.[38]

Bookchin first attracted widespread attention, dropping his former pseudonym of 'Lewis Herber', with *Post-Scarcity Anarchism* (1971). This has been followed by a series of major works, amidst a torrent of articles, many of which have appeared as collections: *The Limits of the City* (1974); *The Spanish Anarchists: The Heroic Years, 1868–1936* (1977); *Toward an Ecological Society* (1980); *The Ecology of Freedom: The Emergence and Dissolution of*

Hierarchy (1982); *The Modern Crisis* (1986); *The Rise of Urbanization and the Decline of Citizenship* (1987).[39]

In Britain, Bookchin is scarcely known outside anarchist circles and not extensively read within them – for one thing, his books are hard to obtain, only *Post-Scarcity Anarchism* having been published in a British edition.[40] In North America the situation is very different, his work rightly commanding considerable attention and his publishers able to excerpt plaudits from a surprising range of periodicals, for example, the *Nation, Science and Society, Canadian Association of University Teachers Review, Toronto Star*, and *San Francisco Chronicle*. *The Ecology of Freedom* was greeted as his *magnum opus*, 'a major achievement, destined to become a classic of contemporary social thought', and 'essential reading not only for anarchists and the left in general, or even environmentalists . . . but for everyone'.[41] The Marxist sociologist Stanley Aronowitz, himself almost entirely unknown on this side of the Atlantic, but author of the impressive *False Promises: The Shaping of American Working Class Consciousness* (1973), ranks Bookchin with 'the most advanced thinkers', Ernst Bloch, Herbert Marcuse, and other members of the Frankfurt School – appropriately it is the critical theorists of the Frankfurt School to whom Bookchin acknowledges particular indebtedness amongst his contemporaries. Aronowitz concluded his review of *The Ecology of Freedom* by maintaining that Bookchin is

> a great utopian, a major builder of a mythic past, a shaker and mover of social consciousness, a preacher, a Ranter. Like Georges Sorel, who argued that the workers' movement of his times required a sustaining myth to mobilize the masses for liberation, Bookchin has provided a sustaining myth of the indestructible spirit and another of the organic civilization to give us the hope to forge ahead. I don't mind these myths. It's too late to believe them entirely, but I'll take Bookchin any time over the prophets of the apocalypse who are concerned only to save our skins, and those who remain mired in the naive belief that science will save us.[42]

Post-Scarcity Anarchism was a selection of writings from the 1960s, *The Spanish Anarchists* had been written in the same decade, and much of *The Limits of the City* dates from the late 1950s. *Toward an Ecological Society* gathered articles from the 1970s. Not until his volumes of the 1980s – although *The Ecology of Freedom* had a lengthy gestation throughout the 1970s – have the readers of Bookchin's books really been able to catch up with where his thinking is currently at. This is important. For

Bookchin's thought is, properly, in continual evolution. To take two very obvious examples, he has come to call his synthesis 'social ecology', which he employs as a synonym for anarchism; and he has centred upon 'hierarchy' in all its forms –

> the domination of the young by the old, of women by men, of one ethnic group by another, of 'masses' by bureaucrats who profess to speak in their 'higher social interests', of countryside by town, and in a more subtle psychological sense, of body by mind, of spirit by a shallow instrumental rationality, and of nature by society and technology[43]

– as the central social problem, the identification of which demarcates anarchism from all other varieties of socio-political radicalism. Finally, Bookchin has the inestimable strength of being able to revise his judgements.[44]

With Bookchin the boundaries between 'theory' and 'practice', as in his chapter on 'New social movements' are, necessarily, transcended (despite the tidy arrangement of the contents of this collection; he has, too, made a typically remarkable excursion into 'history', with his carefully researched study of Spanish anarchism).

By anarchism in 'practice' I understand anarchism in the real world of today – and tomorrow (rather than yesterday: that is the province of 'history') – anarchism in the world of the here and now as opposed to utopian or insurrectionary dreams, what Colin Ward describes as his own field of 'anarchist applications'.[45]

Tom Cahill, very much influenced by Murray Bookchin, examines (in Chapter 9) the co-operative movement which has flourished since the 1970s and contends that it is, in essence, anarchist, although its members are almost entirely unaware of this. He also provides outlines of an anarchist economics, a crucial topic which has been almost completely neglected by libertarian thinkers.

Education, on the contrary, has been a preoccupation of anarchists from the outset – from Godwin through Stirner and Tolstoy to Herbert Read and Paul Goodman. Michael Smith discusses (in Chapter 8) the views, situating them in full context, which Kropotkin expressed when he entered the British debate on technical education in the 1880s, and then boldly proceeds to outline the ideas which Kropotkin might have put forward were he writing in the 1980s.

Leaving aside the matter of the 'new social movements' of the west, is there any mass movement in the world today which can be properly described as 'anarchist'? Anarcho-pacifists have for long pointed to the Gandhian or Sarvodaya movement of India. It is well known that Gandhi was deeply influenced by Tolstoy as well as admiring Kropotkin; and debate has largely centred around the personal politics of Gandhi himself. Geoffrey Ostergaard advances the argument very significantly by examining the ideas of his successor, Vinoba Bhave, concluding that these are certainly anarchist, but cautioning us that there is a major cultural or philosophical difference: 'Indian anarchism is not western anarchism in India.'

Among living writers the subject of anarchist practice belongs to Colin Ward, whose quiet, unspectacular, but very real originality tends to be overlooked.[46] His editorship of *Anarchy* between 1961 and 1970 is generally and correctly acknowledged as outstanding (though, undoubtedly, the 118 monthly issues were a good deal more uneven and bitty than retrospective enthusiasm for a past, unreplaced journal would frequently have a later generation believe).[47] It was in *Anarchy* that he was able to develop his distinctive outlook much influenced by Paul Goodman's work, but in no way derivative, and summarized in his book, dedicated, significantly, to Goodman's memory, *Anarchy in Action*.[48]

The scale of Ward's achievement is fully appreciated by George Woodcock and admirably summarized by him. Colin Ward, he says, develops an effective criticism of 'the argument that we have to wait for fundamental social changes before we can begin the liberation of society. Ward argues that this arises from an erroneous posing of an opposition between existing society and a libertarian future.' Actually, as Ward demonstrates by applying, to society as it exists, Kropotkin's arguments in *Mutual Aid* and Proudhon's on federalism,

> most of our institutions originated in voluntary co-operation and still operate most effectively when that principle is maintained. The factor of free co-operation in fact permeates every sphere of life, even though it is hidden under authoritarian structures which impoverish society by discouraging and de-stroying popular initiatives, by doing things for people instead of letting them do for themselves. 'Do-it-yourself' is in fact the essence of anarchist action, and the more people apply it on every level, in education, in the workplace, in the family, the more ineffective restrictive structures will become and the more dependence will be replaced by individual and collective self-reliance . . .. The more we build and strengthen an alternative society, the more the state is weakened.[49]

One of Ward's favourite statements – and he is a great quoter, *in extenso* – is that by the major German anarchist, Gustav

Landauer: 'The state is not something which can be destroyed by a revolution, but is a condition, a certain relationship between human beings, a mode of human behaviour; we destroy it by contracting other relationships, by behaving differently.' This 'profound and simple' statement is at the core of Ward's anarchism.[50]

Since *Anarchy in Action*, Ward has published a fascinating up-to-date edition of Kropotkin's *Fields, Factories and Workshops* as *Fields, Factories and Workshops Tomorrow* with his own ample introductions and appendices.[51] Otherwise he has largely written books on his particular specialism of housing and urban planning.[52]

Peter Abbs wrote of Colin Ward's contributions to *Fields, Factories and Workshops Tomorrow*:

> the threads of an alternative tradition in political thinking are quietly drawn together: the works of Gandhi, Buber, Paul Goodman, Herbert Read, Lewis Mumford and many others are knitted into one coherent fabric. Here is a suppressed tradition of philosophy and politics, which, as Marxist and capitalist ideology disintegrate or ossify, more and more people will be wanting to consider.[53]

It is a primary purpose of the present collection to draw attention to this latter contention: to demonstrate that anarchism is neither extinct nor crazy but a vital, creative tradition which should be once more (if it ever was) seriously considered by the left in general.

We have had Louis Althusser's *Pour Marx* (*For Marx*) and we have had *For Mao*.[54] This book is *For Anarchism*.

Notes and references

It must be emphasized that the views expressed in this Introduction are those of the editor alone. I am grateful to Sharif Gemie, Carl Levy, and Peter Marshall, among others, for their many helpful, critical comments, only some of which, however, I have incorporated in the final text. I am also indebted to Tom Cahill for providing me with details and copies of some of the reviews of Murray Bookchin's *The Ecology of Freedom*.

1 Cf. David E. Apter, 'The old anarchism and the new – some comments', in David E. Apter and James Joll (eds), *Anarchism Today* (London, 1971), pp. 1–2; Rudolf Rocker, *Anarcho-Syndicalism* (London, 1938), pp. 21–31; Noam Chomsky, 'Introduction' to Daniel Guérin, *Anarchism: From Theory to Practice* (New York, 1970), pp. x–xii (Chomsky's complete text, originally published in the *New*

York Review of Books, 21 May 1970, was reprinted in, among other journals, *Anarchy*, 116 (October 1970)). It should be observed that any association of anarchism with liberalism is furiously rejected by those anarchists who react according to their gut feelings rather than their minds.

2 I believe therefore that the general thrust of George Woodcock's analysis of anarchism since 1939 is correct – *Anarchism: A History of Libertarian Ideas and Movement* (Harmondsworth, 1975 edn), 'Epilogue'; (2nd edn, 1986), esp. 'Preface' and (the new) 'Epilogue'; also *The Anarchist Reader* (London, 1977), pp. 46–56 – as opposed to the sustained criticisms of Nicolas Walter, in *Anarchy*, 28 (June 1963); 'Has anarchism changed?', *Freedom*, 7 April, 1 May, 26 June, 10 July 1976; and, most recently, 'Woodcock reconsidered', *The Raven*, 2 (August 1987).

3 This is an issue which has been surprisingly neglected, with the notable exception of the Dutch pioneer of anarcho-pacifism, Bart de Ligt. See, for example, his *Introduction to the Science of Peace* (London, 1939).

4 Hobsbawm, *Revolutionaries: Contemporary Essays* (London, 1973), p. 83.

5 The American writer James Huneker correctly observed that Stirner 'has left behind him a veritable breviary of destruction, a striking and dangerous book . . . it is dangerous in every sense of the word – to socialism, to politicians, to hypocrisy' – cited by James J. Martin, 'Editor's introduction' to Max Stirner, *The Ego and His Own* (New York, 1963), p. xi.

6 Cf. F. F. Ridley, *Revolutionary Syndicalism in France: The Direct Action of Its Time* (Cambridge, 1970), pp. 25–32. See also my further observations below, pp. 9–10.

7 To be reissued in a new edition entitled simply *Authority and Delinquency* (London, 1988).

8 David Rieff, 'The colonel and the professor', *Times Literary Supplement*, 4–11 September 1987.

9 Howard J. Ehrlich, Carol Ehrlich, David DeLeon, and Glenda Morris (eds), *Reinventing Anarchy: What Are Anarchists Thinking These Days*? (London, 1979).

10 For Cardan/Castoriadis and *Socialisme ou barbarie*, see André Liebich, '*Socialisme ou barbarie*: a radical critique of bureaucracy', *Our Generation*, 12, 2 (Fall 1977); and, for an interesting up-to-date assessment, Sunil Khilnani's brief review of Castoriadis's *Domaines de l'homme*, *Times Literary Supplement*, 12 December 1986 (also Khilnani's 'Politics of honour', *New Society*, 16 October 1987).

While considering modern French libertarian thought it is perhaps worth noting that Situationist theory, which seemed to have so much to offer in the late-1960s, has failed to progress since the publication of substantial theoretical works by its two leading exponents – Guy Debord, *Le Société du spectacle* (Paris, 1967), and Raoul Vaneigem, *Traité de savoir-vivre à l'usage des jeunes générations* (Paris, 1967) (both of which are now available in adequate translations) – and the termination in 1969 of the review *Internationale situationniste* the twelve issues of which, from 1958, were then reprinted in one volume (Amsterdam, 1970)). See, especially, Christopher Gray (ed.), *Leaving the 20th Century: The Incomplete Work of the Situationist International* (London, 1974); and Ken Knabb (ed.), *International Situationist Anthology* (Berkeley, 1981).

It is reported that very interesting work is currently being done in Italy, particularly in connection with the Centro Studi Libertari of Milan and the journal *Volontà* but also in *Rivista anarchica*, yet none has been published in English and it remains in all ways inaccessible.

11 For details of the origins and development of the Anarchist Research Group, see my 'History Workshop 19: Anarchism', *History Workshop Journal*, 22 (Autumn 1986), pp. 199–200.

12 Thompson, *The Poverty of Theory and Other Essays* (London, 1978), pp. 380–4. Similarly the second edition of his monumental *William Morris: Romantic to Revolutionary* (London, 1977), especially 'Postscript: 1976', must be considerably more acceptable to anarchists than the original of 1955. Certainly, Thompson's approval of the work of a French libertarian, Miguel Abensour (2nd edn, pp. 786–802) has attracted the scorn of Perry Anderson in his *Arguments within English Marxism* (London, 1980), pp. 158–62.

13 See, especially, 'Reflections on anarchism', Hobsbawm, *Revolutionaries*, op. cit., and *Primitive Rebels: Studies in Archaic Forms of Social Movement in the 19th and 20th Centuries* (Manchester, 1959), chapter 5; also Nick Rider, Chapter 2 below, 'The practice of direct action: the Barcelona rent strike of 1931', note 1.

14 See, for example, 'Bolshevism and the anarchists', Hobsbawm, *Revolutionaries*, op. cit.

15 In Apter and Joll, *Anarchism Today*, op. cit.

16 *Past and Present*, 41 (December 1968), esp. pp. 141–2. This particular conclusion of Romero Maura's is treated with scepticism by Paul Avrich, *The Modern School Movement: Anarchism and Education in the United States* (Princeton, NJ, 1980), pp. 28–9.

17 Romero Maura, *La rosa de fuego – republicanos y anarquistas: la politica de los obreros barceloneses entre el desastre colonial y la semana tragica, 1899–1909* (Barcelona, 1975).

18 Princeton, NJ, 1977; and Chicago and London, 1982, respectively. Colin Ward, with his typical originality and synthesizing ability, has pointed to the libertarian implications of many of the findings published in recent years by the social historians of nineteenth- and twentieth-century Britain ('The path not taken', *The Raven*, 3 (November 1987) – abridged in the *Guardian*, 12 October 1987, as 'Rebels finding their cause').

19 All published in Princeton, New Jersey. Among Avrich's lesser publications are the documentary collection *The Anarchists in the Russian Revolution* (London, 1973) and the booklet *Bakunin and Nechaev* (London, 1974).* His next book will be a joint study of Alexander Berkman and Emma Goldman and that will be followed by

a full-length re-examination of the case of Sacco and Vanzetti.
20 Avrich, *American Anarchist*, op. cit., p. xiii; *Modern School Movement*, op. cit., p. xii; *Haymarket Tragedy*, op. cit., pp. xiii–xiv.
21 Avrich, *Russian Rebels, 1600–1800* (London, 1973), p. 7.
22 Where, it may be asked, does George Woodcock fit in? In this survey I am principally considering developments of the last fifteen to twenty years at most. Woodcock's history of *Anarchism* on its first publication (1962 in the USA; 1963 in Britain) was an impressive achievement. Twenty-five years on, however, there is need of a replacement, a need actually exacerbated by the unsatisfactory revision for the 2nd edn of 1986 (see Walter, 'Woodcock reconsidered', pp. 181–3). Since 1962–3 Woodcock has, compared with the two preceding decades, written little on anarchism (see the useful bibliography, 1937–76, compiled by Ivan Avakumovic, in William H. New (ed.), *A Political Art: Essays and Images in Honour of George Woodcock* (Vancouver, BC, 1978), pp. 211–48). There is, though, his interesting trilogy on twentieth-century British writers with varying degrees of libertarian commitment: *The Crystal Spirit: A Study of George Orwell* (London, 1967); *Dawn and the Darkest Hour: A Study of Aldous Huxley* (London, 1972); *Herbert Read: The Stream and the Source* (London, 1972). The studies of Orwell and Read both include substantial elements of personal reminiscence, which overlap with passages in *Letter to the Past: An Autobiography* (Toronto, 1982), a volume which contains a detailed account of Woodcock's transition to anarchism and his activism in the 1940s – and ends with his emigration to Canada in 1949. Strangely, *Letter to the Past* has not been published in Britain, but it will appear rather absurd to any reader who is unaware that Canadians consider Woodcock one of their leading men of letters (there is, for example, *A George Woodcock Reader*, edited by Doug Fetherling (n.p., 1980)).
23 London, 1979; reissued with an afterword, Oxford, 1985.
24 Lausanne, n.d.
25 Paris, 1978. The shortest study has been translated as 'From Proudhon to Bakunin', *Our Generation*, 17, 2 (Spring/Summer 1986).
26 See, particularly, Guérin, *Autobiographie de jeunesse: d'une dissidence sexuelle au socialisme* (Paris, 1972); and *Le Feu du sang: Autobiographie politique et charnelle* (Paris, 1977). 'Le feu du sang' is a quotation from Proudhon's *Philosophie de la misère*.
27 Sedgwick, 'Out of hiding: the comradeships of Daniel Guérin', *Salmagundi*, 58–9 (Fall 1982/Winter 1983), p. 219.
28 In a letter to the present writer, 23 September 1986.
29 In Chapter 6 of this book, 'Outline of an anarchist theory of history', note 24.
30 Among them Noam Chomsky. See his 'Introduction' to Guérin, *Anarchism*, op. cit.; and George Woodcock's angry criticism, 'Chomsky's anarchism', *Freedom*, 16 November 1974.
31 Oxford, 1978.
32 London, 1976 (and Cambridge, 1987); and Cambridge, 1982,

respectively. Michael Taylor says, however, in a personal communication, that 'I've never thought of myself as doing research on Anarchism.' For a survey of the already very substantial body of work of this type within contemporary Marxism, see Alan Carling, 'Rational choice Marxism', *New Left Review*, 160 (November/December 1986) (and pp. 25, 62 for Taylor's books).

33 David DeLeon, *The American as Anarchist: Reflections on Indigeneous Radicalism* (Baltimore, Md, 1978), p. 199, goes so far as to claim that Bookchin is 'probably the most systematic and intelligent of all anarchist theoreticians, past and present'.

34 'Listen, Marxist!', Murray Bookchin, *Post-Scarcity Anarchism* (London, 1974). There is a definite convergence between Bookchin's analysis of the contemporary working class and the ideas which have been advanced by E. J. Hobsbawm – in Martin Jacques and Francis Mulhern (eds), *The Forward March of Labour Halted?* (London, 1981), and his continuing articles in *Marxism Today*. See also Alan Wolfe, 'Listen, Bookchin', *Nation*, 29 May 1982.

35 See Colin Ward, 'Introduction' to Lewis Mumford, *The Future of Technics and Civilization* (London, 1986), esp. pp. 11–12.

36 George Woodcock rightly points to the way in which Bookchin has developed Kropotkin's insights in *Fields, Factories and Workshops* but, he criticizes, 'with scanty acknowledgement' (*Anarchism*, 2nd edn, op. cit., p. 422). It should, however, be observed that Bookchin regards William Morris as his 'favourite utopian', and the vision of *News from Nowhere* is therefore highly relevant (*The Ecology of Freedom* (Palo Alto, Calif., 1982), pp. ix, 332–3).

37 Bookchin's Marxist 'intellectual pedigree' has not gone unchallenged. See Clym Yeobright, 'Beginnings for a critique of the thought of Murray Bookchin', *Black Rose*, 8 (Spring 1982); and Murray Bookchin, 'A reply to Clym Yeobright and Peter Kardas', *Black Rose*, 9 (Fall/Winter 1982).

38 See, especially, Bookchin, *The Modern Crisis* (Philadelphia, 1986), pp. 129–61; and *The Rise of Urbanization and the Decline of Citizenship* (San Francisco, 1987), pp. 114–15, 231–8, 268–88.

39 I have given the dates of the first editions of these titles, all published in the United States with the exception of *Toward an Ecological Society* (published by Black Rose Books of Montréal).

40 Most of the American and Canadian editions have been 'distributed' in Britain, yet the distribution has been very poor – only two or three London bookshops being likely to have copies on their shelves – and the prices in any case fairly steep. *Post-Scarcity Anarchism* is additionally familiar to British anarchists since three of its essays had been published by Colin Ward in *Anarchy*: 'Ecology and revolutionary thought', 'Towards a liberatory technology', and 'Desire and need' (*Anarchy*, 69 (November 1966); 78 (August 1967); and 80 (October 1967)). 'Listen, Marxist!' was widely available as a pamphlet.

41 Stanley Aronowitz, 'Past perfect', *Village Voice*; John Clark, *The Anarchist Moment: Reflections on Culture, Nature and Power*

(Montréal, 1984), pp. 215–27 (reprinted from his review in *Our Generation*, which appeared in a slightly different form in *Telos*, 57 (Fall 1983)); review by David L. Westby, *Social Anarchism*, 7 (1984). In contrast, while Peter Cadogan suspected that 'it may have a profound and lasting effect on the thinking of our time' in a careful, detailed assessment in *Resurgence*, 97 (March/April 1983), *Freedom* printed a totally inadequate notice, and I know of only two other British reviews, one by Nicolas Walter in *City Limits*, 1–7 April 1983, the other by 'John Cobbett' in *Solidarity* (New Series), 1, 3 (n.d.), both of which are highly critical, although appreciative of Bookchin's output as a whole. Admittedly, *The Ecology of Freedom* is frequently difficult to understand and the content of its 385 pages poorly structured. Bookchin's mastery has always been fostered by brevity, and it is in hard-hitting polemics and crisp expositions that he has excelled. It is good to know that he has prepared a shorter, more accessible version of *The Ecology of Freedom* – to be published by Black Rose Books in 1988 as *Remaking Society*.

42 Aronowitz, 'Socialism and beyond: remaking the American left, part two', *Socialist Review*, 69 (May/June 1983), pp. 32–4; Aronowitz, 'Past perfect', o. cit.

43 Bookchin, *Ecology of Freedom*, op. cit., p. 4.

44 I am particularly impressed by the revision over twenty years of Bookchin's opinion of Paul Goodman, whose 'pragmatism' he intemperately dismissed in 'Against meliorism', *Anarchy*, 88 (June 1968), pp. 191–2, and whom he now ranks with Kropotkin and Morris as an 'outstanding radical decentralist thinker' ('Social ecology versus "deep ecology" – a challenge for the ecology movement', *Green Perspectives*, 4–5 (Summer 1987), pp. 3, 19).

45 In a letter to the writer, 6 October 1984.

46 Or scorned by those who prefer 'to indulge in windy rhetoric about revolution' rather than, as Ward advocates, 'seek out anarchist solutions' to immediate issues (Colin Ward (ed.), *A Decade of Anarchy, 1961–1970: Selections from the Monthly Journal 'Anarchy'* (London, 1987), p. 279).

47 An example is Raphael Samuel's lengthy review of *A Decade of Anarchy* in *New Society*, 2 October 1987 – but whatever its defects, this generous appraisal of Colin Ward's work to date by a leading Marxist intellectual is heart-warming.

48 London, 1973.

49 Woodcock, *Anarchism*, 2nd edn, op. cit., pp. 420–2. Cf. Ward, *Decade of Anarchy*, op. cit., p. 10.

50 Ward, *Anarchy in Action*, op. cit., p. 19. This is taken from Landauer's classic *Die Revolution* of 1908 and of which, extraordinarily, we still lack an English translation.

51 London, 1974; 2nd edn, 1985.

52 But since Colin Ward regards all his publications as 'looking at life from an anarchist point of view' (letter of 6 October 1984), it is worth listing what I take to be his principal works in this field: *Tenants Take*

Over (London, 1974); *Housing: An Anarchist Approach* (London, 1976); *When We Build Again: Let's Have Housing That Works!* (London, 1985). He has also edited *Vandalism* (London, 1973) and written *The Child in the City* (London, 1978), the sequel to which, *The Child in the Country*, will be published in 1988. His marvellous *Arcadia for All: The Legacy of a Makeshift Landscape* (London, 1984), co-authored with Dennis Hardy, dealing with the 'plotlands' of south-east England – Jaywick Sands, Canvey Island, Peacehaven, and their like – is of much broader interest. Two further collaborative volumes are *Goodnight Campers! The History of the British Holiday Camp* (London, 1986), again with Dennis Hardy, and *The Allotment: Its Culture and Landscape* (London, 1989), with David Crouch.

53 From a review in *The Ecologist*, quoted on the cover of the 2nd edn of *Fields, Factories and Workshops Tomorrow*, op. cit.

54 Philip Corrigan, Harvie Ramsay, and Derek Sayer, *For Mao: Essays in Historical Materialism* (London, 1979). We have also had *For Socialism* (St Louis, Mo., 1978) by, ironically, the anarchist Landauer; but this English title is a mistranslation of *Aufruf zum Sozialismus* (*Call to Socialism*).

* *Anarchist Portraits* (Princeton, NJ, 1988), a collection of Paul Avrich's articles and other shorter items, was published while this volume was in the course of production.

Part I
History

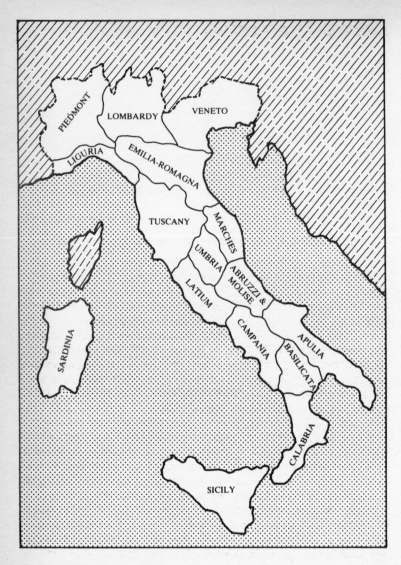

Map 1.1   The regions of Italy
Source: Enzo Santarelli, 'L'Anarchisme en Italie', *Le Mouvement social*, 83 (1973)

1

Italian Anarchism, 1870–1926

Carl Levy

> Se gli anarchici non se ne curano, la storia la faranno i loro nemici.
>
> (Gaetano Salvemini)
>
> If the anarchists are not careful, their enemies will write their history.

These prophetic words of Gaetano Salvemini have until recently been all too true. The history of Italian anarchism has been left mostly to its enemies, and it has only been in the last twenty years, with the development of a less dogmatic dialogue between elements of the Italian left and the emergence of the discipline of social history, that a more balanced account of the movement has been produced. Indeed, one might say that for a long time the anarchist movement suffered an even harsher fate than Salvemini had predicted for it. Until the early 1970s Italian labour and social history concentrated on the origins of political parties, or on the vicissitudes of major party leaders and their theoretical disputes. Those parties or social movements which had been reduced in importance were neglected. Anarchism was forgotten, relegated to a few footnotes generally concerning 'human colour'. It was treated as a millenarian cult, an interesting example of Italian plebeian culture, but hardly deserving close scrutiny.

In this chapter I concentrate on the period before 1914, when the cultural and institutional frameworks for the anarchist movement were established. Then I turn to the period of social upheaval following the First World War (the *biennio rosso*, 1919–20). I conclude with a brief analysis of the anarchists' response to the Bolshevik Revolution and the rise of fascism.

The First International in Italy, 1870–82

My main focus will not be the era of the First International, since this has been studied in great depth elsewhere. The English reader who wants a detailed and solid account of this period should turn to Richard Hostetter's old but reliable book. Rather in this chapter I am more interested in analysing how and why anarchism as a minority movement survived within broader non-anarchist socialist and labour organizations after 1880 until the rise of fascism in the 1920s. Its survival says a great deal about the daily life and culture of various popular social movements in Italy before the establishment of the fascist totalitarian state in 1926 effectively wiped them out.

Therefore in this brief account I shall summarize historical and sociological work on the Italian section of the First International. Further on, I will return to analyse the impact of its best-known leaders (Errico Malatesta, Andrea Costa, and Carlo Cafiero) on the broader left.

The most striking feature of the history of the Italian section of the International must be the rapidity of its growth. There are domestic as well as external factors at work here. Certainly Bakunin's part in the establishment and growth of the Italian section of the First International has been noted and examined in great detail by foreign and Italian historians. While Bakunin and other Russian revolutionaries lived in Italy during the 1860s, and knew the first generation of Italian anarchists very well indeed, most historians now agree that he and others (such as Stepniak) acted as catalysts in, rather than initiators of, the Italian movement. They did not bring a 'new gospel' to left-wing republicans, but they did supply them with an international context within which a native-grown populistic socialism advanced in the 1850s by the Risorgimento martyr, Carlo Pisacane, could evolve with and affect the emergence of anarcho-communist ideology. (Indeed, Giuseppe Fanelli, Bakunin's agent in Spain, was a former associate of Pisacane's and a founder of the important Neapolitan section of the Italian International.)

In short, Bakunin helped accelerate the disenchantment of Mazzinian republicans with their leader while simultaneously steering them towards libertarian rather than Marxist socialism, but the Italian Internationalists were in any case bent in these directions independently of Russian influence. Culturally, socially, and intellectually, Italians were not prepared to agree for long with the suggestions of the London-based General Council of the International. Engels, who interested himself in Italian affairs, ignored or misunderstood the cultural and political content of Italian social radicalism. On the other hand, Bakunin's sensitivities towards rural and artisanal societies such as Italy seemed more attuned to the Internationalists' experiences. Their revolutionary models were not the industrial proletarians of England but rather the mostly artisanal rank and file of the Paris Commune, the 'primitive communists' of the Russian *mir*, the plebeian insurgents of the Spanish First Republic's cantonal revolts, and the Italian tradition of the city-state democracy of the *popolo minuto* (common people).

Disenchanted Mazzinian republicans outraged by their leader's attack upon the 'atheistic' Paris Commune and *garibaldini*, members of Garibaldi's volunteers radicalized by their experiences in the Franco-Prussian War, recruited perhaps twenty to thirty thousand members to the International within a few years. And in his much praised multi-volume history of Italy, a Marxist historian, Giorgio Candeloro, admitted that the International might in fact have been Italy's first mass political party.[1] A social analysis of its membership demonstrates that it was far from being factory-based and proletarian. The lion's share of members were artisans from central Italy and Naples, with a national represent-ation of intellectuals and students, although there were also present primitive worker organizations – the *fasci operai* (local trade-union/political societies of various workers) – which acted as precursors to the modern labour movement.

The parallels with Russia rather than England were certainly more resonant in the minds of the Internationalists when they pondered political strategy. Italian Internationalism was forged during the aftermath of a national liberation struggle within an agrarian society where the concept of 'Italy' was restricted to a small number of intellectuals, urban middle class, and artisans. Social radicalism in the early years of modern Italy was founded not so much upon industrial disputes, even if the first wave of strikes occurred in the early 1870s, as upon a conflict between civil society and the centralizing state.

Indeed, when 'Italy' arrived in the southern countryside, not only was it distrusted, it was physically resisted. During the 1860s the south was bloodied by a ferocious civil war, far more costly than the Risorgimento itself, in which a hostile peasantry opposed what they felt was a foreign, colonizing state. It degraded their religion, forced them to pay heavier taxes, and drafted their sons into a distant army. These 'social bandits' sided with the deposed Bourbons and clergy. Yet if their revolt might be termed 'pre-political' or reactionary, it was part of a broader pattern of discontent which characterized the 1860s. Turin rioted in 1864, when the capital was temporarily transferred to Florence, and in 1866 Palermo was briefly occupied by insurgents. More nationally based social protest occurred in 1869 when a wave of insurrectionary rioting swept the peninsula. It was sparked off by the introduction of a grist-mill tax in order to pay off debts incurred during the wars of national liberation. A few years later, in 1872 and 1873, strikes broke out in Milan, Turin, Florence, and Bologna, accompanied by agitations among sharecroppers and landless labourers in the Po Valley. For many foreign and domestic observers the Italian state appeared on the brink of collapse. And it was within this context that the International grew.

The leadership of the Italian section of the International imagined their revolution as a 'social risorgimento'. With the 1860s in mind the Internationalists believed that the Italian state was gravely weak and could be easily overturned through an armed insurrection. Demonstrative guerrilla action in the countryside, what Errico Malatesta termed propaganda by deed, would convert pre-political revolt into conscious socialist uprising. Pisacane's earlier plans of combining patriotic appeals with a comprehensive agrarian reform based upon a federal political structure were, however, equally unsuccessful when the Internationalists attempted to put an anarcho-communist version into practice. Both a planned national revolt of Internationalists and disgruntled Mazzinians in 1874 and a guerrilla *foco* action in the Matese mountains south of Naples in 1877 ended in disaster. The Internationalists, like Pisacane, confronted bemused or frightened peasants, and these attempts allowed the government to destroy the International. After a mysterious series of bomb explosions and an attempt upon the life of the King by a deranged cook, the International was outlawed in 1879.

The historical verdict passed upon the Internationalist uprisings is usually extremely negative. These incautious attempts, it is argued, undermined the development of a mass-based organization of (libertarian) socialists. Certainly, it must be admitted that in the late 1870s many members of the *fasci operai* were thoroughly alienated from the International's leadership, but none the less historians have been too dismissive of the Internationalist strategy. The recent Risorgimento had been based upon such tactics. Indeed, the middle-class jurors who acquitted the Internationalists after their arrests following 1874 and 1877 must have drawn these parallels. Furthermore, the educated middle-class Internationalists who featured so prominently in these trials, these Italian *narodniki*, were in fact culturally and socially not very dissimilar from those in the state who actively pursued their arrests. Nicotera and Crispi, the anarchists' most zealous prosecutors, were in fact old Mazzinians themselves, who earlier had made their peace with the more moderate Cavour. The young Italian state owed its existence and a good deal of its legitimacy not so much to the great-power negotiations of the Kingdom of Piedmont but rather to the unofficial action of middle-class and artisan armed volunteers. If the anarchist uprisings make more sense with these recent historical events in mind, nor should such a strategy seem entirely illogical to twentieth-century observers. Marxist revolutionaries from Mao to Castro might well have applauded the tactics if not the ideology of the Internationalists.[2]

1880–1914

After the destruction of the International, the Italian anarchist movement failed to create a long-lasting national organization until immediately before the First World War. The government always struck harder at anarchists than it did at the emergent parliamentarian socialists. Anarchism and 'anarchoid' behaviour were identified in criminal terms, quite outside the protection of constitutional guarantees. The anarchists were classified as either terrorists or insurrectionists, and during periods of social unrest they served as scapegoats. After the blanket repression of the late 1870s, the movement once again felt the blows of the state in the middle 1880s during the first massive strike waves of the Po Valley *braccianti* (landless labourers). Later, in the 1890s, as Italian society experienced a grave socio-political crisis caused by an agricultural depression, the collapse of a building boom, financial scandals, and a disastrous war in Abyssinia, the anarchist movement was nearly completely destroyed by the Prime Ministers Crispi and General Pelloux.

While the socialist and republican left was under considerable threat throughout this decade, the anarchists were particularly hard hit due to a series of internal factors within their own movement which I will turn to shortly. However, until the setbacks of the 1890s the anarchists had succeeded in influencing the major labour and socialist political parties which preceded the foundation in 1892 of the modern Partito Socialista Italiano (PSI). In the 1880s and early 1890s the anarchists maintained rather important pressure within the northern Partito Operaio (POI) of 1882–1900, the successor to the *fasci operai* of the 1870s. The POI was largely influenced by an anti-intellectual moderate municipal socialism, yet anarchists, even anarchist intellectuals, such as the then young law student Luigi Galleani, in Vercelli and Turin, and other worker anarchists in Milan, organized modest trade unions of rice weeders, bakers, builders, and factory workers associated with the

POI. In the south, the Fasci Siciliani in the late 1880s and early 1890s were influenced by anarchists at the leadership and cadre levels. This popular Sicilian movement for fairer taxes, land for the poor, free trade unions, and an open and equitable legal system programmatically may well have been an Italian version of Chartism rather than anarchism, yet its basic temper and republican leanings made it a suitable candidate for Internationalist veterans such as Malatesta and Saverio Merlino to approach. Indeed, anarchist exiles, and militants at home, attempted to link the Partito Operaio to the Fasci Siciliani. And when the Fasci Siciliani were suppressed by the military in early 1894, the anarchist quarrymen of Carrara mounted a brief armed rebellion in sympathy.

The anarchists under Malatesta attempted to form a new national party in the late 1880s and early 1890s, but a clandestine meeting in the small Swiss border town of Capolago in 1891 failed to find a solution. However, anarchists were present at the first few congresses of the Socialist Party. In alliance with members of the POI they advocated an anti-parliamentary labour strategy. But the great victories abroad of the legalist and parliamentary German SPD and the widening of the local Italian franchise galvanized support for the socialists' strategy. If an anarchist-type culture of direct action was never discredited in Italy before 1926, neither was voting slighted once increasing numbers of male workers and peasants became enfranchised (see Table 1.1).

Table 1.1   Percentage of total population eligible to vote[3]

1861	1.7
1900	6.9
1913	23.2

The lure of elections, however, was not the only factor undermining the anarchists' revival in the 1890s. As repression mounted after 1894, the anti-organizational and terrorist currents within the movement undermined Malatestan organizational efforts to rebuild internal structures and attempts to create broad non-sectarian united fronts. The 1890s has been characterized as the era of *attentats*, and Italians took a particularly prominent role in English, French, and Spanish terrorist circles. Sante Caserio killed Sadi Carnot, President of France, in 1894; Michele Angiolillo shot Canovas, Prime Minister of Spain, in 1897; Luigi Luccheni, in what was perhaps the most senseless assassination, stabbed to death the innocuous Empress Elizabeth of Austria in

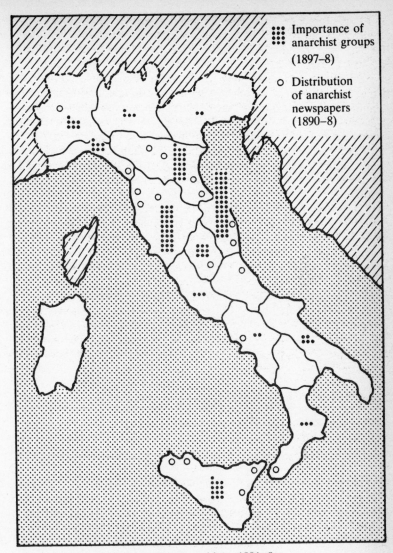

Map 1.2 Geography of Italian anarchism, 1891–8
Source: Enzo Santarelli, 'L'Anarchisme en Italie', *Le Mouvement social*, 83 (1973)

1898; Caetano Bresci executed King Umberto in 1900. An International Anti-Anarchist Conference, sponsored by the Italian government and held in Rome in 1898, accomplished little, but indicated how concerned the Italian authorities were.

It should be borne in mind that some of the Italian assassins received a good deal of sympathy from their compatriots. Sante Caserio's guillotining was subject to a series of popular songs. Angiolillo's crime was justified by pointing to the repression and torture that Canovas and the Spanish government had employed against Spanish comrades. But of all the political assassinations, that of Bresci, the anarchist emigrant from Prato who was sent by the Paterson (New Jersey) colony of anarchist textile workers, received the greatest sympathy. Umberto had awarded General Bava-Beccaris a medal for his efforts at suppressing Milanese protest against the high price of bread in May 1898. His methods had been to use cannon against unarmed men and women, which resulted in several hundred deaths. Even Cesare Lombroso, the anarchist 'cranium-measurer', wrote that, unlike other anarchist attempts during the 1890s, Bresci's was neither the result of degenerate personality nor that of uncontrollable passion but, lamentably, the sad outgrowth of Italian politics.

The anarchists were at the heart of the crisis of the 1890s. Much of the repressive legislation aimed at the anarchists and the left generally arose from failed and successful assassinations. After the suppression of the Fasci Siciliani and the anarchists of Carrara, an anarchist carpenter, Paolo Lega, took a shot at Crispi in June 1894. Three months earlier a tremendous bomb explosion in Rome near the Italian Parliament killed two passers-by. On 1 July, 1894 a Livornese journalist, advocate of a strong state and enemy of the local anarchists, was stabbed to death. The following month Crispi promulgated his anti-anarchist laws, and the penal islands were soon filled with anarchists and socialists.

Anarchists, however, also rallied liberal and socialist opinion against the authoritarian excesses of Crispi. Several anarchists died mysteriously in prison, and others were clearly framed or egged on by *provocateurs*. The resulting scandals discredited Crispi even before his war in Abyssinia went disastrously wrong. But the mysterious deaths of incarcerated anarchists were not limited to the 1890s. Since capital punishment had been abolished except for treason, Bresci was given a life sentence. He only survived several short years in a strict regime until he committed suicide under unclear circumstances.

Although by the turn of the century the exiled Italian anarchists, like the Palestinians of our own day, became synonymous with

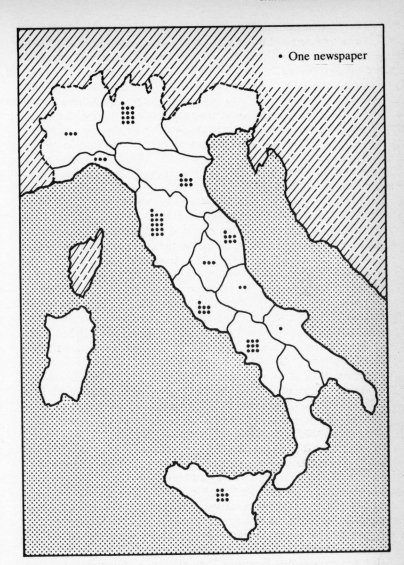

Map 1.3 Distribution of the anarchist press in Italy, 1900–14
Source: Enzo Santarelli, 'L'Anarchisme en Italie', *Le Mouvement social*, 83 (1973)

terrorism, nevertheless, the new century witnessed a decline in terrorism. After 1900 the Piedmontese statesman, Giovanni Giolitti, initiated a more moderate line towards working-class self-organization. Even if more civil libertarian than his predecessors, this characterization can only be used with the greatest of care. Political repression generally spared the more moderate socialists, but the socialist intransigents, the syndicalists, and the anarchists were arrested under a variety of press laws and others restricting freedom of expression and punishing public denigration of the monarchy and police. Giolitti tried to prevent anarchist or syndicalist leaders from emerging in the young labour organizations. While he was perfectly prepared to support moderate-led strikes and occasionally even pressurized employers to settle, he ordered the arrest of anarchist and syndicalist leaders regularly.

While the anarchist movement failed to maintain continuous national organization after the disappearance of the International (national congresses were held in 1891, 1907, and 1915), certain areas became strongholds, where the anarchists through oral traditions and local organizational strength survived periods of repression; and these served as focal points during revivals. Anarchist leaders originated and carried out most of their politics in central Italy. Until fascism Tuscany, the Marches, Umbria, and Rome provided the core of the movement. The repression in the 1890s, and the division of the anarchist movement into mutually distrustful factions of organizationalists and anti-organizationalists, appeared to endanger the anarchists with political extinction. In fact, the anarchists modernized their appeal by partially adapting syndicalist arguments. Through their control of important power bases located in central Italy's Chambers of Labour – Rome, for example, had an anarchist secretariat for most of the Giolittian era – the anarchists were assured of organizational protection.

From these strongholds the anarchists or anarchist-led and -inspired social movements were capable of startling revivals. During the unsettled period opened by the Libyan War (1911) and closed temporarily by Italy's entry into the First World War (1915), and later during the *biennio rosso* (1919–20), this long-standing popularity and organizational presence in Massa-Carrara, Ancona, Leghorn, Piombino, Rome, and the Genoese hinterland acted as a springboard for national revivals. However, as a movement of recognized or dues-paying members, anarchism was modest in size. At its peak of pre-war activity, on the eve of the Red Week of June 1914, the anarchists numbered no more than 8,000, and in 1919–20 the most generous estimate would place membership between 20,000 and 30,000, perhaps in absolute terms surpassing the International. Revivals were, of course, constantly undermined by factional disputes pitting Malatestan anarchist communists, advocating non-sectarian labour organizing, against anti-organizational anarchist communists, who detested the Malatestan insistence upon a separate national anarchist organization; these against anarchists with syndicalist leanings; and all factions against Stirnerite individualists preaching an elitist decadence. It should be stressed, however, that at the grass roots some anarchist militants happily practised eclecticism. One noted railway organizer retained his individualism without being too concerned.[4]

To sum up, by 1914 a pattern of anarchist life had been established, remaining the norm until the fascist squads destroyed the movement's institutional integrity. Local anarchist influence was translated into control of a Chamber of Labour and the appearance of a labour-oriented weekly newspaper. The anarchists supplied cadres and leaders to CGL trade unions and led the railway workers' union (SFI), as they balanced mutually hostile factions of syndicalists and socialists, and their greatest cumulative influence within the fissiparous Italian labour movement was achieved through syndicalism. Gradually its non-anarchist leadership abandoned control of this complex movement; and after the foundation of the Unione Sindacale in 1912 and the defection of its pro-war leadership three years later, the anarchists finally gained control of a workers' organization capable of exercising a significant, if erratic, influence over hundreds of thousands of workers. Nevertheless, if we compare the socialists and the CGL to the anarchists and syndicalists, it has to be conceded that the libertarians remained a junior partner. Anarchism's importance, however, outweighs the sum of its organizational parts.

Anarchist history is harder to follow after 1880 because of the discontinuities of leadership and organization. With the rise of the PSI and its associated trade union federation, the Confederazione Generale del Lavoro (CGL, founded in 1906), after 1900 the history of libertarian socialism breaks down into a study of its influence on other institutions such as the PSI, the CGL, the syndicalist Chambers of Labour, and the Unione Sindacale; studies of regional social history in areas where anarchists maintained continuous physical presence; and the individual biographies of the more prominent national leaders whose reputations transcended anarchism's boundaries.

Leaders, 1870–1914

Middle-class intellectuals played an important – if not decisive – role in the history of Italian socialism. The anarchists were no exception.

Intellectuals involved in the International consciously adopted the heritage of the Risorgimento, especially the conception of a vanguard sparking off national revolt. Errico Malatesta, Carlo Cafiero, and Andrea Costa were trained for professional careers but were drawn into political agitation by the early 1870s. Malatesta came from a landed southern middle-class family and was studying medicine at the University of Naples when he joined the International. Cafiero originated from the Apulian nobility. He gave up a career as a diplomat, sacrificing his family fortune and his sanity for the revolutionary cause. Costa was a product of the Romagnole petty bourgeoisie. He studied law at the University of Bologna and was deeply influenced by the romantic nationalist poet Carducci.

All three young revolutionaries were convinced positivists. Their unusual interpretation of Spencer's and Comte's sociology heightened their distrust of parliamentary politics and statist intervention. They believed that society could be likened to a living organism, where natural growth had been stunted through the combined constraints of private property and the state. In a revolutionary society daily life would be arranged through a free federation of functional organizations. While the Italians were some of Bakunin's closest collaborators, after his death they quickly repudiated his collectivism, believing that only anarchist communism avoided the growth of competition, greed, and inequality.

Carlo Cafiero (1846–92)

Carlo Cafiero was the first Italian popularizer of Marxism. During a visit to London in 1871 Cafiero met Marx and for a brief period was his chief agent in Italy. And even when Cafiero bitterly broke with the Marxists he preserved a strong admiration for Marxian political economy and sociology, interpreting them in terms of positivist and rationalist criteria. In the 1870s Cafiero wrote an Italian compendium of *Capital* which, until after the First World War, remained the standard text for workers and intellectuals alike. And Cafiero's 'positivist Marx' was underlined by the anarchist poet, Pietro Gori's, successive translation of the *Communist Manifesto*.

Cafiero's vulgarization, which Marx praised, was assisted by another anarchist intellectual, Emilio Covelli (1846–1915). He had graduated from the University of Naples and continued his studies in philosophy at the universities of Heidelberg and Berlin. In Berlin he became a student of Dühring and translated his *Critical History of Political Economy and Socialism*, which was the first book in Italy to deal with Marx's *Capital*. Dühring's estimation of Marx's master-work, although severely criticized by Engels, meshed with the positivism of the Italians. Dühring had approved of *Capital*'s main thesis inasmuch as it purported to lay bare the laws of economic movement in capitalist society. His criticism was focused on its Hegelian framework, which diminished, in his judgement, its basically positivist content.

All theoretical niceties aside, Covelli and Cafiero were far from Marx's politics. Covelli had drawn one conclusion from the criminalization of the International. Revolutions were made by criminals or *spostati* (misfits), a term which had originally been associated with the young middle-class activists who had sacrificed their creature comforts for the cause, but was now reinterpreted in a sinister manner. Covelli's response to the government's decision to prosecute the Internationalists using legislation originally designed to suppress the Mafia was to formulate an anarchist terrorist programme, aptly termed by the historian Pier Carlo Masini *illegalismo programmatico*.

From the 1880s until the turn of the century this wreaked havoc in the anarchist movement and was one of the chief reasons why the anarchists lost control of the socialist movement to the PSI. Covelli's *spostati* were idolized by Cafiero, who wrote a rambling theoretical work justifying this revolutionary vanguard of terrorists. Since society defined revolution as criminal, revolutionaries were justified in behaving in an asocial manner.

But other anarchist positivists, notably the poet and criminologist Gori, explained criminality in terms of environmental factors, stressing that the anarchist revolution would eliminate crime by destroying the cruelties of capitalism and the hierarchical society which accompanied it. In this way Gori served as a bridge between the first generation of anarchist positivist intellectuals and the following generation of moderate socialist positivists. It is singularly odd that Cesare Lombroso, who was busy measuring the skulls of Torinese *spostati* during the early 1890s, employed theoretical arguments which Gori not only endorsed but gladly publicized.

Andrea Costa (1851–1910)

Andrea Costa became disenchanted with anarchism in the aftermath of the disastrous attempts at insurrection by the International. It was, in fact, Costa's peculiar transition from revolutionary anarchism to legalistic socialism which can be considered his rather dubious legacy to the pre-fascist socialist movement.

After his desertion from pure anarchism Costa came under the influence of Benoît Malon, who had after Marx and Bakunin the greatest impact on Italian socialism in its formative years. A refugee from the Commune, Malon spent several years in Italy, and his socialism, critical of Marx's centralism but wary of Bakunin's obsession with insurrection, served as a stepping stone for Italian 'revisionist' socialists.

In the spring of 1880 Costa met another disenchanted anarchist – Paul Brousse – while in Paris and announced his change of heart. Costa identified with a wide spectrum of ex-Internationalists, Russian Populists, and early revisionist Marxists who were trying to reconcile collectivism with communism, parliamentary reform with revolution. Stressing decentralization, they pressed for more communal power. Costa applied this strategy to Italy. And in the next forty years communalism was used by revolutionary and moderate socialists alike. By the 1880s the franchise had been extended far enough so that in certain areas socialists could capture local government. Reformist socialists used this communalism in a Fabian sense and gained power in the Po Valley's governments. On the other hand, syndicalists before the First World War, and maximalist socialists in its aftermath, interpreted it in a revolutionary sense. The control of local government was the first step towards socialist power. In both interpretations communalism reflected a diffuse anti-statism which affected many strands of the Italian left.

Costa's other tactical invention plagued the PSI for forty years. In the 1880s he devised the idea of maximum and minimum programmes for his local socialist party. Costa's maximum programme was full anarchist communism; his minimum programme of reformist collectivism was especially geared to the peculiar problems of the Po Valley. And even if Costa became more reformist as time passed, the psychology of maximalist socialism, its attempts at reconciling reformist parliamentarian policies with revolutionary rhetoric, can be traced back to the former anarchist.

Errico Malatesta (1853–1932)

By the end of the 1870s only Errico Malatesta remained devoted to anarchism. Malatesta was the leader of the Italian anarchist movement during its most important years. While other leaders of the International changed their opinions or abandoned politics altogether, Malatesta remained firm to his original convictions for a half-century. He did so by modifying his optimistic approach, substituting one of the more sophisticated versions of anarchism.

From the 1880s until the world war, Malatesta was perpetually in exile. His appearances in Italy were of short duration, but this did not diminish his impact on the Italian anarchist movement. Malatesta, even with the desertions, deaths, and madness of comrades continued in his Mazzini-like role, attracting into his circle every new generation which entered the anarchist movement. In this sense his connection with three generations of anarchists, as Enzo Santarelli notes, made the history of Italian anarchism largely coincidental with his own political biography.[5]

Between the 1880s and the turn of the century Malatesta developed a two-pronged strategy. On the one hand, he sought to unify the anarchist and anti-parliamentarian socialists into a new anarchist socialist party. With the lack of a national socialist party before the 1890s, Malatesta and his followers hoped to galvanize the elements of regional socialist groups (the Fasci Siciliani, the Revolutionary Socialist Party of Romagna, and the Partito Operaio) into a new anti-parliamentary socialist party.

By the 1890s, however, Malatesta realized that anarchism was a minority movement within the Italian left. Anarchists for Malatesta had to prod the socialists into insurrection and remain a revolutionary conscience afterwards during socialist reconstruction. Malatesta defined this type of anarchist communism as 'anarchism without adjectives'. It was a concept which he had developed with a group of Spanish anarchist intellectuals in the process of mediating between mutually hostile collectivists and communists. Stressing tolerance within the libertarian movement, Malatesta hoped that Marxist socialists would permit the anarchists liberty for their own movement in post-revolutionary society. When Malatesta returned to Italy, briefly in 1897 and 1913 and permanently in 1919, he strove to create revolutionary united fronts which embodied these themes.

Malatesta, on the other hand, was one of the first anarchists to stress a syndicalist strategy. Although the Neapolitan anarchists were actively organizing in the 1870s, and Malatesta led a similar drive in Florence in the middle 1880s, neither of these attempts revealed a particular sensitivity for the specific problems of the daily labour movement. Labour organizations were used more generally as recruiting agencies for the political anarchist movement.

When Malatesta emigrated to Argentina in the late 1880s and involved himself in founding its labour movement, and later when he lived in London during the 1890s and experienced the mass mobilization of the New Unionism, his more sophisticated view on the role of trade unions took shape.

The 1890s were a turning-point. From London, Malatesta and his followers proclaimed their strenuous opposition to terrorism and anti-organizational theories. And by the late 1890s Malatesta transferred the example of the New Unionism to Italy. He introduced the concepts of cacanny, the boycott, the sympathy strike, and the general trades union in the simple language of his workers' newspaper, published in Ancona (1897–8).

But in the twentieth century, when the international syndicalist movement threatened to denature anarchism, and in Italy syndicalism actually became a faction of the PSI, Malatesta struggled to keep the anarchist movement autonomous. He believed in trade-union unity, but felt that syndicalism divided rather than united the workers. Syndicalism was a tactic whereby anarchism could remain a serious alternative for workers; Malatesta did not believe that it was an end in itself.

It should also be recalled that Malatesta never neglected the countryside. His most popular pamphlet was a dialogue between two peasants entitled *Fra contadini*, translated into eleven languages, first published in 1884. Here, Malatesta, the anarcho-communist, does not press for unconditional socialization of their land, realizing that Italian sharecroppers and peasants would have to be won over via voluntary co-operative projects. It was in fact a message he repeated in vain to fellow anarchists as well as syndicalists and socialists in the years immediately before the March on Rome in 1922, since fascism would find a good deal of popularity amongst these very groups when they felt threatened by calls from the left for the socialization of the land.

During the 1880s and 1890s, Malatesta and his collaborator F. S. Merlino (1856–1930) began to revise the theoretical bases of anarchism. On the one hand, anti-organizationalism bred from the optimistic and scientistic socialism of Kropotkin had led anarchists into an uncritical praise of spontaneity. On the other, Malatesta and Merlino realized that their own doctrines had been too immersed in the sociology of Marx. Merlino, Italian anarchism's greatest theoretician, intended to show, through his pioneering studies of the modern Italian state, that bureaucracy and the state could have an independent effect on the economic structure of society.

Merlino was a revisionist socialist *ante litteram*. And during his exile in London (1884–94) he developed the chief points which Bernstein would popularize at the turn of the century. Both Merlino and Malatesta wanted anarchists to involve themselves in the workaday world of the labour movement, pushing for reforms which they felt would maintain the morale of the working classes. By winning gains through direct action they felt the fascination for state socialism and parliamentarianism would be weakened.

Merlino eventually abandoned a strict anarchist position, but he amplified revisionist socialism in the process. Back in Italy his theoretical journal, *Rivista critica del socialismo*, acted as a major international conduit for the revisionist debate at the turn of the century. His importance was perhaps greater for the development of Sorel's and Bernstein's socialisms than for Italy where the debate was muddled at best. Curiously enough, Malatesta and Merlino helped lay the groundwork for the French syndicalist movement. Malatesta converted Pouget to syndicalism, and influenced Pelloutier's libertarian socialism. Merlino converted Sorel from an orthodox Marxism to a position approaching syndicalism. And later Merlino and Malatesta laid the seeds for the growth of Italian syndicalism.

During the first decade of the twentieth century Malatesta's closest intellectual collaborators were Pietro Gori (1865–1911) and Luigi Fabbri (1877–1935). Gori, criminologist, positivist and star defence lawyer for the anarchist movement, can be defined as anarchism's cultural organizer. He composed some of the most popular songs of the Italian labour movement, and his poetry became a popular form of propaganda. Although he was a libertarian, his positivist determinism made him the anarchist equivalent to the purveyors of Second Internationalist scientific socialism.

Luigi Fabbri, a younger man, born in the first generation after the Risorgimento, became the unofficial ideologist of Malatestan anarchism. Both Gori and Fabbri kept anarchism intellectually alive. Fabbri, too, was a cultural organizer. His work in the Ferrer School, as well as in the anti-clerical and birth control movements, widened anarchist influences outside the confines of the labour movement; and he had close contacts with small groups of women anarchists who stressed neo-Malthusianism and anti-militarism.

This network of anarchist intellectuals gave the movement an international orientation, but also preserved its influence within

Italian culture. Malatesta's popularity on his return in 1913 and 1919 was not a freak occurrence. His fame had been nurtured through a network of cultural organizers, instrumental in the formation of a generation of socialist and libertarian self-educated workers. And another, more obscure, network connected regional and local anarchist movements to the exiled leader. In this case a small group of artisans and skilled workers from the Marches, Tuscany, and Rome provided a direct link with the anarchist rank and file and the wider labour movement. These 'cadres' of the anarchist party performed long years of organizational work in Italy; they kept the local anarchist newspapers running, and represented the anarchist point of view in trade unions and Chambers of Labour. They were not theoreticians, but activists. Most had experienced exile and the penal islands, but unlike Malatesta had spent most of their lives in Italy.

Malatesta remained connected to both intellectual and working-class anarchists. He was one of the very few middle-class Italian socialists who consciously 'declassed' himself and remained a skilled worker for the rest of his life. Trained as a gas fitter and electrician, he plied his trade until nearly 80 years of age. Togliatti noted in his obituary of Malatesta that the anarchist had remained a popular figure because he reflected the aspirations and the life-styles of artisanal Italy.[6] But he also modernized his anarchism, remaining a symbol of Italian socialism in industrial areas during the *biennio rosso*.

The 'warrior anarchist': Amilcare Cipriani (1844–1918)

Although Amilcare Cipriani was closely associated with the anarchists from the late 1870s to 1900, his politics defy exact definition. However, through his spectacular deeds he personified the anti-dynastic 'subversive' during the last decades of the nineteenth century.

A Romagnole of relatively well-off commercial origins, he fought with Garibaldi's volunteers at Aspromonte. Later he participated in a failed Greek republican revolution and then fought in the 1866 war. He was made a colonel during the Paris Commune and was transported to New Caledonia, where he lived until amnestied in 1880. From 1880 to 1882 he helped Malatesta, Cafiero, and other Internationalists re-establish the International in Italy. He was arrested by the Italians in 1882 and given a 25-year prison sentence under extremely harsh conditions for the murder of three men during a late-night banquet in the Italian colony in Alexandria in 1867. The circumstances surrounding the incident are far from clear, and the fact that he was tried in Italy fifteen years later and given virtual solitary confinement made him an object of the protests of radical liberals, socialists, republicans, and anarchists. Indeed, he was elected as a deputy to Parliament at Ravenna and Forlì in 1886, two years before his release from prison.

In the early 1890s Cipriani helped the anarchists organize a national presence and served another one-year prison sentence after his arrest at Rome's May Day riots of 1891. He seemed to be particularly intimate with the leaders of the Fasci Siciliani. Internationally he represented the Italian anarchists at several congresses of the Second International. From the turn of the century he lived in Paris, where he died in poverty in 1918.

While Cipriani's life may have been a godsend for journalists, his pronouncements and his ties with certain French republicans did not endear him to the leading anarchists. Malatesta always thought of him as muddle-headed and impulsive. His advocacy of a Union of Latin Peoples and his pronounced anti-German sentiments may have jarred on Malatesta, but these, and his leadership of an international brigade in support of Cretan insurgents against their Turkish overlords in 1897, were congenial to much of Italian 'subversive' political culture. Cipriani foreshadowed the rhetoric and actions of those left-wing interventionists who would split the 'subversives' in 1914–15. And it is not surprising that one of Cipriani's strongholds, Forlì, was the birthplace of another 'subversive', Benito Mussolini. (See the note on *sovversivo* or 'subversive' on pp. 75–6.)

The exile network

Although Malatesta was the leader of Italian anarchism for most of its important years, for most of his adult life he lived abroad. He was not alone.

The history of Italian anarchism in exile has yet to be written. From the First International to the downfall of fascism, exile was a constant and important episode in the history of the movement. Exile shaped the lives of three generations of leaders and followers; it circulated new ideas and forms of labour organization back home; it allowed Italians to play a major role in the formation of other national socialist and labour movements. Between the fall of the Paris Commune and the outbreak of the First World War, an international community of socialist, anarchist, and syndicalist exiles played a crucial role in the formulation of these ideologies and in their propagation in Europe and beyond.

The Italian anarchist movement was particularly internationalist in outlook due to the fact that it was constantly being forced into exile. This tradition was almost as old as the movement itself, and it was the heir to the longer history of exile during the Risorgimento. Mazzini and Garibaldi need only be mentioned to make the point.

The suppression of the International in the 1870s began the first mass exile of anarchists. They established small communities in the Balkans and the Levant, in France, Switzerland, Spain, and London. Many travelled to the western hemisphere, where notable communities arose in Latin America, particularly in Argentina but also in Peru and Brazil. In the United States anarchist influence existed in the midst of the large centres of immigration, among the miners of Illinois and Pennsylvania, the textile workers of Paterson, New Jersey, and Lawrence, Massachusetts, and in the great cities: New York, Boston, Philadelphia, Chicago, and San Francisco. The anarchists defended immigrants from exploitation by unscrupulous members of their own communities, from political bosses and the sweating system. Later, many Italians were active in the formation and development of the IWW; and in South America, Italian anarchist communists and syndicalists virtually started the labour movements of Argentina, Brazil, and Peru single-handedly. In France and Switzerland the Italians worked through local anarchist movements or started Italian language groups. Even in the Balkans the Italians appeared as the first advocates of anarchism.

While the anarchist movement rapidly assumed international dimensions, the Italian exiles always kept Italian problems foremost in their minds. But exile extended their horizons and created hidden organizational and financial mobilization networks, which explains to a great extent why the movement could suddenly snap back to life in Italy after years of torpidity.

Equally, however, it was the political opportunity structures and the social space ceded to them by the Partito Socialista Italiano and the labour movement which permitted exile mobilization networks to find an available constituency.

The Socialist Party, labour organizations, and the anarchists, 1900–14

By 1914 anti-statism had become overwhelmed by an electorally oriented socialist party. The anarchists remained a weaker party; paradoxically, however, their values retained notable support at the grass roots. Anarchism's symbols and language dominated

Italian socialist culture. Unfortunately the dearth, until recently, of serious studies concerning Italian socialism as popular culture has obscured this fact. While this is a problem of great interest in itself, I can only present the reader with a broad outline of a popular socialism which can best be defined as 'the second socialist culture'. By this I mean a network of institutions bound together by sentiments of localism, anti-statism, and *operaismo* (workerism). It collided repeatedly with the Italian state, and during serious crises even with the more centralized institutions of the labour and socialist movements themselves. However, this 'second socialist culture' should not be romanticized; individuals flitted in and out of it, and reformists were not alien to its customs and cadences. I will now examine the peculiarities of the major institutions of Italian socialism in reference to this admittedly unstable 'second socialist culture', in order to indicate the cultural and social milieu of the anarchists, the context in which their message and modes of political behaviour prospered.

The Socialist Party

The PSI was a predominantly northern party, attracting urban workers, artisans, and landless labourers but failing to organize the southern peasantry. It had a rather low membership (approximately 30,000 to 50,000 before 1914) and was greatly dependent upon middle-class activists and parliamentary deputies from the professional classes to keep functioning. Since voting was restricted until 1913, the PSI relied upon a middle-class electorate to win seats in Parliament (29 in 1903, 52 in 1913). The party became a symbol for the growing socialist movement, but it never eradicated the libertarian influence at the grass roots.

Certainly the overwhelmingly important Socialist Parliamentary Group (GPS), which for all intents and purposes became a party within a party, was not capable of representing the disenfranchised. Socialist deputies exhibited the same prejudices against mass democracy as other educated middle-class Italian men of their era. In his definitive history of the party, Gaetano Arfé has described this political philosophy as more liberal than democratic, more an expression of the patriotic legacy of the Risorgimento, one which assumed the natural ascendancy of a reformist elite in order to make the Italian nation, than of immediate and full democratic participation by all Italian adults in their political affairs.[7] The GPS was therefore infused with a Fabian-like parliamentary reformism and decidedly suspicious of all extra-parliamentary affairs.

On the other hand, the left wing's power was permanently restricted by its inability to displace the GPS. While reformists were continually elected to Parliament under a system of restricted suffrage, the left could only mount ineffectual campaigns against their influence in the party. In any case, the left's leadership was socially a mirror image of its reformist adversaries. Both Arturo Labriola's syndicalists and Enrico Ferri's intransigents were led and organized by professors. And even Mussolini's revolutionaries were decidedly overweighted with lower-middle-class journalists and school teachers. Manual-working-class and trade-unionist voices were rarely heard at party congresses and even less so in Parliament. If professionals dominated in Parliament, revolutionary journalists, through their occasional control of *L'avanti!*, the PSI's national organ, could bypass the reformists. Under the editorship of Ferri, and more openly Mussolini, syndicalists, anarchists, and other generic 'subversives' were encouraged to present their case to the socialist rank and file. Moreover, reformists never developed a highly organized party bureaucracy or network of nationally organized cultural institutions. The PSI never came close to equalling the German SPD, with its party school and extensive Marxist press; while the Italian socialist youth movement, which supplied an increasingly large percentage of all socialists, openly flirted with anarchists and syndicalists. In sum, one can say that before 1914 the PSI relied upon libertarian symbols and literature to educate its youth. Small wonder that the anarchists and syndicalists continued to receive a fair hearing in many party circles up to and beyond 1914.

Trade unionism

While modern trade unionism only grew under the more benevolent conditions fostered by Giolitti's government, even so only a very small percentage of the working population – 10 per cent in 1914 – was unionized. Italian trade unionism lacked the decades of organizational life found in northern European labour movements. In fact, only in the last few years before the war did the trade-union federations based on the Second Internationalist model become a reliable barometer of worker discontent, or even a satisfactory channel through which to conduct strikes. The vertical national federations never matched the popularity of locally based Chambers of Labour nor the direct knowledge of conditions possessed by the internal commissions, the shop-floor factory committees. And in contrast to more established labour movements, unofficial strikes remained more common, with political aims intruding in response to an invariable 'proletarian massacre' (*strage proletaria*). If, therefore, the PSI did not follow the Second Internationalist model faithfully, nor did the broader labour movement compared with its British, German, or French counterparts. Since the trade unions were so weak, localistic institutions, such as the Chambers of Labour, mobilized broader support for objectives which were political in character. Anti-clericalism, anti-militarism, and republicanism generated greater support than simple economic strikes.

Certain peculiar factors therefore clearly made the Italian labour movement unusual. A low percentage of unionization was joined with factional and sectarian tensions arising between socialist, syndicalist, anarchist, republican, and Catholic trade unionists. Furthermore, the national federations faced the centrifugal force of regionally or even municipally based labour organizations. Federation membership fluctuated wildly. Even FIOM – the federation of metal workers – only achieved relative stability in 1913. Most workers, even a skilled industrial membership, could simply not afford a dues system required to maintain a modern trade-union bureaucracy.

The local ramifications of the labour movement remained the most popular and respected. Such institutions – the Chamber of Labour, the constituent peasant leagues of the Federterra (the socialist agricultural workers' union), the worker circles of the trade unions, and the factory internal commissions – tended to exercise political and economic roles. This lack of discrete economic and political institutions set Italy apart from the Second Internationalist model.

From the 1890s onwards, labour organizations posed economic and political demands. The structural constraints of Italian capitalism had much to do with this. Inflation and underemployment remained two major problems. And local labour organizations fought a bitter battle to be able to establish labour-hiring offices which would control the labour market and realize fuller employment for the working class. In the early twentieth century, and with greater insistence as time progressed, Chambers of Labour and factory internal commissions questioned the employer's absolute power in the workplace. And their representatives felt that they had the right to dispute the employer's new investment decisions and the introduction of new production techniques.

The constraints of Italian capitalism also further undermined the national federations. They were particularly exposed to the cyclical downturns of the economy and faced disastrous times when a period of economic adversity arrived. And in periods when inflation combined with unemployment, such as the economic crisis of 1911–13, the reformist programme of the national federations nearly collapsed. Then syndicalism and anarchism won widespread support amongst many different strata of the working population – including skilled metal workers.

The lack of economic security reduced the margins in which the CGL could operate. Its foremost leader, the former anarchist Rinaldo Rigola, envisaged an Italian version of British Labourism gradually supplanting the PSI. But as long as the CGL remained dependent on the national federations, which were still being established, there only remained the Federterra, which relied on the GPS and greeted Rigola's plans with hostility.

On the eve of the First World War the national labour movement and the PSI were unable to supplant the tradition of localism. The confluence of political and economic functions in grass-roots labour organization, and the failure of the PSI and the CGL to establish a lasting link, gave the syndicalist and anarchist movements, and a more diffuse libertarian tradition, a great deal of social space in which to prosper.

The Chambers of Labour

The Chambers of Labour (*camere del lavoro*) were the most important and accessible institutions affecting working-class daily life. The Chambers began as institutions promoting class reconciliation, being funded by major municipal governments in the 1890s to serve as labour exchanges. By the early twentieth century, however, following the pattern set by the French *bourses du travail*, they had become autonomous organizations. Their major tasks were to represent the working class on a territorial basis, to control the labour market, and to organize sympathy strikes and boycotts during provincial industrial disputes. Their importance was magnified since the pre-war national federations were weak and therefore could not, and were not inclined to, represent the myriad of occupations which were deemed to be outside their jurisdiction or considered unorganizable. The extreme heterogeneity of the Italian working class was partially overcome through the offices of the Chamber, and this institution was closely associated with *operaismo*. Indeed, it was the Partito Operaio which had originally transplanted the French *bourses du travail* to Italy, though the home-grown *fasci* had been an anticipation.

By supplying the local working class a sense of unity which joined together the skilled and unskilled, as well as the rural and urban workers, the Chambers gave the disenfranchised a sense of political involvement and a taste for self-management. And by being closely aligned to localism and extra-parliamentary politics, they were natural forums for anarchists and syndicalists.

The Chambers were not limited to economic or strictly political functions. They served equally as cultural centres: holding festivals, running educational programmes, and acting as neighbourhood meeting places. The political will of the Chamber was expressed in the recurrent public meeting – the *comizio* – held for many different reasons, from commemorations of past labour struggles, to protests against 'proletarian massacres', or as expressions of solidarity with the international labour movement.

At a *comizio* a certain ritual was followed. The assembled crowd would pass *ordini del giorno* (resolutions). These informal resolutions were treated as plebiscites by the local labour movement. They could decide whether a strike would continue or cease, and any study of popular unrest in Giolittian Italy always connects the spread or cessation of industrial conflict with the results of *ordini del giorno*.

The Chambers also sponsored, or gave shelter to, anti-clerical and anti-militarist movements. Anti-militarism was perhaps the most significant force through which the anarchist movement mobilized working-class support. Anti-clericalism was an almost equally important conduit of libertarian influence. In 1909 the execution of the Spanish anarchist educationist Francisco Ferrer by a conservative-clerical Spanish government led to the second largest pre-war protest movement. The anarchists directed this tremendous wave of protest, which mobilized northern industrialized workers, and rudely shattered the social compact which the moderate CGL had been nurturing with industrialists. But anti-clericalism also served as a unifying issue that joined together radical Freemasons, republicans, socialists, and libertarians. Indeed, one of the most popular pre-war socialist newspapers was Guido Podrecca's crude anti-clerical sheet *L'asino*, which reached the then tremendous circulation of 100,000 copies weekly.

Ferrer's educational theories also informed some of the Chambers' attempts at instituting workers' education. The Università Popolare, based in the Chambers, relied on Ferrer's rationalist-positivist Modern School, and anarchists remained a significant minority within them.

General strikes

Through the general strike the institutions of the second socialist culture revealed their hidden strength. Throughout the Giolittian era the general strike became an integral feature of national political life, recurring in staccato fashion from 1904 to 1914. Italy experienced general strikes in 1904, 1905, 1906, 1909, 1911, and 1914. A general strike would usually start with news of a fresh 'proletarian massacre' – perhaps the killings of southern peasants or northern striking workers – which would start things off. Then as local solidarity strikes spread, more killings would occur. For a day or so the CGL and the PSI would lose complete control of the situation. But the chain of seemingly spontaneous strikes would exhaust themselves, never achieving national co-ordination. At times the GPS would use the dramatic events to pressurize the government to restrict the police. And Socialist deputies might apply a policy of 'collective bargaining through riot', squeezing government funds out of Rome to support workers' co-operatives.

The actual spread of the rolling general strike has never been fully examined. I would argue, and I shall return to this point when I examine the unrest during the *biennio rosso*, that the second socialist culture acted as an unofficial grapevine. And in such situations even very small groups of individuals prepared to follow direct action could sway thousands of angry demonstrators. In such dramatic situations anarchists gained control of mass movements even if they were a mere handful.

The general strike, and the cycle of violence which accompanied it, became a regular occurrence in pre-fascist Italy. 'Proletarian massacres' and the ensuing arrests of strikers were the chief causes of general strikes. But other reasons caused their outbreak as well. The rising cost of living could mobilize a crowd rapidly. And here something of that 'moral economy of the crowd' which E. P. Thompson has identified for an earlier period of British history functioned well into twentieth-century Italy. In fact, the chief upheavals of post-Risorgimento Italy, from the *macinato* (gristmill) riots of 1869 to the violent confrontations which studded the late 1880s and 1890s, and on to the events of the Red Week and the *biennio rosso*, were either caused by *fiscalismo* (taxes on items of popular consumption) or the abrupt rise in bread prices. But the defence of political rights was intertwined with what were apparently bread riots. The conviction by the *popolo minuto* (common people) that their rights of assembly were endangered could start protest. Louise Tilly has shown how the agitations leading up to Milan's *fatti di maggio* (riots of May) in 1898 were in fact sparked off by the announcement that workers would no longer be permitted to demonstrate in their traditional meeting places.[8] In the twentieth century, when industrial disputes became regular occurrences, these older types of protest intermingled with the economic general strike. The general strike therefore was never a mere dropping of tools, but contained elements which occasionally exploded into local popular uprisings.

Syndicalism

On several occasions I have mentioned linkages between anarchism and syndicalism. But since it is an extremely complex and perhaps the most misunderstood aspect of the pre-war Italian labour movement, syndicalism deserves greater discussion. Until very recently Italian historians have ignored its wide-ranging effects on the pre-war socialist movement, and even today very little has been written on its connections with the emergence of the post-war factory council movement. There has been far too much emphasis on syndicalist intellectuals and national organizers, while the dynamics of individual local movements have been studied in isolation. The continuous re-emergence of syndicalist themes in the Italian labour movement has been overlooked because its leadership was notoriously inconsistent and lacked the staying power of more mainstream socialists. But syndicalism, and for that matter anarchism, relied little on its national leadership for its long-term vitality. My attempt at sketching the outlines of a second socialist culture has been motivated to show how libertarian values found a congenial home in the heart of the Italian socialist and labour movements, even if anarchist and syndicalist organizations remained weaker than their socialist counterparts.

Perhaps the best way to approach the complicated history of pre-war syndicalism is to begin by highlighting its anomalous origins. Unlike other syndicalist movements, the Italian variation coalesced inside a Second Internationalist party. Supporters were partially drawn from socialist intransigents fearful that the party would accept ministerial posts in Giolitti's cabinet. This anti-ministerialism was deepened by the example of France, where the socialists had entered into a Dreyfusard cabinet at the turn of the century and had apparently been overshadowed by their Radical partners. But the Italian anti-intransigents' anti-Giolittianism meshed nicely with the southern syndicalist intellectuals' pronounced republicanism; both expressed a fear that Giolitti, using the German model, would initiate a programme of Bismarckian statist reforms aimed at incorporating the northern proletariat into an undemocratic, monarchist-bureaucratic state. Another component of the emerging syndicalist movement, which lent it a popular base and its proletarian *élan*, was the remnants of the Partito Operaio.

Finally, syndicalism gathered supporters from the growing jurisdictional disputes between the Chambers of Labour and the emerging national craft unions. While the cameralists had a history stretching back through the *fasci*, the unionists had depended on the intervention of the PSI to help them get off the ground. Cameralism was deeply influenced by the libertarian tradition, and, as I have previously pointed out, Malatesta and Merlino had laid the foundations for an 'apolitical' socialism based on such institutions.

Syndicalism, probably because of these variegated roots, was even less capable than the mainstream socialists of providing consistent leadership. Its theoreticians were marginalized within the party before their official expulsion in 1908. The foundation of the CGL in 1906 had effectively caused their downfall. It had been created, at least in part, to give the newer craft federations like FIOM greater power to control the more localistic Chambers of Labour, but equally important was the desire to centralize labour movement leadership, preventing the grass roots from abusing the general strike weapon.

It was only with the defeat of syndicalism as a party faction that it appeared in the more conventional costume of pure direct action, shunning, for the most part, parliamentary strategies. Before, syndicalism had more in common with the verbally intransigent Kautskyite social democrats.

After 1906, a younger generation of labour organizers, in many ways socially different from their predecessors, became particularly active in the Po Valley. In those provinces where the more reformist Federterra was prevented from organizing due to employer resistance, syndicalist labour organizers gave the movement a new lease of life. If the first syndicalists had concentrated their efforts at winning the northern urban working class to their cause, their successors, in a series of spectacular agricultural general strikes (Parma, 1907; Ferrara, 1908), achieved an initial success in the countryside. They had gained a following amongst the rural workforce by embarking on a shrewd policy which combined militant opposition to employer anti-trade unionism with alliance building. Success was due to the ability to include the sharecroppers in wider struggles of the landless labourers. But with victory, the organizers threw caution to the winds and initiated a new cycle of demands that antagonized allies and enemies alike. The employers responded by creating anti-strike agrarian federations, while the sharecroppers, particularly the Catholic strata above the landless labourers, were frightened by syndicalism's new emphasis on the proletarianization of the entire rural working population.

Successive defeats in Parma and Ferrara, coupled with the new prestige the CGL gathered in these years, severely eroded syndicalist strength. The movement was riven by dissensions. And it failed to gain new adherents outside a rump of agricultural Chambers of Labour, which were more homogeneously composed of landless labourers.

With the failure of its labour organizing, many of syndicalism's chief advocates even plumped for entry into the CGL; others adopted positions as independent candidates for Parliament. And to confuse matters further, some syndicalist intellectuals, through their ties with Sorel and the elitist sociological school, helped to generate, or sympathetically endorsed, the new Nationalist movement which, while largely extraneous from working-class organizations, bore similarities to the populist and republican rhetoric of the southern syndicalist intellectuals. Nationalism transposed the techniques and tone of syndicalism from a concentration on the modern proletariat to one which praised the aggressive entrepreneur and the patriotic industrial worker. Productivist leanings linked the two movements. But Nationalism claimed that a 'proletarian Italy', i.e. a young European nation state, would only generate the necessary productive capital to fuel a new corporate society of entrepreneurs and disciplined workers through imperial conquest.

And, ironically, it was the Nationalists who endorsed and lent their publicizing talents to the movement for the formation of industrialist and agrarian associations which would tame the 'anti-productive' socialist and syndicalist trade unions. Along with the labour syndicalists they shared a distaste for the corrupting compromises of Giolittianism, and both set out to undermine the stability of the system.

The new employer federations, particularly after 1909, began to adopt a much more aggressive stance towards the moderate CGL. With the post-Libyan crisis, CGL policies which sought to work out a *modus vivendi* with northern industry went by the board. Earlier experiments at allowing greater factory democracy were toned down; now industrialists were forced to modernize production, so as to alleviate the pressures of a profit squeeze caused by war-generated inflation. Factory discipline became the order of the day. And Giolitti's even-handed approach, so thought the industrialists, had given socialist and syndicalist labour unions too much power, undermining their efforts.

In 1910–11 a series of bitter strikes in the company towns of Piombino and Terni heralded a cycle of massive industrial disputes in Milan and Turin during 1912 and 1913. The syndicalist labour organizers scored remarkable advances in industrial areas. But, as in the previous agrarian strikes, syndicalism's organizational strength remained short-lived. Massive support for the syndicalist Unione Sindacale was due more to a combination of CGL weakness, in front of the employers' offensive, and a meshing of 'second socialist culture' traditions with some of syndicalism's chief ideological planks than to a complete conversion.

The Unione Sindacale Italiana (USI) was founded in 1912 and brought together the older agricultural Chambers of Labour with a new stratum of industrial unionist organizers. By 1913, the USI already had a membership of 102,000, half the size of the CGL. But significantly, CGL numerical superiority depended on its control of the Federterra's huge membership. In industrial areas the contest was much closer, and in some places CGL workers went over *en masse* to the USI.

However, the USI remained an inherently unstable organization. Disputes between industrial unionists and cameralists repeated, in a fashion, the earlier struggle between craft federations and Chambers of Labour. The industrial unionists wanted greater centralization, whilst the cameralists envisaged the USI as little more than a confederation of syndicalist Chambers of Labour.

In the end this dispute was overwhelmed by other events. The Red Week left many syndicalist leaders disillusioned with direct action. Instead these syndicalists advocated a combined policy of direct action with a drive to win communal elections. Such a strategy, all nuances aside, was little different from the one which Po Valley socialists had been implementing for twenty years. Exactly what the syndicalists had in mind was never tested, since the war intervened.

From Red Week to interventionist crisis, 1914–15

The Red Week (*settimana rossa*) revealed the extent to which anarchists were still a significantly popular force in Italy. The rising in June 1914 exposed a grave crisis of authority and legitimacy not only within the political ruling class but equally within the elites of the PSI and the socialist labour movement.

The events leading to the Red Week were connected to an anti-militarist campaign that had been largely co-ordinated through the Chambers of Labour. The linkages between anti-militarism and

Map 1.4 Insurrectionary areas and anarchist predominance in Italy, 1914–20
Source: Enzo Santarelli, 'L'Anarchisme en Italie', *Le Mouvement social*, 83 (1973)

anarchism were long-standing. In the 1880s and 1890s anarchists and former anarchists (such as Andrea Costa) were some of the most outspoken opponents of Italian military adventures in Eritrea and Abyssinia. In the early 1900s anarchists and syndicalists mounted a new anti-militarist campaign influenced by Hervé's in France and the growth of an anti-militarist International. Throughout the 1900s anti-militarist *ordini del giorno* followed on the heels of 'proletarian massacres'.

The Italian invasion of Libya on 19 September 1911 reinforced the campaign. On 30 October at the 'Cialdini' barracks in Bologna, a soldier, Augusto Masetti, who in civilian life had been a bricklayer from the anarchist-influenced rural neighbourhood of the Bolognese (S. Giovanni in Persiceto), shot at and wounded his colonel whilst the officer addressed troops departing for Libya. Masetti accompanied his act with the cry 'Viva l'anarchia' and was placed in a lunatic asylum so as to avoid a trial which may have resulted in the death penalty. Masetti and another anarchist anti-war soldier became the enormously popular symbols of anti-militarism. Anarchists helped to organize anti-war demonstrations and tried to prevent troop trains leaving the Marches and Liguria for their embarkation points.

By 1914 a small group of libertarian anti-militarists, assisted by the Socialist Youth Federation, had grown to 20,000. An anarchist protest (held on 7 June, a national holiday to commemorate the monarchist constitution) against the army's special punishment battalions led to two deaths.

The Red Week foreshadowed the *biennio rosso* of 1919–20. First, what stands out is the continual importance of anti-militarism as a popular mobilizer. It is enough to emphasize that the anarchist-dominated united front of anti-militarist committees numbered over 20,000 members. Second, the anarchists were extremely active in anti-dynastic alliances of radical republicans, 'rebel' socialists, and syndicalists, just as they were in the 1890s and would be in 1919–20. And republicanism, anti-militarism, and anti-clericalism were entrées into radical politics for a generation of northern industrial workers, who later were active in 1919–20 and played prominent roles in the foundation of the Communist Party in 1921. Finally, the frenetic activity of Errico Malatesta was essential for coalescing (as it had been in 1897 and would be in 1920) non-sectarian alliances. His popularity amongst younger workers rivalled, and may have exceeded, the attraction of Benito Mussolini; and the melding of different and sometimes confusing 'subversive' movements into one grand coalition was certainly not very different from what Malatesta had just experienced amongst

London's syndicalists, suffragettes, and Irish nationalists. He, for one, drew apposite parallels.

The Red Week witnessed the declaration of self-governing republics by small towns in the Marches, the capture of a general in his car outside Ancona, and the rapid spread of general strikes from Rome northwards. These were characterized by particularly violent clashes between strikers on the one hand and security forces and Nationalist vigilantes on the other.

However, within nine months Italy was on the verge of war, and important leaders of the Red Week, such as Benito Mussolini, but also including some well-known syndicalists and anarchists, became the most vociferous advocates of intervention on the side of the Allies. I have mentioned how syndicalists' attraction to Mazzinian and Sorelian ideologies may have predestined their route. Anarchists, too, were not immune. Some of Mussolini's earliest interventionist allies were Stirnerite anarchists whose access to printing presses magnified their influence beyond their actual numbers.

In addition, other more persuasive influences were at work amongst the anarchist rank and file. In August and September 1914, when France appeared in danger of being overrun by Germany, older linkages with republican France were recalled by many anarchists. Garibaldi was remembered, but perhaps more important was the living example of a veteran of the Commune, Amilcare Cipriani, the 'subversive' whose residence in Paris and long spells in Italian prisons in the 1880s linked popular anti-militarism with notions of just wars fought against reactionary states. Malatesta had been suspicious of Cipriani since he gathered a group of volunteers to fight for Crete against the Turks in 1897. But in the autumn of 1914 Malatesta was again in his London exile, and the Italian anarchist and syndicalist movements were disoriented by the outbreak of European war just two months after the Red Week. Leading anarchist newspapers such as the Malatestan *Volontà* of Ancona and *Il libertario* of La Spezia displayed signs of confusion, expressing uncertainty as to how anarchists might respond to a possible Austrian invasion of Italy. Indeed, the 1914 national anarchist congress was postponed to January 1915, so the anarchists could clarify their position *vis-à-vis* the left interventionists. Even if most of the Italian population was opposed or indifferent to the war, some anarchists in late 1914 and early 1915 could not resist the appeal of sentiments which claimed that France was fighting for civilization against German authoritarian barbarism. However, by the late spring of 1915, as violence between interventionists and anti-interventionists escalated in

Italian streets, neither Mazzinian nor Sorelian nor Francophile influences were so strong as to undermine the anti-militarism of the movement as a whole.

The USI was also severely wounded in the ensuing interventionist dispute. The war was seen as the only alternative now that the proletariat had proven it could not move beyond 'anarchist' risings. Through war, syndicalists argued, the European working class would be prepared for an international revolutionary cataclysm. The irrational aspects of syndicalism came to the forefront. War was pictured alternatively as a democratic crusade or as revolution; and the verbal violence so characteristic of syndicalist speakers now found its most congenial outlet.

The USI lost its two most important bases – the powerful Parma Chamber of Labour, which followed its Mazzinian leadership into a pro-war position, and the Unione Sindacale Milanese, stronghold of the industrial unionists, which also turned out to be swayed more by Mazzinian arguments than by socialist internationalism or pacifism. But the remaining Po Valley cameralists and a nucleus of Ligurian industrial unionists were faithful to the anti-war platform which anarchists inside the USI had adopted.

It was now that the anarchists, led by the Romagnole Armando Borghi, gained control of the USI. Borghi (1882–1968) had become one of the leading advocates of anarchist involvement within the USI. He earned his living as a journalist on a variety of anarchist newspapers before 1914. At first an individualist, he later embraced syndicalism through his encounter with Italian anti-militarist syndicalists and his reading of Fernand Pelloutier. From 1914 to 1922 he was the chief editor of *Guerra di classe*, the organ of the USI. With the war, membership shrank to 50,000, but the USI retained and deepened its grass-roots support in Liguria and Apulia. When conditions worsened, as the war dragged on, it began quickly to regain strength.

The world war, 1915–18

Historians now agree that most of the politically radical and apolitical dissent which affected wartime north and central Italy from the summer of 1916 to governmental repression in late 1917 and early 1918 can be attributed to food shortages and military discipline in the factories. To the extent to which these rather ill-co-ordinated protests were openly political, anarchists played a significant and disproportionate role.

The government kept the movement under close surveillance from 1916 to the end of the war. However, even with government spies and the earlier wounds of the interventionist crisis, by August 1916 the anarchists were capable of holding a clandestine meeting in Ravenna, representing a selection of groups from northern and central Italy.

What chiefly concerned the authorities were detailed reports by provincial prefects of attempts at revolutionary united fronts. From the summer of 1916 the authorities believed that the 'rigid' faction within the PSI (young, and not so young, intransigent anti-war socialists) would soon achieve an insurrectionary alliance with the anarchists and the USI. Several events in the summer and autumn of 1917 reinforced these concerns.

In late August 1917 five days of rioting by Torinese workers and housewives left fifty civilians shot dead by the army, drafted in to suppress one of the most serious incidents of social protest in western Europe during the war. Although the initial spark was undoubtedly severe bread shortages, and the government's own efforts to blame socialist and libertarian agitators were implausible, nevertheless it now seems clear that, once the riots began, young socialists and anarchists organized largely spontaneous protest. The *fatti* of August 1917 must also be seen against a backdrop of a year's semi-legal and clandestine anti-war propaganda. Anti-war protest had begun when young anarchists demonstrated illegally in the summer of 1916, after an officially sanctioned meeting held to demand the release of the Italo-American 'Wobbly', Carlo Tresca, awaiting execution in Minnesota.

Even if many historians and Gramsci underline the apolitical aspects of the *fatti*, few would dispute the openly political importance of the clandestine meeting of 'rigid' socialists in Florence in the autumn of 1917. The government feared that, if the 'rigids' were capable of greater unity, A Red-Week-type alliance was that much closer. But attempts at such libertarian-socialist alliances in Rome, Milan, Turin, or Florence varied from city to city. Undoubtedly prefects' reports had been written under the influence of general unease caused by the dramatic domestic and international events of 1917. The social and political turbulence generated by war weariness, the Russian Revolutions, and inept provisioning of basic foodstuffs probably exaggerated their fears. If the Florence meeting of 'rigid' socialists did include local socialists with very close links to Armando Borghi and other anarchists who now steered the USI, these alliances never achieved national co-ordination. Attempted united fronts were built on shaky foundations.

Although Giacomo Serrati, the editor of *L'avanti!*, who had spent twenty years fighting anarchists and syndicalists in Italy and abroad, started a friendly correspondence with Luigi Fabbri in 1916, the anarchist intellectual could not agree to fusion or incorporation with radical anti-war socialists since this would have inevitably resulted in their domination by the numerically superior socialists.[9] Moreover, if Malatesta was fully aware of the revolutionary potential of the disastrous rout of the Italian army at Caporetto, and in a private meeting in London cited Lenin's strategy of turning world war into revolutionary civil war, the anarchists in Italy (especially railwaymen) only succeeded at great cost in disseminating a few pamphlets to front-line troops. Besides, apolitical southern peasant infantry were unlikely targets for anarchist arguments. Nor did Italy have the geographical space within which an Italian Lenin might consolidate his revolution as he bargained with triumphant Habsburg and German generals. What, however, the anarchists did succeed in achieving during the war was the creation of an 'underground' railway which smuggled socialist and anarchist deserters into Switzerland, where they were hidden by the Italian exile communities.

Attempted left-wing wartime alliances (*fasci rivoluzionari*) not only reflected Italian habits and foreshadowed similar short-term ventures during the *biennio rosso*; they also were part and parcel of continent-wide alliances of syndicalists, anarchists, and socialists fostered by the ecumenical influence of the Russian Revolution. Italian political behaviour therefore became intertwined with the pre- and early history of the Third International.

The anti-war, international socialist gatherings at Zimmerwald (1915) and Kienthal (1916) received a mixed response from Italian anarchist leaders and intellectuals because syndicalists and anarchists had been excluded, although the second Swiss conclave was better received because its concluding statement seemed so much more intransigent, and appeared to transcend parliamentary strategies. The Italian anarchists' Ravenna congress met to discuss, among other things, the movement's attitude towards a possible new radical socialist International, to which Kienthal pointed; and one well-known anarchist, Pasquale Binazzi, predicted a new era of cordial relations between anarchists and syndicalists. He envisaged an international organization open to all working-class anti-war elements, replacing the discredited and exclusively parliamentary Second International. Binazzi's conception of the new International circulated widely throughout the Italian left in 1916–17. In Turin a leading working-class 'rigid' socialist explained to a large May Day audience in 1916 that anti-parliamentary syndicalism would return corrupted socialist politics to their Marxist sources. At another meeting that year he called for a

Unione dei Lavoratori del Mondo, as the successor to the discredited Second International, echoing intentionally or otherwise Binazzi and Malatesta. In December 1917 the Florentine socialist editor of *La difesa* defended a similar conception of the International, linking it with the anti-parliamentarian and largely Malatestan anarchist position advanced at the London Congress of 1896 of the Second International. But these efforts, just like the proposed *fasci*, brought harsh responses from other maximalists such as Serrati, Amadeo Bordiga, and Gramsci.

Nevertheless the Russian Revolution seemed to lessen rather than accentuate ideological differences. It is undoubtedly true that at first the Bolshevik Revolution brought 'rigid' socialists and libertarians closer together. Much of the socialist left and the anarchist movement adapted a sovietist interpretation of the Bolshevik Revolution which blurred ideological boundaries. The role of the party was downgraded absolutely, or interpreted in a way which was far from the realities of Leninist theory and practice. While Gramsci, for instance, stressed the need for a party to differentiate socialists from anarchists, and he had little admiration for national anarchist leaders or intellectuals such as Fabbri or Malatesta, his wartime and *biennio rosso* versions of the party were not, in fact, very different from Malatesta's version of an anarchist 'party'. Gramsci, at least until the summer of 1920, imagined the party not as a Leninist vanguard but a co-ordinating force amongst the rank and file's factory councils and soviets. The party articulated electoral choices, but did not necessarily guide with an iron hand popular direct action. There is little in fact which separates Gramsci's anti-Jacobin councilism from the notion that the young anarchist intellectual Camillo Berneri advanced in the summer of 1919, when he described the Russian Soviet Republic as a system of *autogoverno* (self-management). Gramsci was far from alone in approaching anarchist-like strategies even if most socialist leaders and activists retained pride in their own party organization.

The *biennio rosso*, 1919–20: patterns of protest

The *biennio rosso* has long been pictured as a complex sociopolitical crisis that finally destroyed the already ailing liberal state. These years are characterized by much higher (if short-lived) levels of trade unionization, the dramatic growth of the Socialist Party, and the introduction of universal male suffrage and proportional representation. Popularly based Catholic and socialist parties became significant actors in Parliament, replacing pre-war liberal notables. But this major revolution in the political system was accompanied by an extraordinary number of northern industrial strikes, land occupations in the south, and extra-parliamentary direct action by the Nationalist right and the socialist and libertarian left. The *biennio rosso* concluded with a month-long occupation of engineering and automobile factories in September 1920.

The Prime Ministers Orlando Nitti and Giolitti were not unsympathetic to a reform of political or industrial relations. But none would permit libertarian-socialist alliances to threaten the Italian state. So that, if at the end of the war the government was forced to release detained socialist and libertarian leaders, once again Rome and provincial prefects feared that a post-war version of the Red Week united front from below might be an immediate threat. They were particularly concerned about the activities of Armando Borghi in Italy and Errico Malatesta in London during the spring of 1919. They, it was thought, might well supply the national leadership or inspiration for a post-war revolutionary front. But by themselves neither the anarchists (whose members may have climbed to 20,000-plus by 1920) nor the USI (whose members on paper were at least 500,000 by 1920) could have been successful, since at their height during the *biennio rosso* the PSI and the CGL had 250,000 and over 2,000,000 members respectively. What the political elites quite rightly feared was the combined impact of libertarian ginger groups and charismatic leaders such as Malatesta upon a highly charged and dissatisfied populace.

Malatesta's re-entry into Italy was delayed for as long as possible. His requests for a new passport were at first denied, and the British authorities made certain that he could not board any ships. However, it was this policy which in fact generated the very type of non-sectarian united front from below that the Italian government so feared.

In April 1919 the first national congress of the Unione Communista Anarchica was held. (In 1920 it changed its name to the Unione Anarchica Italiana.) The April congress was the first public national meeting of the anarchist movement since 1915. Delegates, mostly from reconstructed northern and central federations, demanded the unconditional return of Malatesta. And throughout the spring and summer of 1919 demonstrations demanding his return accompanied opposition to Italian intervention against the Bolsheviks abroad. Maximalist socialists, such as Serrati, anarchists, and the leadership of the railway workers' union (SFI) and the Unione Sindacale often shared platforms. Even if the leaders were in fact privately quite suspicious of each other, their joint appearances gave the initial impression to the massive crowds assembled that here was a new united front in the making.

Although most former interventionists would join the bloody purge of the left in the autumn of 1920, boundaries were still ill-defined in late 1919 and early 1920. And Malatesta's clandestine return to Italy at Christmas 1919, organized through the intervention of the pro-war Mazzinian merchant navy trade-union boss, Guiseppe Giulietti, led to one of the most bizarre, if unsuccessful, political alliances of the period.

Giulietti admired Malatesta and had in fact met him before the war. He was also a devoted follower of D'Annunzio and supplied his legionnaires with arms and food after they seized the contested town of Fiume on the new Yugoslav border. Since many of the 'social' interventionists attracted to D'Annunzio and Mussolini's movement in the spring and summer of 1919 were former leftists, Giulietti hoped to reconcile unorthodox left socialists and anarchists with their former comrades. In January 1920 a series of meetings occurred between the recently arrived Malatesta, Giulietti, and maximalist socialists concerning a possible march on Rome.

With the monarchy's credibility strained by the war, and Parliament unable to translate the claims of socialists or Catholics into effective legislation, this potential alliance of peasants, workers, and disgruntled middle class would have indeed been a threat to the regime. However, several factors conspired against this march on Rome. It is nearly impossible to imagine how the exaggerated nationalism of large sectors of the middle class could have been reconciled with the militant ritualistic internationalism of the left. But, if such an alliance hoped for any success, it would have also had to pose not revolutionary but what socialists might term transitional demands. The demands for constitutional changes through a constituent assembly generated enormous sympathy in Italy, but were unacceptable to slogan-bound maximalist socialists even if Lenin himself had used a similar movement for his own ends. Certainly some of the anarchists, such as Malatesta, may have seen the tactical utility, but on the whole purity of principles prevented them from indulging in what was deemed constitution-mongering. Finally, even if we suppose that this march on Rome had been successful at expelling Nitti from power, it is exceedingly difficult to imagine socialists and D'Annunzio sharing it. The most likely outcome might have been a military counter-coup and the installation of an authoritarian state on lines earlier proposed by conservative political figures in the 1890s. Less likely, but still plausible, might have been an Italian-style Peronism, with D'Annunzio playing the populist dictator, ruling an Italian right-wing authoritarian state whose trade unions and social policies might have contained somewhat more radical substance than Mussolini's future confection. Certainly in early 1920 Mussolini himself realized both the comical and the dangerous aspects of the enterprise and steered clear so as to keep his future options open. But he and other bourgeois commentators on this murky affair actually believed that the greatest winner would have been Malatesta!

Such gross overestimation of Malatesta's and the anarchist movement's strength in early 1920 says a great deal about their popularity in the middle of the two years of social unrest. Anarchist strength during the *biennio rosso* can largely be understood by recalling the pre-war protest cycles. These were merely enlarged and deepened after the war, but not significantly changed. Three types of issue congenial to anarchists mobilized massive social protest and political strikes during the *biennio rosso*. First, inflation, including the rising price of basic necessities such as bread, caused popular explosions of anger. Types of protest associated with 'pre-modern' bread riots had, as I have shown, previously been anarchist issues. Many historians of the *biennio rosso* claim that the most revolutionary moment during this cycle of social protest occurred in May and June 1919 when the so-called cost-of-living riots spread rapidly from central to northern Italy. Frightened shopkeepers handed in the keys to their shops to the local Chambers of Labour; and for several days many Italians lived under a condition of dual power. Second, anti-militarism and anti-imperialism mobilized an equally vociferous protest in July 1920, recalling similar events six years earlier during the Red Week. A mutiny of troops refusing to leave the port of Ancona for Italian-occupied Albania involved anarchists, who mounted a fierce armed resistance to its suppression for two days. Following the suppression of the uprising and mutiny, anarchist- and USI-led campaigns throughout Italian industry, against war material being manufactured and shipped to Albania or the Whites and Allied troops fighting in the Russian Civil War, received such widespread support as to make the CGL and socialist leadership quite anxious that their rivals might be stealing their thunder and their supporters. Third, the arrival of Malatesta at Christmas 1919 repeated the pattern already discerned in the spring of 1914. From January to the summer of 1920 Malatesta drew large crowds wherever he spoke. His meetings also provoked further 'proletarian massacres', which in their turn increased social tensions throughout northern Italy.

Geographically and industrially, anarchist strength was reflected in its sustained presence in central Italy but equally in the anarchist control of syndicalist Chambers of Labour in industrial Liguria. The anarchists and syndicalists also held something of a monopoly in the rather small Italian mining industry (marble quarries and lignite mines). In certain areas of the Po Valley, anarchists maintained a presence amongst landless labourers, though they were generally overshadowed by the socialists. In Apulia, anarchists worked within the powerful syndicalist peasants' leagues. However, prominent syndicalists endorsed an electoralist strategy and were supported by their rank and file, although at the same time some of the most serious insurrectionary rioting occurred within their strongholds during 1920 and 1921.

Ideologically, anarchism retained important links with anti-clericalism and republicanism. But, interestingly enough, many of Bordiga's fellow abstentionist 'scientific socialists' were more willing to work with the anarchists than their highly sectarian leader. Although *ordinovisti* (followers of Antonio Gramsci's *L'ordine nuovo*) did not really spread beyond the confines of Turin, anarchist militants within the factory council movement did have influence amongst anarchist and socialist activists in the Ligurian industrial city of Savona.

Just as, before the war, anarchists and syndicalists had displayed their greatest strength within modern industry in Italian 'company towns', so too, during the *biennio rosso* in Piombino, Sestri Ponente, and Terni, thousands of workers enrolled in the Unione Sindacale. In such locales economic and political life was dominated by one great anti-union trust, like ILVA or Ansaldo, or had state industries, such as arsenals and armaments factories, where the law restricted strikes. Normal economic disputes in both cases rapidly degenerated into violent confrontations. Moreover, these towns (and the Apulian agro-towns) were characterized by segregated workers' districts which had few municipal amenities. The working class faced a small middle class composed of wholesalers and retailers whose inflationary prices caused great hardship and anger. Industrial production may have been modern, but it was in a precarious situation as peacetime conversion exposed workers to massive redundancies or shortened working weeks. The locally segregated working class had to contend with unemployment *and* galloping inflation. The merchant and the trust became objects of their wrath.

While these objective conditions may to some extent explain the success of the libertarians in Liguria, Tuscany, and Apulia, equally the anarchists or syndicalists may have had the best industrial organizers available. Riccardo Sacconi, Alberto Meschi, and Giuseppe Di Vittorio, to name three prominent examples, recruited thousands of miners, industrial workers, and landless labourers into the USI because they were effective at winning limited economic demands during hard-fought disputes. It was their apolitical or neutral stance which allowed them to unite socialist, anarchist, syndicalist, and republican workers in a common effort.

The major areas of social protest from the spring of 1919 to the summer of 1920 followed the contours of anarchism's political geography. Strike and protest waves were sparked off from La Spezia (the cost-of-living riots) and Ancona (the 1920 mutiny) and then spread to the northern industrial triangle.

The disturbances during the *biennio rosso* were also like their pre-war counterparts in being of short duration. Just as before 1915 sectarian barriers vanished temporarily as relatively small groups of anarchists, syndicalists, and left socialists provided *ad hoc* leadership, so after a few days socialist parliamentarians and the by now immeasurably stronger trade-union leaders regained the upper hand. Within the two-year pattern of protest the anarchists remained one of the few left-wing groups prepared to support insurrection, and even attempted through united fronts to provide the extra-party frameworks to fulfil this goal. Certainly one of the great strengths of the anarchist movement must have been its lack of bureaucratic organization. The anarchists could not be blamed for suffering from the bureaucratic inertia which fatally weakened their socialist competitors. But their greatest weakness arose from this very strength. If anarchists reflected a radical non-sectarian temper, they also lacked a national organization capable of capturing many potential converts. Most serious for the anarchists was their inability to overcome long-standing internal divisions. Even Malatesta's enormous popularity could not bring internal unity. Although the Unione Anarchica Italiana held successful non-sectarian meetings in 1920 and the creation of an anarchist daily, *Umanità nova*, in Milan, boosted the presence of anarchists, with Malatesta's newspaper nearly supplanting *L'avanti!* as the preferred journal of the Milanese left in the 'hot summer' of 1920, anti-organizationalists such as the recently returned Luigi Galleani were suspicious. (Galleani (1861–1931) had lived in North America for nearly twenty years until his deportation during the Red Scare of 1919. Through his newspaper, *Cronaca sovversiva*, he developed an anti-organizational anarcho-communism which sometimes rivalled the influence of Malatestan anarchism amongst Italian immigrants.)

But the old quarrel between *malatestiani* and *galleanisti* was not the only internal dispute at hand. Milanese individualists, and their supporters elsewhere, were not thrilled by 'party' anarchism. Conflicts erupted between Torinese anarchists who considered themselves non-sectarian minorities within the CGL and the cadres and leaders of the USI. Even within the USI itself, relations between 'pure' syndicalists and anarchists were rarely excellent.

In sum, the anarchists never posed a credible alternative to the socialists because of uneven national representation, lack of solid institutions, and internal squabbling. They also failed to supplant the lure of extended suffrage which their supporters in the 'second socialist culture' happily endorsed. For many rank-and-file leftists direct action and electoralism were not discrete strategic choices. Anarchism could never guarantee state patronage and possible industrial and land reforms, which still remained highly popular goals even in the midst of social upheaval.

Support for direct action movements may have given anarchists a role to play in the *biennio rosso*. However, popular support for extra-parliamentary strategies on the part of socialist sympathizers was not without its ambiguities. The chief obstacle to an insurrectional strategy was in fact the profoundly pacifist spirit which dominated the core values of the Socialist Party. If in theory maximalism, *ordinovismo*, or *bordighismo* (the faction following Amadeo Bordiga's abstentionist Marxism) preached the necessity of violence, their chief proponents were appalled when popular violence occurred in 1919 and 1920. Riots were usually considered unconscious hooliganism having little to do with the struggle for revolutionary victory. At other times the violence was considered premature since the vanguard party and/or urban soviets had yet to be created.

Yet the failure of anarchist-type direct action goes deeper than the betrayal of timid or prudent leaders. While their rank and file had decades of experience calling general strikes in response to 'proletarian massacres', or employing sabotage and violence during bitter strikes – indeed, even reformists amongst the landless labourers were old hands at vine-cutting and coercion of non-striking tenant farmers – the movement as a whole lacked a definite tradition of armed struggle.

Italy was neither tsarist Russia nor even Spain. It was a constitutional liberal state, something the anarchists learned to recall with some nostalgia in the 1920s and 1930s. Even if the anarchists had suffered waves of exile and repression since the 1880s, and militants were detained without trial or murdered by security forces during the *biennio rosso*, the movement nevertheless succeeded in organizing on a wider scale during this period than ever before. The heavy-handed liberal state never intended to annihilate the 'subversives'. Instead it was the post-war crisis itself that unsettled the liberal state and overwhelmed the socialists and anarchists, which then allowed an old 'subversive' to teach the state some new tricks. Benito Mussolini's movement of sustained private violence in collusion with sympathetic local prefects and police or army officers, followed by the rapid replacement of pulverized labour or popular cultural institutions with fascist counterparts, was a break with earlier forms of repression engineered by the liberal state. The left was neither prepared for insurrection nor alert to the novelty of fascism's reactionary mass movement.

Neighbourhood anarchism in Turin

Turin was the scene for one of the most significant and characteristic areas of anarchist presence during the *biennio rosso*, revealing not only the ways through which anarchists affected broader social and labour movements but equally the very limits of their influence. In order to understand the importance of the Torinese anarchist movement it is necessary to engage in a little micro-history.

After the episodes of the International, the Partito Operaio, and Crispian repression, the movement did not reappear until the years after 1905. There are few continuities between the Torinese pioneers of the 1870s and 1880s and the younger generation, but it was the generation of 1910 which finally revived the movement's fortunes, and revived them in a distinctly modern industrial setting. Within the new jerry-built suburbs of Turin this anarchism found a constituency. Immigrants from the nearby Vercellese and Biellese carried within them memories of the anarchism – and of organizers such as Galleani – of the 1870s and 1880s, into a new social setting to provide factory anarchism with an opportunity to exercise an influence out of proportion to the actual number of adherents.

At the centre of the new anarchism of Turin was the Gruppo Barriera di Milano – a mere dozen or two of car and foundry workers – who maintained a tradition of militancy in local factories stretching from 1910 to 1922. They had the advantage of being a fairly homogeneous group of skilled workers intimately associated with that industrial revolution which had transformed Turin from the somnolent aristocratic ex-capital of Italy and the Kingdom of Piedmont into the city of Fiat.

The growth of Torinese socialism after 1910 was based upon two face-to-face institutions congenial to the anarchists: political clubs and factory internal commissions. And since anarchist symbols and culture remained acceptable and readily digested by radical and not so radical working-class socialists, so anarchism's influence was far greater than mere number-crunching might suggest.

The influence anarchism exercised upon the Torinese working class from 1910 to 1922 was closely associated with the Ferrer School located in Barriera di Milano, founded after the execution of the Spanish libertarian educationist in 1909. Indeed, the violent demonstrations in the wake of his death can be considered this generation of 1910's baptism by fire.

The Ferrer School played an analogous role to socialist workers' clubs in other neighbouring suburbs: they acted as second homes and schools for many self-educated industrial workers. And the Ferrer School acted as a 'proletarian university' and gathering point for young left-wing socialists and libertarians. It can be considered part of a wider contemporary European tendency to marry self-education and radical-left (especially syndicalist) politics. In many respects it bore striking resemblances to the British Plebs League and the libertarian schools located within the French *bourses du travail*. During its decade of existence it attracted scores of pupils who later played prominent roles in the chief industrial conflicts and battles which extended from the anarchist-organized car workers' strike of 1912, through the uprising of 1917, and onwards to the famous strikes of 1920.

Neighbouring socialist clubs which doubled as socialist circles (the lowest level within the PSI's organization) did not seem to mind anarchists in their midst. Anarchists and socialists shared the experience of youth and expressed a rather austere puritanism. Less drinking and gaming occurred in the political clubs of the new generation.

The anarchists and socialists also shared similar tastes in reading. Battista Santhià, future Communist militant, recalled how young socialists were immersed in anarchist classics. Kropotkin's *The Conquest of Bread* was extremely popular, Louise Michel's account of the Paris Commune, the anti-militarist pamphlets of Gustave Hervé, and the semi-clandestine *Rompete le file* (Break Ranks), an anti-militarist newspaper, were read by all. Paolo Robotti, a future power in the Communist Party, then a barely literate factory worker, remembered that, although he and his comrades spoke of Marx, it was only because they had a portrait of him in the hall of their club. But, he continued, to claim they knew Marxism would be an exaggeration, because Marx's books were indigestible, too voluminous for their intellectual diets. Instead the young socialists read Cafiero and Gori.

Student reading preferences at the Ferrer School differed little from the socialist clubs or for that matter Milan's *biblioteche popolari*. Along with the obligatory Jules Verne, Jack London, Emile Zola, and Anatole France, pupils used Most's *The Religious Pest* as an 'atheist's textbook'. Attempts at understanding Marx's dialectical materialism were not very successful, but the political differences between Marx and Bakunin were spelt out.

In Turin the anarchists were considered by socialist club members as *purer*, if slightly utopian, socialists. And recent ethnographic and oral-historical research suggests that throughout Italy, and even in areas without notable anarchist presence, the anarchists were admired for their high ideals and considered the intellectuals of the 'second socialist culture'. Within Turin anarchists played an important role in the emergence and growth of the factory council movement in 1919 and affected the ideological and political coloration of the greatest intellectual amongst a younger generation of socialist radicals, Antonio Gramsci.

Without the political and organizational contributions of two worker anarchists, Maurizio Garino (1892–1976) and Pietro Ferrero (1892–1922), it would be difficult to imagine how Gramsci and the *Ordine nuovo* group could have popularized their distinctly libertarian, if Marxist, conception of council communism to the workers of Fiat and other engineering factories of Turin. Ferrero was a trade union activist who became secretary of the locally powerful branch of FIOM, while Garino was another highly skilled factory worker whose presence at factory council meetings and street demonstrations is noted throughout the *biennio rosso*. Both were self-educated organizers of the Ferrer School and maintained close contacts with *L'Ordine nuovo*.

Another anarchist who was a thinker rather than an activist published extensively in Gramsci's journal. Pietro Carlo Mosso (1893–1945), a Fiat technician, contributed significantly to Gramsci's peculiar mixture of libertarianism, productivism, and Marxism. Unlike many middle-class socialists and anarchists, he possessed a technical rather than a literary education. However, not only was he a technician, he was also something of a philosopher. And it was through Gramsci's and Mosso's mutual acquaintance with the Torinese philosophy professor, Annibale Pastore, that they became friends.

Since the cutting edge of Gramsci's post-war radicalism was a belief that Italian capitalist elites had sacrificed any legitimacy they held as the war transformed them from entrepreneurs to plutocratic profiteers, so an alternative mass-based form of entrepreneurial or productivist drive would have to be found to replace the capitalists'. For Mosso (and Gramsci), Taylorism was just such a value-free technique which could be transferred to socialized, self-managed factories. And in a series of articles commissioned by Gramsci, Mosso the Kropotkinite outlined a libertarian form of Taylorism which Gramsci employed in his own articles in 1919 and 1920.

With the aid of the anarchists, the local factory committees were transformed into factory councils in the autumn and winter of 1919. However, neither the employers nor the trade-union and Socialist Party elites were keen on Gramsci's or the anarchists' expansive interpretations of their duties. Employers precipitated a general strike in Turin in April 1920 which limited the growing encroaching control of the factory councils. The leadership of the CGL and the PSI refused to help the Torinese. Gramsci and the local socialists were forced to rely on the help of the USI, the anarchists, and the SFI (railway workers' union). Without the support of national anarchist and syndicalist solidarity networks Turin's general strike would have been completely isolated.

Gramsci and the Torinese socialists were placed in a delicate position by seeking Borghi's or Malatesta's support, yet being simultaneously increasingly critical of libertarian ideology. With the libertarians, *ordinovisti*, and maximalists in disarray, only the reformist leader of FIOM, Bruno Buozzi, could settle with the victorious employers in April 1920.

Between the end of the April strike and the occupation of the factories, the left, which was to take a leading position in the Communist Party in January 1921, was incapable of seizing the initiative. Bordiga and his followers were far too sectarian, the *Ordine nuovo* group started to disintegrate after the failed strike, and the maximalists were tied hand and foot to reformist trade-union leaders. Furthermore, the entire Marxist left became increasingly alarmed by the growth of the anarchists and the USI, who benefited from the Ancona rising and the anti-Albanian- and Russian-interventionist campaigns. In the summer of 1920 even Turin witnessed the rapid spread of USI influence in factories. Nevertheless, Gramsci and his closest allies probed and analysed the libertarian left that summer. They sought out Malatesta in Milan, expressed sympathy for the Anconans, and even sent representatives to a large anti-Russian-interventionist meeting organized by the Unione Anarchica Italiana (UAI) in Florence in August. Notwithstanding these moves Gramsci and the remaining *ordinovisti* remained suspicious of the libertarian left outside of their own home-grown Torinese contacts.

Failure

The occupation of the factories in September clarified the situation. The libertarians were unable to lead this defensive movement, which was steered by reformist trade-union leaders. At most, the anarchists could have created a *fait accompli* in Liguria by seizing government offices or launching some sort of insurrection which would have forced the socialists' hand. In the event some of Gramsci's Torinese anarchist allies convinced them to await the inconclusive decision of an 'estates general' of the left in Milan. Without larger national organizations, the anarchists and USI might be able to tap their 'second socialist culture' networks; but on the national level they remained as mere ginger groups.

In October 1920, after the factories were evacuated, Giolitti arrested the entire leadership of the USI and the UAI. The socialists did not respond, disoriented by the first fascist attacks in Bologna and Ferrara, distracted by internal doctrinal problems which foreshadowed the emergence of the Communist Party in January 1921. The socialists more or less ignored the persecution of the libertarians until the spring of 1921 when the aged Malatesta and other imprisoned anarchists mounted hunger strikes from their cells in Milan. But an anarchist terrorist bombing of a crowded Milan theatre at the height of the campaign lost the anarchists the widespread sympathy they appeared to be gaining. Mussolini took this opportunity to sack the offices of *Umanità nova*, although it soldiered on until the March on Rome from an office in that city.

The anarchists played important roles in the Arditi del Popolo in 1921, a grass-roots united front alliance which might have succeeded in resisting the fascist squads if the sectarianism and timidity of the socialists and Communists had not sabotaged their efforts. Finally, in a last desperate gamble, the anarchist-led railway workers' union helped organize the more bureaucratically structured Labour Alliance in 1922, but this too lacked unity and came too late.

Anarchism, communism, and fascism

For Malatesta and others the real confrontation with Bolshevism only occurred after 1921 with the emergence of Comintern Leninism. But both Fabbri and Malatesta consistently denounced the conception of the dictatorship of the proletariat. And in July 1919 the revived theoretical journal of Malatestan anarchism, *Volontà*, initiated a long bitter debate about this within the Italian anarchist movement. Many Italian anarchists were attracted to this expedient. Indeed, like a great many Italian socialists they believed that the Bolshevik dictatorship would be dismantled once the Civil War was won. Malatesta thought otherwise and sent a message to his Italian comrades:

> In reality one is dealing with a dictatorship of a party; and a very real dictatorship with its decrees, penal sanctions, executions and above all its armed force that today helps defend the revolution from external enemies, but tomorrow will help impose the dictators' will on the workers, stop the revolution, consolidate and defend new interests of a new privileged class against the masses. Even Bonaparte helped defend the French Revolution against the European reaction, but in defending it he strangled it. Lenin, Trotsky and comrades are certainly sincere revolutionaries, and they will not betray what they take as revolution, but they are preparing the governmental apparatus which will help those who follow them to profit by the revolution and destroy it. They will be the first victims of their methods, and with them, I fear, the revolution will collapse. History repeats itself, *mutatis mutandis*: and the dictatorship of Robespierre brought Robespierre to the guillotine and prepared the way for Napoleon.[10]

After Kronstadt, after the sectarian policies of the Italian Communists, and after the recognition of Mussolini's regime by the Soviet Union, Malatesta could only declare in his obituary of Lenin in 1924 that his death should be celebrated as a holiday rather than commemorated in mourning. Anarchist intellectuals were roasted in the Communist press. Between 1921 and 1926 the anarchist rank and file were driven out of factories and forced into poverty. The anarchists probably suffered greater violence proportionate to their numbers than other political opponents of fascism. (In December 1922, six weeks after the March on Rome, local fascists brutally murdered several Torinese anarchists, syndicalists, and socialists. Pietro Ferrero was caught in the vendetta and dragged tied to a car down Corso Vittorio Emanuele. His battered body could only be identified from his Green Cross identification card.) Simultaneously, the USI collapsed as fascist squads and rivalries with internal Communist minorities wiped out its fragile organization.

In the last months before Mussolini suppressed all opposition the anarchists Gino Lucetti and Anteo Zamboni nearly assassinated him. Zamboni was lynched by an enraged mob in Bologna on

31 October 1926. In November, using his attempt as a pretext, Mussolini destroyed the final vestiges of the liberal state.

Anarchists were driven into exile, placed on the penal islands, or, if too famous like Malatesta, placed under a species of house arrest. Anarchists were active in Paris and elsewhere in the 1920s and 1930s. They planned several unsuccessful attempts on Mussolini's life. They even maintained a clandestine presence in Torinese factories in the early 1930s. Some gave in and swore allegiance to the regime, and others fought on during the Civil War in Spain, where the brilliant Camillo Berneri was assassinated, most probably by the Stalinist secret police.

During the Resistance the anarchists organized several partisan bands in the Milanese and Massa-Carrara areas; and the movement even enjoyed a brief revival in the post-war period as dissident Communist workers, disenchanted by Togliatti's moderate and bureaucratic politics, joined the libertarians and Trotskyists in a short-lived alliance. But these circumstances were temporary. When a mass movement of rank-and-file workers again appeared on the scene in the late 1960s and early 1970s, the New Left addressed them in strictly Leninist or Marxist language. It has only been with the demise of that New Left and its replacement with social movements emphasizing life-style and Green politics that the anarchist message, in entirely different surroundings, is again heard. But perhaps this post-industrial educated middle class's greatest gift to the memory of the anarchist movement has been a new generation of historians and social scientists capable of opening their ears and eyes and observing a much neglected part of their country's turbulent past.

When and where did the libertarians begin to lose their impact on the broader labour movement? The break in generational continuity occurs in the early 1920s when anarchism's grip on local political cultures begins to loosen. A younger generation of militants in the anarchist seedbeds of the Marches and Liguria turned to the Communists. As anarchist intellectuals increased their criticisms of the Soviet Union's repression of the Russian movement, younger Italian anarchist workers switched allegiance to the Socialists or Communists.

If we can fairly easily date the weakening of anarchism, the reasons for its permanent eclipse demand greater study. Here I shall only advance several hypotheses. First, as I have mentioned earlier, the anarchists, and for that matter a good deal of the left, were neither intellectually nor organizationally prepared to withstand the fascist counter-revolution. Second, the Communists as representatives of the 'first workers' state' attracted militants who otherwise might have become anarchist sympathizers. And the Communist Party's organization and international logistical support guaranteed it a continuity the anarchists could never maintain. In short, the Communists could compete with the anarchists as the most radical yet, at the same time, the most efficient left-wing party. Third, the anarchist exile during Mussolini's regime lasted over twenty years – far longer than shorter spells experienced under his liberal predecessors. And between 1925 and 1945 the anarchists lost their greatest leaders (Malatesta, Fabbri, and Galleani) and one possible replacement (Berneri). Younger popular leaders did not emerge in 1945. During exile, moreover, the influence of the anti-organizationalist and individualist anarchism of the American, *L'adunata dei refrattari*, undermined internal cohesion. Finally, perhaps of greatest importance was surely the gradual disappearance of the isolated working-class popular cultures that had been the anarchists' natural home. Fascism not only destroyed popular working-class organizations and historical memories; but by modernizing capitalism Mussolini's regime unwittingly introduced the first exemplars of American mass culture. The culture of the radical autodidact was replaced by an urban culture rooted in the myths and realities of geographical and social mobility. Recent oral history of Turin demonstrates how the generation of the 1920s looked beyond their industrial suburbs to the capitalist heart of Turin. And this dream of mobility flourished openly after the fascist regime collapsed. Whether or not it was more satisfying than the anarchists' remains an open question.

Notes and references

Sovversivo

A definition of the term *sovversivo* can be found, in the notes by Franco Andreucci, ' "Subversiveness" and anti-fascism in Italy', in R. Samuel (ed.), *People's History and Socialist Theory* (London, 1981), pp. 199–204. 'Subversiveness' and the 'subversive' are said to grow out of the dreams and vendettas of the Italian 'pre-industrial' and 'pre-modern'. But Andreucci hedges his bets:

> One could call it [subversiveness] an old tradition in the history of the Italian people, one which is difficult to define. It was an attitude, a mood, which spread to the borders and even outside the borders of the labour movement, in the strict sense of the word. Subversiveness has always been something more than a simple feeling of spontaneous rebellion against the state.
>
> (p. 201)

Perhaps it was adopted by the left as a badge of honour, since the authoritarianism and heavy-handedness of the forces of law and order affected the entire opposition outside the liberal ruling elite.

Due to limitations of space, the following footnotes have been kept to an absolute minimum. For somewhat greater detail see the select bibliography that follows.

1 G. Candeloro, *Storia d'Italia moderna,* Vol. VI (Milan, 1972), p. 54.
2 See M. Clark, *Modern Italy 1871–1982* (London, 1984), p. 75.
3 R. J. Goldstein, *Political Repression in 19th Century Europe* (London, 1983), p. 9.
4 The railway worker was Camillo Signorini. See Luigi Fabbri to Max Nettlau, Montevideo, 31 January 1931, Max Nettlau Archives, no. 91, International Institute of Social History (IISH), Amsterdam.
5 E. Santarelli, *Il socialismo anarchico in Italia* (Milan, 1973 edn), p. 40.
6 'Errico Malatesta', *Lo stato operaio*, 10 August 1932.
7 G. Arfé, *Storia del socialismo italiano (1892–1926)* (Turin, 1965), p. 158.
8 L. Tilly, ' "I fatti di maggio". The working class of Milan and the rebellion of 1898', in R. J. Bezucha (ed.), *Modern European Social History* (Lexington, Mass., 1972), pp. 124–38.
9 Serrati's correspondence with Fabbri is in the Luigi Fabbri Papers, IISH.
10 Although printed elsewhere, the complete letter is in the Fabbri Papers, IISH: Malatesta to Fabbri, 30 July 1919.

Select bibliography

English sources are extremely limited. Richard Hostetter's unfinished history of Italian socialism is very comprehensive for the first period: *The Italian Socialist Movement*, Vol. I, *Origins (1860–1882)* (New York, 1958). For the story up to 1894: N. Pernicone, 'The Italian anarchist movement: the years of crisis, decline and transformation (1874–1894)', PhD thesis, University of Rochester, 1971. For the era of the *biennio rosso* (1919–20): M. Clark, *Antonio Gramsci and the Revolution That Failed* (London, 1977).

My forthcoming London PhD concentrates on the Torinese case (1910–22), but I do try to give a general overview: 'Gramsci, and the Italian libertarian movement during the *biennio rosso, 1919–20*'.

One of the best thematic overviews in Italian is Enzo Santarelli's *Il socialismo anarchico in Italia* (Milan, 1959 and 1973 (revised edn)). It is interesting to observe how the Communist Santarelli's account loses much of its Stalinist flavour between the 1959 and 1973 editions. The latest and most accurate account is in chapter 5 of the 1973 edition, translated from E. Santarelli, 'L'anarchisme en Italie', *Le Mouvement social*, 83 (1973), pp. 135–66. Pier Carlo Masini's history promises to be the standard work but as of today it still has not been completed, his first two volumes taking the story up to 1906: *Storia degli anarchici dal Bakunin a Malatesta (1862–1892)* (Milan, 1974); *Storia degli anarchici italiani nell'epoca degli attentati* (Milan, 1981).* Gino Cerrito has also written a brief account from a Malatestan position, covering the period 1881 to 1914: *Dall' insurrezionalismo alla settimana rossa* (Florence, 1977). Cerrito's and his student Adriana Dadà's accounts are mixtures of antiquated history of ideas and ideological polemics. They do not stand up to either Santarelli's social historical account or Masini's more popularly written volumes. Dadà's major account runs from the First International to the present, and in it the pre-1926 period is severely underweighted: *L'anarchismo in Italia: fra movimento e partito. Storia e documenti dell'anarchismo italiano* (Milan, 1984). Her shorter contribution to a historical textbook is more satisfactory: 'Gli anarchici italiani fra guerra di classe e reazione', in G. Cherubini (ed.), *Storia della società italiana*, Vol. 21 (Milan, 1982), pp. 375–406 (this covers the period 1914–26). For an excellent general account of the Red Week of 1914: L. Lotti, *La settimana rossa* (Florence, 1972). Armando Borghi's memoirs, *Mezzo secolo di anarchia (1898–1945)* (Naples, 1954), are charming.

The literature in English on Italian syndicalism is uneven. A book which concentrates on the syndicalist intelligentsia and is too impressed by its intellectual and moral coherence is: D. D. Roberts, *The Syndicalist Tradition and Italian Fascism* (Chapel Hill, NC, 1979). For overviews of syndicalism's political *and* social history: C. Bertrand, 'Revolutionary syndicalism in Italy, 1912–1922', PhD thesis, University of Wisconsin, 1969; T. R. Sykes, 'The practice of revolutionary syndicalism in Italy, 1905–1911', PhD thesis, Columbia University, 1973; C. Bertrand, 'Italian revolutionary syndicalism and the crisis of intervention', *Canadian Journal of History*, 10 (1974), pp. 349–67; R. Webster, *Industrial Imperialism in Italy 1908–1915.* (Berkeley, Calif., 1975); T. R. Sykes, 'Revolutionary syndicalism in the Italian labour movement: the agrarian strikes of 1907–08 in the province of Parma', *International Review of Social History*, 21 (1976), pp. 186–211; F. M. Snowden, *Violence and Great Estates in the South of Italy: Apulia, 1900–1922* (Cambridge, 1986).

The Italian literature concerning syndicalism has expanded dramatically since the early 1970s. See, especially: A. Riosa, *Il sindacalismo rivoluzionario in Italia* (Bari, 1976); G. B. Furiozzi, *Il sindacalismo rivoluzionario italiano* (Milan, 1977); Maurizio Antonioli's account in M. Antonioli *et al.*, *Sindacao e classe operaia nell'età della seconda internazionale* (Florence, 1983).

There are a number of path-breaking essays on Italian anarchism and syndicalism in *Ricerche storiche*, 5 (1979); 11 (1981); 12 (1983); and in *Movimento operaio e socialista* and *Volontà* from the 1970s to the early 1980s (see especially essays by Maurizio Antonioli, Lorenzo Gestri, Ugo Sereni, Gian Biagio Furiozzi, Maria Malatesta, Giovanni Procacci, Alceo Riosa, and Maurizio degl'Innocenti).

For short biographical sketches: F. Andreucci and T. Detti (eds), *Il movimento operaio italiano dizionario biografico*, 5 vols. (Rome, 1975–8).

In English one can find information on Malatesta in: V. Richards (ed.), *Errico Malatesta. His Life and Ideas* (London, 1965); C. Levy, 'Malatesta in exile', *Annali della Fondazione Einaudi*, 15 (1981), pp. 245–70.

Local social history studies with the emphasis on anarchism and syndicalism include the following books: E. Santarelli, *Le Marche dall'unità al fascismo* (Milan, 1964); P. Bianconi, *Il movimento operaio a Piombino* (Florence, 1970); P. Favilli, *Capitalismo e classe operaia a Piombino 1861–1918* (Rome, 1974); L. Gestri, *Capitalismo e classe operaia in provincia di Massa-Carrara. Dall'unità all'età giolittiana* (Florence, 1976); M. Marmo, *Il proletariato italiano a Napoli in età liberale* (Rome, 1978); V. Mantovani, *Mazurka Blu. La strage del Diana* (Milan, 1979), a superb study of anarchists in Milan during the *biennio rosso*; D. H. Bell, *Sesto San Giovanni: Workers, Culture and Politics in an Italian Town, 1880–1992* (New Brunswick, NJ, 1986); Snowden, op. cit. For the Torinese case: Levy, forthcoming PhD, op. cit.; P. Spriano, *Storia di Torino operaio e socialista. Da De Amicis a Gramsci* (Turin, 1972); S. Musso, *Gli operai di Torino 1900–1920* (Milan, 1980). There are also the following articles: G. Bianco and C. Constantini, ' "Il libertario" dalla fondazione alla guerra mondiale', *Movimento operaio e socialista*, 6 (1960), pp. 99–112; C. Constantini, 'Gli anarchici in Liguria durante la Prima Guerra Mondiale', *Movimento operaio e socialista*, 7 (1961), pp. 9–122; G. Bianco, 'L'attivita degli anarchici nel biennio rosso (1919–1920)', *Movimento operaio e socialista*, 8 (1962), pp. 110–25; M. Antonioli, 'Il movimento anarchico milanese agli inizi del secolo', in Various Authors, *Anna Kuliscioff e l'età del riformismo* (Rome, 1978), pp. 275–90.

For socialism: J. Miller, 'The Italian Socialist Party, 1900–1914: an organizational study', PhD thesis, University of Illinois 1974; A. Riosa, *Il movimento operaio tra società e stato. Il caso italiano nell'epoca della II Internationale* (Milan, 1984); P. Spriano, *Storia del Partito Communista Italiano*, 5 vols. (Turin, 1967–75); R. Martinelli, *Il Partito Communista d'Italia 1921–1926* (Rome, 1977).

* A third volume of Masini's history of anarchism was published too late to be used in this chapter.

2

The practice of direct action:
the Barcelona rent strike of 1931

Nick Rider

Conventionally, the image given of the path taken by the Spanish anarcho-syndicalist union, the CNT, following the establishment of a democratic republic in April 1931 has been, put very broadly, that almost from the inauguration of the new regime it came under the domination, particularly in Catalonia, of the most intransigent wing of anarchism, organized in the Iberian Anarchist Federation (FAI). This then sought immediate confrontation with the regime, launching a wave of maximalist, purely ideologically motivated, insurrectionary activism, without any intermediate objectives, a round of 'mindless revolutionism' that served only to destabilize the Republic and fritter away the strength of the CNT itself. No clear explanation is generally given of the process through which these radical elements came to the fore in what was an open, mass organization and in which, as several recent writers have pointed out, a great many of the membership were not by any means committed anarchists, it frequently being suggested that this was due to internal organizational machinations or fortuitous circumstances rather than to any more direct appeal to any section of the working class.

This image carries with it several assumptions. One is that the Republic of 1931 was indeed a genuinely democratic regime that did offer adequate means of expression for legitimate grievances, against which radical anarchists, without any previous provocation, launched actions of a kind that no government could be expected to tolerate, and which left the government with no alternative but to take repressive measures against the CNT. Another idea implied by this argument is that radical anarchism consisted entirely of an inflexible, purist ideology, a vaguely mystical 'Idea' still heavily imbued with millenarianism, in many ways unchanged since the introduction of anarchism into Spain in the 1860s and lacking, above all, any sense of development, any sense of strategy or tactics, and any concern for immediate, practical needs and aims. Often allied with this image is the argument that, in order to explain the apparent anomaly of the strength of anarchism in industrial Catalonia, stresses the stagnation and immobility of the Spanish economy, including Catalan industry, and of rural Spain, suggesting that anarchism in the cities was simply carried over from a backward countryside, as something of a survival of pre-industrial forms of conflict. These ideas seem to put forward a vision of the new migrants into the city, and of the Catalan working class in general, whenever they were identified with anarchism, as being peculiarly inflexible and predetermined; that is, to suggest that, rather than develop their forms of organization and action in accordance with experience and circumstances, they were liable to react only in a largely unreflecting manner and in terms of pre-existing, near-atavistic prejudices and fixed ideas. Conversely, it is rarely ever suggested that any of these modes of action could have formed part of attempts to respond imaginatively and dynamically to the practical demands of an urban environment.[1]

However, over and above the more apparent weaknesses in these arguments – notably the fact that only a very small proportion of the migrants into Barcelona came from the heartlands of rural anarchism in western Andalusia[2] – a closer examination of the record of the CNT reveals that in fact both the theory and, more importantly, the practice of all sectors of the CNT were in continual evolution; and that, alongside the more familiar preoccupation with ideology, a constant effort was made by different groups of union militants not only to build up a revolutionary movement but also, simultaneously, to come to terms with a rapidly changing social situation and respond to the apparent needs of the working class. In this chapter I shall deal with one example of this effort, in an area that was a primary social problem in Barcelona in the 1930s, housing, and which was of equal importance in the developing relationship between the Republic and the mass base of the CNT. In order to understand this process it is first necessary to look at the development of Barcelona in the first thirty years of this century.

Far from being a period of continuing stagnation and backwardness, that between 1910 and 1930 was one of enormous change in Spain, and intensive urbanization. In only fifteen years, between 1915 and 1930, the population of Barcelona, in particular, officially increased from 619,083 to 1,005,565 – that is, by some 62 per cent – and during the 1920s the city was one of the fastest-growing in Europe.[3] This rapid change was an integral part of the social and political crisis that would reach its climax in the Civil War of 1936.

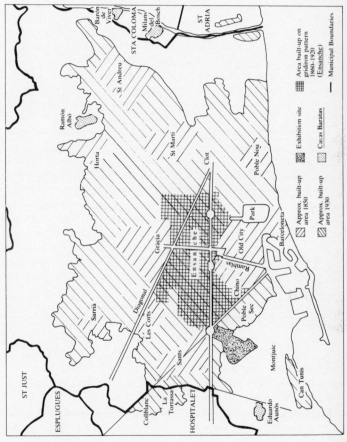

Map 2.1 Barcelona, showing districts mentioned in text and the groups of Cheap Houses (*Casas Baratas*).

The increase in the population of Barcelona was principally caused by two great waves of immigration, the first of which was associated with the boom set off by the First World War. The war opened up enormous possibilities for the Spanish economy, principally in the shape of exports to the belligerent countries, and stimulated an almost unprecedented wave of industrial expansion. Catalan industry, in particular, was permitted to break out of its excessive dependence on a sluggish and outmoded textile industry and diversify into more modern, technically based sectors such as engineering, chemicals, and electrical machinery. As Carme Massana has put it, it was between 1900 and 1930 that Barcelona acquired 'a truly industrial economic structure'.[4] At the same time, however, this sudden acceleration in the economy had a tremendous destabilizing effect on the whole country, producing massive inflation, rising far in advance of wages, that made life intolerable for large sections of the rural population and set in motion migration to the cities in numbers that, despite the boom, still exceeded the capacity of industry to absorb them.

Industrial expansion slowed down after the war, but, nevertheless, this exodus continued. In the case of Barcelona, which during the 1920s became the largest city in Spain, this second wave of immigration was attracted less by any industrial growth than by the massive public works projects associated with the International Exhibition of 1929. Several authors have indicated how the Exhibition was initially conceived by conservative Catalan nationalists as a means of mobilizing state and private capital to realize their ideal of Barcelona as a great modern city, equipped with modern systems of transport, energy, and so on.[5] In the Exhibition as it eventually materialized, however, many other sectors were to be equally influential, with different or very much more limited ideological motivations, notably the regime of General Primo de Rivera, which adopted it as a prestige operation, and several major financial interests. As a result it took on still more of the character of a capitalist project, a speculative operation in which state funds, the almost uncontrolled credits provided by the dictatorship, would be used to permit the maximizing of private profit.

Hence, while the official bodies occupied themselves in the building of the monuments and parks of the Exhibition and of an urban infrastructure conceived only as great avenues and transport systems, they did nothing to provide housing for the masses of immigrants who would come to build them. The only official initiative in this field was the four groups of so-called 'Cheap Houses', 2,229 in total, which were by no means sufficient to satisfy the demand and were in any case, according to the future Republican Mayor of Barcelona, no more than a reproduction 'in reinforced concrete of the primitive shack'.[6]

In consequence, the rapid growth of the city was accompanied by an acute housing crisis, in which the condition of housing available in Barcelona to the working class degenerated, while its price spiralled. In the absence of official initiatives the provision of housing was carried out by private landlords and, particularly, by the great many small landlords. The Chamber of Urban Property of Barcelona, membership of which had been obligatory for all landlords since 1920, had 97,853 members in the whole province in 1931, out of a total population of around 1,760,000. Of this membership 80 per cent, nearly 79,000, received an annual income from property lower than, at the most, 880 pesetas, and a great many received much less than this.[7] In value terms, much the greater part of property was held by major landlords, who were the chief beneficiaries of the revaluation of property produced by the Exhibition in the central areas of the city, but nevertheless ownership was also extremely fragmented, particularly in the working-class districts. Despite the vastly increased demand for housing, such small landlords disposed of very little capital with which to build, and the result was the appearance of an enormous amount of unplanned, substandard housing.

This new housing took various forms. One of the first manifestations of the housing crisis was the spread of shanty towns. In 1922 the then Director of the Municipal Hygiene Institute, Dr Pons Freixa, counted 3,008 shanties in Barcelona, with 15,552 inhabitants, although these figures had to be taken as provisional since the groups of shanties were growing out of all control.[8] The majority of these shanties were not built by the inhabitants themselves, nor were they occupied for free; around Barcelona there was very little land without an owner, and rent nearly always had to be paid for shanties, no matter what their condition might be. In addition, Pons Freixa denounced the appearance of shanty 'industrialists', who rented plots of land to build shacks and let them out at abusive rents, making 'an almost always usurious profit'. This 'industry' was not a matter of a few speculators, as, since massive profits could be made with only limited capital, an 'endless number' of people had entered into it, including many 'of very modest condition'.[9]

The situation changed slightly during the second wave of immigration, and indeed, as much of the capital accumulated during the industrial boom filtered into property, small landlords were able to take part in a veritable boom in building that occurred

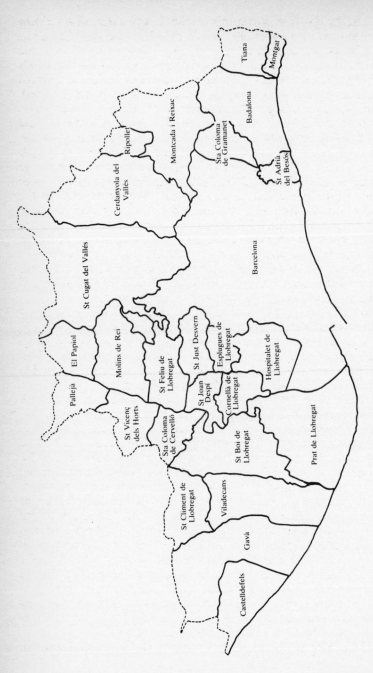

Map 2.2 Barcelona and the surrounding area.

during the 1920s. It was in this period, in particular, that building spread over into the smaller municipalities around the Barcelona city boundary, notably Hospitalet, Santa Coloma and Sant Adrià del Besós, the populations of which grew extraordinarily quickly within a very few years.[10] Though not shanties, the greater part of this housing was still of very low quality and grossly overcrowded, consisting, according to the architect N. M. Rubió i Tudurí, of no more than a mass of 'brand-new slums'.[11] Also, even this amount of building was not sufficient before the insatiability of the demand, and other, inferior forms of housing continued to spread. The number of shanties kept growing, reaching, according to one estimate, 6,000, housing 30,000 people, in Barcelona by 1927, with many more in the surrounding towns.[12] Within the city, in the older districts, virtual shanties were built on roofs, and flats were subdivided to the limit. In addition, on the initiative and due to the necessity of the tenants themselves, the practice of taking in subtenants was extended, as Rubió i Tudurí put it, 'to the limits of its elasticity', with in some cases seven or eight families in space designed for one.[13] In 1927 one observer estimated that around 100,000 people lived as subtenants in Barcelona.[14]

With this pressure on housing, and the lack of effective legal controls under the Dictatorship, an increase in the price of housing was inevitable. After the inflationary period of the war, working-class wage levels were more or less stable during the 1920s. Thus, in 1930 the average daily wage for a manual worker continued to be around 10 pesetas, as it had been for most of the decade. Similarly most retail prices, having fallen somewhat from their peak reached at the high point of inflation, remained relatively stable during this period.[15] Rents, on the other hand, registered an increase of between 50 and 150 per cent. The *Anuari estadístic* of Barcelona for 1920 gives 20 pesetas as an average monthly rent for a working-class family, and in 1922 Pons Freixa found that the most common rents for shanties were between 15 and 20 pesetas.[16] In 1931, however, the CNT Commission that organized the rent strike claimed that the normal rent for a flat was 50 pesetas,[17] and this does not seem at all exaggerated. Notes in the press refer to rents of 50, 60, 66 pesetas or more in working-class districts, and of 30 pesetas for a virtually uninhabitable shanty.[18] Also, figures taken from a register of vacant housing made by the City of Barcelona in 1934 show that the largest single group, 3,152, was that of rents between 50 and 150 pesetas a month, while for less than 50 pesetas there were only 450, less than for any other group apart from the luxury flats of 200 pesetas or more.[19]

Everything seems to confirm that there had been a massive

increase in rents, despite the theoretical validity of the Rent Decree of 1920, which authorized only increases of 10 per cent for each period of five years since 1914.[20] Indeed, it can be seen that housing, previously relatively cheap, had come to be a major problem in a working-class budget; at the same time, there had been a sizeable increase in the relative wealth of those of the lower middle class with urban property, a fact that had great potential consequences for social relations.

In addition, it should be pointed out that a situation like this gave ample room for abuses of all kinds. Pons Freixa noted that the rents of shanties were not subject to any market logic, and much less to any legal norms, but were determined entirely by 'the ambition of the landlords', since the desperation of the tenants obliged them to accept anything that was offered. Hence, such anomalies could occur as the fact that one could often pay *more* for an 'infected hovel' than for decent housing. Also, entirely illegal evictions were carried out, either by simple force or with the connivance of local officials.[21] Similar abuses were seen in more 'regular' housing. To give only one example, in 1933 another public health official wrote that in Barcelona some 20,000 houses or flats, housing 100,000 people, lacked running water because 'miserly' landlords refused to connect it, despite the fact that this had been obligatory in the Municipal Regulations since 1891, and that this was one of the main reasons why typhoid fever was still endemic in the city.[22] In effect, it would appear that a large part of the working-class housing of Barcelona functioned within a black economy, and that the inoperativeness of legal controls was virtually the norm in working-class districts.

The response that the elements of the CNT gave to this situation should be considered in the context of the widespread awareness in the movement that in the years leading up to the *coup d'état* of 1923 they had entered into a dead end. On the one hand, the CNT had achieved the primary objective of any syndicalist movement, that of mobilizing a majority of the working class, becoming by far the largest such movement in the world. However, the militant unionism of those years had ended in a rising spiral of violence, in which they were always at a disadvantage, while the achievement of wage increases had not brought real changes in living standards, due to inflation. In addition, there was also a strong awareness among many militants that the movement had not been able to go beyond a purely labour context and extend its influence to other areas of society. On the contrary, a great part of even the union base of the CNT had been reduced to the level of passive spectators as the organization had become locked into a desperate, exhausting struggle involving only the most dedicated militants against the police and the gunmen of the right, and its strength had been withered away. However heroic, the results of such a struggle, either in purely practical terms or for the building up of a genuinely participatory social movement, were seen to be simply not proportional to the prodigious effort involved. The 1920s were years of intense debate among all sectors of the CNT as they struggled to remedy the evident weaknesses of the movement.

One aspect of these debates, the most familiar, was the in many ways purely theoretical dispute between, broadly, the 'syndicalist' and 'radical anarchist' wings of the CNT, as they each strove to give a particular orientation to the organization, or more precisely to prevent it being controlled by other tendencies that they considered to be harmful deviations. Another, however, was the concern, seen among militants in all the main tendencies, to find new methods, more broadly based than those of straightforward industrial conflict, that would, within its libertarian structure, increase the movement's effectiveness, its implantation in society, and its resilience before repression. This concern led to considerable discussion of the nature of one of the basic principles of the CNT, that of direct action, and of the need to extend its practice in order for the workers' movement to become a genuine alternative system of social organization capable of dealing independently with all kinds of social problems. An open letter sent by a number of radical anarchists held in the Barcelona prison in 1925 spoke of the need for anarchist ideas to leave the 'abstractions of thought' and be given immediate practical form in the agitation of the movement.[23] From another wing of the CNT, the leading syndicalist Joan Peiró criticized the organization's excessive dependence on industrial strikes and urged that it should establish 'district committees' to organize action around any matter of concern to the working class, not just labour questions, so that direct action could become 'mass action' and a universal form of social agitation and organization.[24]

In practical terms this concern was reflected in a belief that the movement should try to give answers to all the urgent problems of the working class, of which, it was generally agreed, housing was one of the most acute. This attitude was expressed soon after the Berenguer government, appointed after the fall of Primo de Rivera in January 1930, permitted the re-emergence of the CNT. Shortly after the reappearance of the Barcelona CNT newspaper, *Solidaridad obrera*, in September the same year, an article announced a forthcoming campaign on rents. The imbalance between earnings and what was indispensable to live, it said, was unbearable, and in this the primary factor was that of rents, which had reached intolerable levels. Despite this, however, the subject was hardly spoken of, and it was necessary to expose it, because there was no other question that could be of so much interest to so many families, including many of the lower middle class, civil servants and so on, who were usually opposed to the workers' organization. In order to defend both workers and the people in general, the paper was going to launch a campaign of denunciation of housing abuses.[25] It was temporarily banned shortly afterwards, however, and this campaign did not materialize. Nevertheless, in the succeeding months there were more indications of this concern. Thus, in January 1931 another article said, referring to the established practices of the workers' movement, that 'we have tried to put up dykes against the exploitation of the producers, but we have almost entirely forgotten to combat exploitation in the field of consumption'. It went on to describe how building and property produced profits far superior to those of industry, and how rents consumed a third of earnings. 'We believe', it said,

> that there is a magnificent field for action here; great masses of the population, indifferent to the struggles carried on by the unions and often enemies of union demands when these make themselves felt through prolonged strikes, would understand actions of this kind and unite their voice of protest to ours.[26]

In early 1931 there were already local tenants' movements in some districts of Barcelona. The general protest movement, however, came out of a meeting of the CNT Construction Workers' Union of 12 April 1931, the same day as the municipal elections that would bring in the Republic. There, Arturo Parera, a building worker and radical anarchist, proposed the creation of the 'Economic Defence Commission of the Construction Union', which would study 'the expense that corresponds to each worker for the wage earned. For example: on the question of rents, no more will be paid than that which has a relation to the income of the family concerned.' The Commission was established with the proviso that it could be expanded to include the other unions and to deal with other problems as well as rents. Among its first members were Parera and Santiago Bilbao, who would be the most visible 'figures' of this movement.[27]

Immediately afterwards came the proclamation of the Republic, something that caught most of the CNT and many of the Republicans themselves by surprise. Here it is necessary to point out that the Republic, after fifty years of agitation in which it had always signified the opposition to the dominant regime, aroused expectations among the working and lower middle classes that were as broad as they were ill-defined, and the assumption was general that, even if it were not a regime of total equity, it would at least bring an end to repression and permit the free expression of popular discontents. Moreover, these expectations had been encouraged to the maximum over the preceding months by republican politicians, and by none more so than by the Catalan Republican Left, the Esquerra Republicana, absolute victors of the elections in Catalonia, whose propagandists had presented a prospect of sweeping change following a change of regime.[28] In a society that was traditionally heavily authoritarian, something that had only been accentuated by seven years of Dictatorship, the apparent breakdown in the structure of authority produced a general outburst of accumulated social resentments. For the unions, this meant a massive intensification in their activities. In only one month, May 1931, 105,000 new members were admitted into the Catalan region of the CNT,[29] and, on 28 May, *Solidaridad obrera* said that 'the unions have been taken by assault by the workers', who sought immediate solutions to their problems.[30] A wave of strikes began that, continually increasing in intensity, overflowed from union structures and escaped from the control of union committees. The rent campaign was to take place within this atmosphere of generalized agitation, and the repression it attracted was also part of the general 'restoration of authority', a phrase that would become an authentic fetish for the respectable classes and press at this time.

The Economic Defence Commission of the Construction Union first presented its basic demand, for a 40 per cent reduction in rents, to the public in the massive CNT meeting held on 1 May. However, the real launching of the campaign came in three articles that appeared in *Solidaridad obrera* on 12, 13, and 15 May.

The announcement of the campaign, the first article said, had aroused a great deal of expectation among the working class, but there was considerable confusion about what exactly they were proposing. There was, it went on, a general desire for immediate material improvements, which, while entirely comprehensible, could make people act in unthinking and unproductive ways. It was necessary to find a means of organizing action to secure these immediate needs that was in accordance with the principles and organization of the CNT and which would enable the people to resolve, effectively and by their own actions, their most urgent problems, which were, the Commission believed, unemployment, the cost of housing, and the cost of food.

On unemployment, they proposed – and it should be remembered that they were still referring principally to the building trades – that on an agreed day the unemployed should enter sites and factories and demand the taking on of 15 per cent more workers. It was made clear that this would not be just an act of protest or of revolutionary provocation, but would be genuinely designed to achieve its declared object and oblige contractors to put into circulation the capital they had lying idle, thus increasing demand and reactivating the economy. This would not suppose any fundamental break with the capitalist system, if those newly arrived in power were prepared to act with energy and goodwill.

On rents, the Commission presented the grounds for their demand of a 40 per cent reduction, explaining how landlords had taken advantage of the housing crisis to increase their return on capital to, they claimed, between 8 and 16 per cent, and how one of the major causes of Spanish economic stagnation was the high proportion of capital retained in non-productive sectors such as property. On food prices, they proposed the formation of local defence groups, through which the working class could control prices directly, imposing reasonable prices and exposing speculators.

By achieving these minimum demands, people would improve their own situation at the same time as they learnt how to organize themselves through the actual practice of direct action, until such time as they were able to carry out the hoped-for 'total change'. This would come 'when we understand that we are in a condition to assume this responsibility'. That is, it was implicitly accepted that a revolution was not immediately practicable. The important thing, however, was that people should get used to self-organization and to solving their own problems. While this would necessarily produce conflicts, these did not have to cause insuperable problems with the Republic, if this was truly a liberal regime. The Commission said that 'we will put forward without exaggerations reasonable measures for resolving adequately whatever matters there are in which the sufferings of the people demand rapid solutions', and it would be 'madness' if capitalism or the state were intransigent before these demands.[31]

It could be alleged that this apparent belief in the possibilities of the Republican regime was no more than a manipulation on the part of some radical anarchists – both Bilbao and Parera were prominent members of the FAI – who sought out conflicts with the object of provoking violent incidents and insurrectional actions. This would have been peculiarly Machiavellian, given the effort expended on the campaign, and was emphatically not the attitude of those who took part in it at the grass roots. Moreover, if one leading radical activist, Juan García Oliver, has written that from the first he was seeking to provoke as many violent incidents as possible so as to destabilize the Republic,[32] there is little indication that this was a majority opinion. Many radical anarchists, including such influential figures as the Urales family, felt that the movement was in no state to undertake any large-scale initiatives, and that its immediate priority was to build up its strength and expand. Similarly, they also seem to have shared in the expectation that the Republic would at least give the CNT sufficient room to allow this to take place.[33]

In their articles in May the Construction Union Commission also said that they were in contact with the other CNT unions with the object of becoming a representative body of the whole local organization, and asked that sympathizers with the campaign should place their names on a register, so that they might know how many people they could count on. It was not necessary to be a member of the CNT. This process of organization would last a long time, too long for the Commission, but nevertheless they excused it by virtue of the overwhelming work of reconstruction that at that time was borne by all the union committees. This work would be lightened, they said, precisely by the definitive establishment of the Commission, since it could take charge of the most immediate material questions and leave the committees to their more strictly administrative duties. Thus, as well as other things, it would contribute to remedying the growing disorder in the organization of the CNT.[34] Again, the attitude shown by the Commission here contrasts with a commonly presented image of radical anarchists in the CNT as being unconcerned with organizational problems.

In the meantime, resistance to landlords had begun spontaneously. On 4 May a group of workers re-installed an unemployed family evicted from a house on the south side of Barcelona. *Solidaridad obrera* applauded this 'generous action'. On 23 June, in Hospitalet, when local people re-installed another evicted family, their action was 'greatly discussed' in the district.[35] The number of similar incidents would increase in the following weeks.

The active campaign of the Economic Defence Commission, however, began with a series of meetings held in all the working-class districts of Barcelona and the surrounding towns at the end of June and the beginning of July. In the Barceloneta district, near the docks, for example, on 1 July, some 1,500 people heard various speakers accuse landlords and traders of systematically robbing the people, with the complicity of the authorities. According to *Solidaridad obrera*, the crowd consisted predominantly of women.[36] Here it is interesting to point out that, since in Catalonia there was a strong tradition that working men gave their wages complete to their wives, rent paying was generally a woman's responsibility, and in fact in all the incidents associated with this campaign women played a very prominent role.

This series of meetings culminated in a mass rally held on 5 July in the Palace of Fine Arts, where the following demands were accepted as the basis of the campaign:

- that the equivalent of an extra month's rent demanded by landlords from new tenants as security should be taken as rent, so that no more should be paid for the month of July;
- that after then rent should only be paid with a 40 per cent reduction;
- that the unemployed should not have to pay any rent.

It was also agreed that, if landlords refused to accept the reduced rent, tenants should declare themselves on rent strike and pay nothing, always making clear that they did so as part of the general campaign. At the same time, it was also decided that action on food prices should be left until after the rent question had been resolved, while unemployment would be better dealt with by the individual unions. The work of the Commission thus became concentrated entirely on the rent campaign.[37] Their demands were quickly made known through leaflets distributed in working-class districts, and it is evident that the response was immediate and widespread.

This provoked an equally immediate reaction from the principal landlords' organization, the Chamber of Urban Property. First on 15 July they denounced the appearance of the Commission's leaflets, saying that they could not believe the CNT was responsible for such a thing, which would cause alarm and prejudice the consolidation of the Republic. On the 16th the President of the Barcelona Chamber, Joan Pich i Pon, visited the Civil Governor, the appointed official responsible for the administration of policing, to inform him of the concern that existed and to request the support of authority.[38] On the 20th an assembly was held of all the Chambers of Catalonia, at which it is clear that the general mood was both highly concerned and extremely aggressive. The hall had to be altered to admit the 'extraordinary attendance', above all of small landlords.

Pich and the other speakers laid great emphasis on the sufferings of small landlords, saying that they were already weighed down by taxes, that they were workers who had saved a little capital with years of labour, and that in a Republic they should be protected by the law. Only the courts, they declared, could order reductions in rent. It was proposed that the Civil Governor be asked not to permit any acts of propaganda for the campaign, as being 'against all social, legal and juridical order', and at the end of the meeting it was agreed that a permanent committee be established to carry out any actions necessary for the defence of property. Also, Pich i Pon and a delegation would go to Madrid to seek the support of the central government.[39]

Already in this assembly one can see what was to be the main characteristic of the reaction of both the landlords and the authorities. There was not at any time any attempt to consider the matter as a social and economic problem for which solutions should be sought, but instead it was viewed as a campaign of delinquency, a violation of the rights of property, and so essentially a police problem. On 30 July the Chamber's Committee requested not only the prohibition of all propaganda for the rent strike, but also that those responsible should be arrested, as would be 'all those who hold public or private meetings to agree together with the object of committing a crime of any kind'.[40] There was not, therefore, any attempt to negotiate, but only an immovable determination to restore social discipline. Later in the campaign the Economic Defence Commission did propose a negotiated solution, but was ignored.[41]

In the preceding weeks social tensions had been intensifying in the whole of Spain. On 6 July the national telephone strike, the first major confrontation between the CNT and the Republican government, had begun. More and more clashes occurred between union militants and the police, and the government returned to the old practice of arresting strikers solely on 'governmental order', without any judicial process, fixed sentence, or right of appeal. This had always been considered one of the most oppressive practices of the Monarchy, the disappearance of which, it had been reliably assured, would follow immediately on the change of regime, and its revival had a profound impact among the working class. On the 20th, in protest at the shooting of a striker by police, a general strike, which ended in considerable violence, was declared in Seville, and Miguel Maura, the Interior Minister, was already talking of the need to ban the CNT.[42]

Hence the representatives of the Barcelona Chamber of Property found a receptive atmosphere in Madrid. Largo Caballero, the socialist Labour Minister, said he considered the rent campaign 'absurd',[43] and Maura and Fernando de los Ríos, the Justice Minister, promised Pich that they would give instructions to facilitate the rapid processing and carrying out of evictions of rent strikers.[44] Meanwhile, in Barcelona on 22 July a bomb exploded in an underground telephone line in the centre of the city, causing no deaths or injuries but considerable damage. Though responsibility for the bomb was by no means clear, it was immediately attributed to the telephone strikers. On the same day the Civil Governor, Carlos Esplá, prohibited all meetings of the telephone union. At the same time, however, he also banned a rally of the Economic Defence Commission, although nothing was said to explain what connection they had with the bomb. On the 27th the local prosecutor began legal action against the Commission's leaflets, as 'seditious propaganda'. In effect, from this time on the Commission was not permitted any public propaganda outside of the press, and so a good part of the Chamber of Property's requests had been satisfied almost immediately.[45]

The Commission, however, responded by urging rent strikers not to be discouraged or be intimidated by threats of eviction, since, they said, they had received a great deal more support than they had expected, and if there were enough of them they could flood the courts.[46]

It is very difficult to estimate the number of people who took part in the rent strike. Due to the destruction of Spanish records that occurred during the Civil War there is very little documentation available. The Municipal Courts, responsible for evictions, do not have any records from the time, and the archives of the Chamber of Urban Property were destroyed by the revolutionaries in 1936, something that is itself significant. The Commission said that in July there were 45,000 and in August over 100,000 rent strikers.[47] Even if this is taken to be exaggerated and cut by half, it is still a large number in a city of just over one million. The extreme reaction of landlords and authorities, and the memories of the participants, suggest that it was very widespread. One CNT militant, who then lived in the Clot district of Barcelona, remembers that the response 'could not have been more unanimous', since the objective was readily understandable to everybody. According to another, from Hospitalet, at one time 'a large majority' ceased paying.[48] The Commission pointed out that the strike did not demand the terrible sacrifices of industrial strikes, but instead gave people an immediate benefit. As Bilbao wrote later in the campaign, even if they achieved nothing else, by not paying rent for four months the strikers would have saved themselves 12 million pesetas.[49] Hence the strike could gain in strength over time, rather than exhaust itself.

From the incidents mentioned in the press it appears that the areas where the strike was strongest were the outer working-class districts of Barcelona and those in the surrounding towns, notably Sants, Poble Nou, and Clot in Barcelona, La Torrassa in Hospitalet, and Santa Coloma. There were rent strikers in all the working-class districts of Barcelona, however, while some towns further away from the city also set up their own Economic Defence Commissions.[50] Mass meetings having been prohibited, communication was maintained between the strikers at district level. The Commission had local committees in many districts, and it was made known that one could go to the local union halls and libertarian clubs to find people to help in resisting evictions. Often, though, this was not really necessary: 'When something was going to happen, we knew by word of mouth. . . . All the kids used to go,' one woman remembers.[51] The resistance was based in a strong sense of community solidarity. The Commission recommended that people should insult and remonstrate with the workers who carried out evictions, and on 26 August a crowd nearly lynched two men who had obeyed the orders of a judge to help in clearing a house in Hospitalet.[52] Also, people were reminded 'not to abandon those evicted'. According to the CNT militant Severino Campos, in cases where tenants could not be re-installed the Commission took charge of finding them other housing.[53] Here it should be remembered that it was already traditional among CNT militants to take in others who for one reason or another needed shelter.

With this popular base the movement proved extremely difficult to suppress. In the meantime, the number of incidents at evictions was increasing. Also, even when evictions were carried out without problems the authorities did not have sufficient forces to mount a permanent guard on each vacant house, so there was nothing to prevent tenants being re-installed at a later time.[54]

From the end of July onwards one does not see in official policy towards the strike anything more than an ever greater deployment of repressive measures. On 30 July the Assault Guards, the new Republican police, intervened in an eviction for the first time.[55] This repressive policy hardened above all after the appointment as Civil Governor of a conservative lawyer, Oriol Anguera de Sojo, on 3 August. Anguera let it be known that he considered the campaign to be simply illegal, and would not tolerate it. On 17 August, Santiago Bilbao was arrested on governmental order, and was to be held until well into 1932. The justification given was that he had ridiculed authority by speaking on the rent strike at a meeting of the textile union, thus evading the prohibition on the Commission's own meetings.[56]

At the same time, an increasingly direct role was assumed by the

Chamber of Urban Property. Its Committee was continually in contact with the authorities, and above all with the Civil Governor, who promised them that all necessary assistance would be given in evictions. On several occasions the Chamber would request and obtain police protection even in cases where the Municipal Courts did not, and in October would establish its own service of men and lorries to carry out evictions themselves, since the municipal employees whose job it was to do them often did not do so because they felt intimidated or were themselves union members.[57]

The Defence Commission, for their part, seemed rather surprised by the ferocity of the reaction they had provoked, reaffirming the realistic nature of their demands and indicating a willingness to negotiate that contrasted sharply with the intransigence of landlords and authorities. They had wanted, they said, to achieve 'the maximum benefit with the minimum of effort' and correct the abuses of the Dictatorship, but were treated only as 'trouble-makers'.[58] As they repeatedly pointed out, they were a committee of the CNT, a legal organization. From early August onwards, the Commission published a series of revelations of the tax frauds committed by landlords, who, they claimed, habitually declared in tax only half or less of their actual rents, which thus could rise entirely outside any legal control. They had imagined, they said, that in a Republic the law would be the same for all, but had found that, whereas landlords were allowed to swindle both their tenants and the state, they were labelled as criminals simply for protesting.[59]

The Chamber of Urban Property naturally denied all of these allegations. Nevertheless, in the administrative section of the annual report of the Chamber itself for 1932 there is an item which, in effect, amply confirms the rent strikers' accusations. This section, an internal document that dealt with the collection of the Chamber's own membership fees, states that an actual majority of landlords made false declarations of their properties to the tax and census authorities and to the Chamber itself, that they gave false identities and tried to conceal their own addresses, that it was 'almost impossible' to know how many properties were held by each landlord, and that the information in the majority of rental contracts (leases) was also false.[60] Once again, then, the evasion of legal and fiscal controls appears to have been virtual standard practice among landlords.

By late August tension was reaching its height between the CNT and the Republican authorities in Barcelona, centred, particularly, on the emotive issue of the prisoners held on governmental order.

In this situation, of vital importance for the future relations between the CNT and the regime, the rent strike seems to have been particularly important. It was claimed in *Solidaridad obrera* at the time that Anguera de Sojo had said that he was prepared to free all the 'governmental' prisoners *except* Bilbao, something that is also maintained today by Severino Campos.[61] Also, in a later statement justifying his hard line, Anguera de Sojo mentioned specifically three things which he did not think could be tolerated: the use of coercion against the freedom of labour, 'violent campaigns' like 'the offensive to make tenants stop paying rent', and the circulation of unauthorized leaflets.[62] At the end of August the fifty-three CNT members in the Barcelona prison declared themselves on hunger strike to demand the release of those held without trial.[63] This led to a riot in the prison, on 2 September, and outside a general strike broke out in protest at the treatment of the prisoners. In the prevailing atmosphere of tension, it ended in violence. Afterwards, even stricter restrictions were placed on the activities of the CNT, and over three hundred arrests were made. These new prisoners, virtually all of them held on governmental order, were, as much as any fixed ideological position, to constitute an almost insuperable obstacle to any reconciliation between the CNT and the regime.

Within the general official hard line, the repression of the tenants' movement also tightened after the September strike. Federica Montseny claimed in *El luchador* that activists involved in the rent campaign were arrested on any kind of pretext.[64] More police protection was provided at evictions, and the police took to breaking or impounding the belongings of those evicted to prevent further reoccupations.[65] Also, on 2 October the Chamber of Property's own lorries began operating. Finally, Anguera de Sojo demanded the names of the Defence Commission from the CNT Local Federation, and, when the latter refused to co-operate, gave it a heavy fine.[66] From that day, 12 October, onwards the Commission could no longer even publish statements in the press, and went underground.

Even so, the strike continued, as resistance had also hardened. One landlord was threatened with pistols at an eviction.[67] In a letter to the Interior Minister of 17 October the Chamber of Urban Property denounced the existence of a 'state of anarchy' in the 'outer districts' of Barcelona. In another letter of the same day, to the Civil Governor, they described an incident a few days previously when, despite the presence of the Assault Guards, who were there at the request of the Chamber, 'a crowd . . . of pregnant women and children' had prevented an eviction from being carried out. The officer commanding the Guards had declined to attack the women, and the Chamber pointed out to the Governor the gravity of the situation for the 'principle of authority and the necessity of maintaining order' if the law could be ridiculed in this way.[68] This invulnerability of women would not last, however. To carry out an eviction in Poble Nou on 21 October eighty Assault Guards were sent, who closed off the street, and when a demonstration of women began to form, the Guards charged. The eviction was completed.[69]

What really seems to have broken down the strike, however, was the practice of arresting tenants who went back into their houses after being evicted, even when they claimed not to be responsible for their own re-installation. Tenants were easy to locate, and once it became clear that the authorities were actually prepared to arrest them in significant numbers morale seems to have sagged. The level of active resistance fell notably in November. Also, some tenants may have been led to abandon the strike by the hope that the new Rent Decree, of December 1931, would enable them to obtain redress through legal means, an expectation that would prove to be illusory.[70] The Chamber of Property, in any case, felt able to congratulate itself in December that the rebelliousness was 'virtually terminated'.[71]

Nevertheless, the strike never entirely ended in many districts, but continued in a more or less underground form, since the non-payment of rent, occasionally leading to violent incidents, would be endemic in many areas and a chronic source of conflict throughout the Republican period. This was particularly the case in La Torrassa in Hospitalet, and in the municipal 'Cheap Houses', both of them major centres of radical anarchist influence.[72] Neither was the strike a total failure elsewhere, as many landlords, unable to carry on without receiving any income, had made separate agreements with their tenants, conceding them a reduction or at least wiping off the arrears built up during the strike.[73] As a result, many tenants felt they had at least won a moral victory. The Chamber of Urban Property, for their part, did not feel able to relax their vigilance and at the end of the year announced that, to take advantage of the information acquired during the strike, they had made up a register of evicted tenants, which all landlords should consult before letting property. The register would be kept up to date, since the collaboration had been secured of the Municipal Courts, which would send on details of any new eviction cases.[74]

The anarchist historian Abel Paz believes that the popular

mobilization begun in the rent strike formed the basis for many subsequent anarchist campaigns.[75] Other witnesses also remember the strike as being the initiation into the anarchist movement for many people, above all among the young, who would play a major role in the conflicts of the following years.[76] In all, it presents an image of radical anarchism much more complex than the conventional one of an unthinking 'putschism'. In contrast, it appears here as a movement that, in addition to possessing a revolutionary ideology, was also capable of mobilizing action around objectives firmly rooted in the life and conditions of the working class. Similar agitation was also undertaken, for example, against the suppression of street trading, an essential supplement to their income for many of the poorer working class, and against gas prices. It was this ability periodically to identify and express widely felt needs and feelings that, together with its strong presence at community level, formed the basis of the strength of radical anarchism, and enabled it to build up a mass base of support. Similarly, agitation of this kind can be seen not to have been simply the result of a hangover of rural ideas and attitudes, but to have arisen out of an effort precisely to respond, from the position of the poorer working class, to the problems experienced in the city, and specifically to those created by intensive and uncontrolled urbanization of the kind that had taken place in Barcelona. Equally, 'direct action' appears not as any abstract ideological proposition but as an entirely practical form of action for sectors of the working class with urgent needs and little hope of obtaining satisfaction by other means.

The manner in which this specific campaign was carried forward also contrasts with the established image. There were, undoubtedly, many among the different groups into which even the radical wing of the CNT was divided who were more concerned with a more abstract conception of anarchism. The leading figures in the rent campaign, nevertheless, who were also, as has been said, prominent members of the FAI, revealed a clear awareness of a social situation, considerable tactical agility and flexibility, and a willingness to make use of legal channels, such as the denunciation of tax fraud, when it appeared that they could have practical effect. Faced with the conventional opposition between reformism and revolution, they appear, in effect, to have put forward a third alternative, seeking to obtain immediate practical improvements through the actual development, in practice, of autonomous, libertarian forms of self-organization, in such a way that they would, it was hoped, be beyond the power of the structures of the state to recuperate them.

The impact of the rent campaign was all the greater because belief in the essential justice of its demands was so widely shared. The Republic was generally seen as a historic opportunity to rectify the injustices long accumulated under a reactionary regime, and in particular to correct the abuses of the Dictatorship, an impression that had been fully encouraged by Republican politicians. Given these expectations it was not surprising that the transition to a new regime was accompanied by a wave of strikes and other agitation, without any great need for provocation by ideological agitators. In Barcelona, it was widely recognized that the grossly exploitative state of the housing market was one of the most scandalous of the abuses of recent years, and indeed members of the Catalan Republican Left had specifically suggested that action in this area would follow rapidly upon a change of regime.[77] In the rent campaign, therefore, anarchist militants were organizing not around revolutionary demands, but around the expectations associated with the Republic itself, and among a population many of which did not previously have any fixed attitude of opposition to the regime.

The Republican authorities, however, showed themselves inflexible once these demands were made. Many tenants evidently expected some intervention in their favour from the Catalan Republican Left. However, among the confused ideological baggage of even the more reforming elements in the party there was a notable reluctance to place real restrictions on the property of the lower middle class; more importantly, among the lower-middle-class base of the party there were many who were themselves major beneficiaries of the building boom of the preceding years. The vague promise of an inter-class reformism thus rapidly broke down once the contradictions built up in the development of the city began to emerge. If elected politicians prevaricated, the judicial and police system of the state, on the other hand, directed in an entirely traditional manner, showed itself to possess much greater effective social power. It was a traditional liberal criticism of the Spanish state machine under the Monarchy that it was excessively subservient to oligarchical interest groups, simply responding to their wishes rather than developing an independent policy. In the situation created by the Barcelona rent strike, the state administration, above all at local level, can be seen to have functioned in an essentially similar manner, its policy consisting of little more than placing its forces at the disposal of a business organization, the Chamber of Urban Property, to restore social discipline.

It should be remembered that the status quo with regard

to housing in Barcelona was one of widespread and near-institutionalized illegality, in which the law as a system of regulation of property relations was often wholly ineffective, a fact, moreover, that was no secret but was frequently denounced by many sectors well to the right of the CNT.[78] By insisting, in the name of legality, on the overriding priority of social discipline, therefore, the state authorities were defending this situation and allowing it to continue. Those who became involved in the rent strike and similar campaigns responded to the reality of this situation, rather than to the ostensible legalism of the Republican regime. The frustration of the initial hopes of change, and the swift reversion of the regime to traditional repressive methods, fatally undermined the position of those within the CNT who favoured a *rapprochement* between the union and the Republic and, in contrast, raised the standing of radical militants, who were identified, among other things, as refusing to compromise in the defence of interests in every way as concrete as those defended by more 'moderate' groupings. This situation thus provided the natural background for a rapid radicalization of the poorer working class. In turn, this established a social base for the growth in prestige of a more definedly revolutionary anarchism, found among sectors of the working class who came into conflict with the institutions of the Republic not for purely ideological reasons, but for very practical causes based in the inability of these institutions to provide constructive solutions to the problems created by the rapid economic development of the preceding years.

Notes and references

1 'Mindless revolutionism', Raymond Carr, *Spain 1808–1975* (Oxford, 1982), p. 624. This basic image, albeit with differences of detail, is found in all the standard works in English, such as Carr; Gerald Brenan, *The Spanish Labyrinth* (Cambridge, 1943); Hugh Thomas, *The Spanish Civil War* (London, 1977, revised edn); Gabriel Jackson, *The Spanish Republic and the Civil War, 1931–1939* (Princeton, NJ, 1965); and Stanley Payne, *The Spanish Revolution* (London, 1970). Later works, more critical towards the Republic, such as Ronald Fraser's *Blood of Spain* (London, 1979), nevertheless still emphasize the essentially ideological and inflexible nature of radical anarchism. The diversity of ideological commitment among the grass roots of the CNT is stressed in Colin Winston, *Workers and the Right in Spain, 1900–1936* (Princeton, NJ, 1985), and in much of the recent work produced in Catalonia, notably Enric Ucelay da Cal, *La Catalunya populista* (Barcelona, 1982), and Pere Gabriel, 'Classe obrera i sindicats a Catalunya, 1903–1920', PhD thesis, University of

Barcelona, 1981. The explanation of anarchist influence, and above all that of radical anarchism, in Spain in terms of industrial and rural backwardness was first developed extensively in the 1920s by Marxist critics of the CNT such as Andreu Nin and Joaquin Maurín, and then by the Catalan historian Jaume Vicens Vives – *Cataluña en el siglo XIX* (Madrid, 1961). It is reflected in the writings of E. J. Hobsbawm on Spain – *Primitive Rebels* (Manchester, 1959); *Bandits* (London, 1969); and the article 'The Spanish background' (1966), included in *Revolutionaries* (London, 1973) – as well as in many of the standard works previously mentioned.

2 Only 2.5 per cent of non-Catalans resident in Catalonia in 1930 were from western Andalusia. Principal regions of origin of migrants were Valencia (36 per cent), Aragon (21 per cent), and eastern Andalusia (10 per cent), areas where, if anything, anarchist influence spread from Barcelona, rather than vice versa – J. A. Vandellós i Solà, *L'immigració a Catalunya* (Barcelona, 1935), p. 62. For more extensive criticism of conventional interpretations of Spanish anarchism, see Joaquín Romero Maura, 'The Spanish case', in D. E. Apter and J. Joll (eds), *Anarchism Today* (London, 1971).

3 *Gaseta municipal de Barcelona* (1934), Estadística, p. 7.

4 Carme Massana, *Indústria, ciutat i propietat* (Barcelona, 1985), p. 65.

5 See particularly Francesc Roca, *Política econòmica i territori a Catalunya, 1901–1939* (Barcelona, 1979); and Ignasi Solà-Morales, 'L'Exposició International de Barcelona (1914–1929), com a instrument de política urbana', *Recerques*, 6 (Barcelona, 1976).

6 J. Aiguader i Miró, *El problema de l'habitació obrera a Barcelona* (Barcelona, 1932), p. 10. On the 'Cheap Houses', see also T. García de Castro, 'Barrios Barceloneses de la dictadura de Primo de Rivera', *Revista de geografía*, 8, 1–2 (Barcelona, 1974).

7 Figures based on membership lists in Cámara Oficial de la Propiedad Urbana de la Provincia de Barcelona (CPUB), *Memoria de 1931* (Barcelona, 1932), pp. 359–60. It should be pointed out that these lists and figures are based on the tax returns made by the landlords themselves and so, since tax evasion was notoriously common, almost certainly underestimate the true wealth of landlords. They can, though, be taken to give a broad indication of the distribution of property. The approximate exchange rate at that time was £1 = 4.8 pesetas.

8 F. Pons Freixa and J. M. Martino, *Los aduares de Barcelona* (Barcelona, 1929), p. 52.

9 Ibid., pp. 62–4.

10 The populations of the municipalities most affected by immigration increased in the following manner:

	Population 1920	Population 1930	Proportional increase
Hospitalet de Llobregat	12,360	37,650	204.61%
Santa Coloma de Gramanet	2,728	12,930	373.97%
Sant Adrià del Besós	1,073	6,515	507.18%

Source: La població de Catalunya 1936 (Barcelona, 1937).

11 N. M. Rubió i Tudurí, *La caseta i l'hortet* (Barcelona, 1933).
12 J. Aiguader i Miró, 'El problema de les barraques i dels rellogats', *Butlletí del Sindicat de Metges de Catalunya* (Barcelona, May 1927).
13 Rubió i Tudurí, *La caseta*, op. cit.
14 Aiguader i Miró, 'El problema de les barraques' op. cit.
15 For wage levels and price indexes, see *Anuario estadístico de España* (1931), pp. 541, 549.
16 *Anuari estadístic de la ciutat de Barcelona* (1920), p. 676. Pons Freixa and Martino, *Los aduares*, op. cit., pp. 54–5.
17 *Solidaridad obrera*, 25 September 1931.
18 *Solidaridad obrera*, 5, 7, and 13 August and 10 and 17 October 1931.
19 *Gaseta municipal de Barcelona* (1935), p. 42.
20 J. M. Cardelús Barcons, *El decreto de alquileres* (Barcelona, 1932).
21 Pons Freixa and Martino, *Los Aduares*, op. cit., pp. 54–8.
22 Dr Lluís Claramunt i Furest, *La iluita contra la febra tifòidea a Catalunya* (Barcelona, 1933), pp. 205–6. Mortality due to typhoid fever in various European cities in 1932 was as follows (deaths per 100,000 of the population): Berlin, 1; Berne, 0.9; Brussels, 1; Hamburg, 0.7; London, 0.6; and Barcelona, 22.8 (ibid., pp. 189–200).
23 'Carta abierta a los camaradas anarquistas', *La protesta* (Buenos Aires), 29 March 1925, reproduced in A. Elorza, 'El anarcosindicalismo español bajo la dictadura, 1923–1930', *Revista de trabajo*, 39–40 (Madrid, 1972), pp. 318–23.
24 For the ideas of Peiró, see *Trayectoria de la CNT* (1925) and *Ideas sobre sindicalismo y anarquismo* (1930), reprinted in *Pensamiento de Juan Peiró* (Mexico, 1959).
25 *Solidaridad obrera*, 19 October 1930.
26 *Solidaridad obrera*, 15 January 1931.
27 *Solidaridad obrera*, 18 April 1931.
28 To give only one example, at one meeting during the April 1931 campaign Jaume Aiguader, later Mayor of Barcelona, suggested that the changes then being carried out in Soviet Russia were only an

'anticipation' of what was projected by the Esquerra (*El diluvio*, 7 April 1931).

29 *Memoria* of the Catalan Regional Congress of the CNT, 31 May to 1 June 1931 (Barcelona, 1931).
30 *Solidaridad obrera*, 28 May 1931.
31 *Solidaridad obrera*, 12, 13, and 15 May 1931.
32 Juan García Oliver, *El eco de los pasos* (Barcelona, 1978), pp. 114–17.
33 The Urales family, centred around Federico Urales, Soledad Gustavo, and their daughter Federica Montseny, published *La revista blanca*, one of the most important of Spanish anarchist magazines, the weekly *El luchador*, and several books. Urales initially wrote enthusiastically about the possibilities offered by the new regime. For their attitude to the Republic, see *El luchador* and *La revista blanca*, April to December 1931.
34 *Solidaridad obrera*, 5 June 1931.
35 *Solidaridad obrera*, 5 May 1931; *El día gráfico*, 24 June 1931.
36 *Solidaridad obrera*, 3 July 1931.
37 These demands and the resolutions of the meeting are contained in a leaflet preserved in the Institut Municipal d'Historia of Barcelona (Arxiu de Fulls Volants, 1931).
38 CPUB, *Memoria de 1931*, p. 469; *El día gráfico*, 16 July 1931.
39 CPUB, *Memoria de 1931*, pp. 257–61.
40 Ibid., p. 477.
41 They proposed the establishment of a Joint Commission to determine, with technical assistance, the value and an acceptable rent for each property (*Solidaridad obrera*, 12 August and 10 October 1931).
42 See *El día gráfico* and *La vanguardia*, 7 to 25 July 1931.
43 *La vanguardia*, 23 July 1931.
44 CPUB, *Memoria de 1931*, p. 263.
45 *La vanguardia*, 23 and 28 July 1931; *La publicitat*, 23 July 1931.
46 *Solidaridad obrera*, 31 July 1931.
47 *Solidaridad obrera*, 5 and 8 August 1931.
48 Interviews with Joan Pujalte, 22 May 1984, and 'Joan Roca' (pseudonym), 30 May 1984.
49 *Solidaridad obrera*, 15 October 1931.
50 In, for example, Sabadell and Calella (*Solidaridad obrera*, 3 September 1931; and CPUB, *Memoria de 1931*, p. 482).
51 Interview with Concha Pérez Collado, 22 May 1984.
52 *Solidaridad obrera*, 28 August 1931.
53 Interview with Severino Campos, 5 June 1984.
54 Information from personal interviews.
55 *Solidaridad obrera*, 31 July 1931.
56 *Solidaridad obrera*, 27 August and 9 September 1931.
57 CPUB, *Memoria de 1931*, pp. 255–74, 443–510.
58 *Solidaridad obrera*, 20 August 1931.
59 *Solidaridad obrera*, 31 July, 5 August, 20 and 25 September 1931, etc.
60 CPUB, *Memoria de 1932*, pp. 48–57.

61 *Solidaridad obrera*, 28 August, 1 and 9 September 1931; interview with Severino Campos, 5 June 1984.
62 *El día gráfico*, 6 September 1931.
63 Fifty-three, according to a statement published in *El luchador*, 35 (4 September 1931). Of these fourteen were held without charge, according to a report to Madrid by the Civil Governor, 2 September 1931 (Archivo Histórico Nacional (Madrid), Gobernación Series A, file 7A, dossier 1).
64 *El luchador*, 41 (16 October 1931).
65 *Solidaridad obrera*, 24 September 1931; Hospitalet Municipal Archive, Correspondència de 1931, box 2 – Juzgados, letter of 28 August 1931.
66 *El día gráfico*, 13 October 1931.
67 *El día gráfico*, 2 October 1931.
68 CPUB, *Memoria de 1931*, pp. 265–7, 270–3.
69 *Solidaridad obrera* and *El día gráfico*, 22 October 1931.
70 In June 1932, after an intensive campaign by all the Chambers of Urban Property in Spain, led particularly by Pich i Pon and the Barcelona Chamber, the government agreed to modify the Decree, drastically reducing the right of tenants to a review of rental contracts (Cardelús Barcons, *El decreto*, op. cit.).
71 CPUB, *Memoria de 1931*, p. 507.
72 The construction of the municipally-owned 'Cheap Houses' in 1928–30 and the body that administered them, a semi-autonomous trust, were among the most notorious examples of corruption under the Primo regime. Following the establishment of the Republics the tenants began action to demand rent reductions and basic services. The ensuing conflict intensified throughout 1931. As in the broader campaign CNT militants and those of the Construction Union in particular made up most of the prominent activists. By the beginning of 1932 a stand-off situation had virtually been established in which the authorities still refused formally to concede rent reductions, but in practice were unable to enforce payment. This situation would continue, with virtually no rent being paid, up to the Civil War in 1936, and in fact the houses became something of a no-go area to the police and the authorities in general, and a preserve of the CNT. Many CNT militants gravitated to them, and the FAI magazine *Tierra y libertad* was produced from a house in the Ramón Albó group.
73 Information from personal interviews.
74 CPUB, *Memoria de 1931*, p. 510.
75 Conversation with Abel Paz, June 1984.
76 Information from personal interviews.
77 See, for example, the 'Manifest d'estat Català', *L'opinió*, 140 (13 March 1931); also J. Aiguader i Miró, 'Els obrers al municipi', *L'opinió*, 142 (27 March 1931).
78 To give one example, see the occasional column '¡Estos Caseros!' ('These landlords') run in the Republican newspaper *El diluvio* during 1931.

Part II
Theory

3

Marxism and anarchism

Daniel Guérin

In a discussion of the relationship between Marxism and anarchism, we are confronted by several difficulties. The first one is, what do we really mean by the word 'Marxism'? Which 'Marxism' are we talking about?

Let me explain immediately that what I mean by 'Marxism' is all of the writings of Karl Marx and Friedrich Engels themselves. I exclude the works of their more or less faithless successors, who have usurped the label of 'Marxists'.

Such, in the first instance, is the case of the distorted Marxism of the German Social Democrats, of which the following are some examples.

During the first years of the Social Democratic Party in Germany, in Marx's lifetime, the Social Democrats launched the slogan of a so-called *Volkstaat* (People's State). Marx and Engels were probably so happy and proud to have at last, in Germany, a mass party drawing inspiration from them, that they displayed a strange indulgence towards it. It took Bakunin's furious and persistent denunciation of the *Volkstaat* and at the same time of the Social Democrats' collusion with the bourgeois radical parties for Marx and Engels to feel obliged to repudiate such a slogan and such a practice.

Much later, in 1895, the ageing Engels while writing his famous preface to Marx's *The Class Struggles in France*, was to make a complete revision of Marxism in a reformist direction, putting the accent on the use of the ballot paper as the ideal way, if not the only way, to take power. Engels himself, therefore, was no longer 'Marxist' in the sense that I understand it.

Next, Karl Kautsky became the equivocal successor to Marx and Engels. On one hand, in theory, he made a show of keeping within the bounds of revolutionary class struggle, while in fact covering up the successively more opportunist and reformist practices of his party. At the same time, Eduard Bernstein, who also saw himself as a 'Marxist', called for more frankness from Kautsky and openly renounced class struggle, which according to him was out of date, in favour of electoralism, parliamentarianism, and social reforms.

Kautsky, on the other hand, considered it 'entirely wrong' to say that socialist consciousness was the necessary and direct result of proletarian class struggle. If he was to be believed, socialism and class struggle did not generate one another. They arose from different premises. Socialist consciousness came from science. The carriers of science would not be the proletariat, but the bourgeois intellectuals. By them would scientific socialism be 'communicated' to the proletarians. To conclude: 'Socialist consciousness is an element imported from outside the proletarian class struggle, and not something which springs from it spontaneously.'

The able theoretician in German Social Democracy who remained faithful to the genuine original Marxism was Rosa Luxemburg. Nevertheless, she had to make plenty of tactical compromises with the leadership of her party. She did not openly criticize Bebel and Kautsky; she did not enter into open conflict with Kautsky until 1910, when her ex-tutor dropped the idea of the mass political strike; and above all she tried hard to dissimulate the strong links with anarchism of her conception of the revolutionary spontaneity of the masses, resorting to the pretence of vituperations against the anarchists.[1] Thus she hoped not to alarm a party which she was attached to both by conviction and, it must be said, for it is now known, by material interests.[2]

But, in spite of variants in presentation, there is no real difference between the anarcho-syndicalist general strike and what the prudent Rosa Luxemburg preferred to name the 'mass strike'. In the same way, her violent disagreements, the first with Lenin in 1904, the last in the spring of 1918, with Bolshevik power, were not very far from anarchism. The same applies to her ultimate ideas, in the Spartacist movement, at the end of 1918, of a socialism powered from the bottom up by workers' councils. Rosa Luxemburg is one of the links between anarchism and authentic Marxism.

But authentic Marxism was not distrusted only by German Social Democracy. It was altered in a great measure by Lenin. He considerably increased certain of the Jacobin and authoritarian traits which already appear from time to time, although not always, in the writings of Marx and Engels.[3] He introduced an ultra-centralism, a narrow sectarian concept of the Party (with a capital P), and above all the idea of professional revolutionaries as leaders of the masses.[4] Not many of these notions can be found in

Marx's writings, where they are no more than embryonic and underlying.

Nevertheless, Lenin violently accused the Social Democrats of having reviled the anarchists, and, in his little book *The State and Revolution*, he devoted a whole section to paying them tribute for their fidelity to the revolution. This quite important point is usually burked by the blind or dishonest followers of Lenin and rabid detractors of anarchism.

Nowadays 'Marxism' has become a commonplace word in reactionary political jargon, used to designate all kinds of non-democratic, non-genuinely socialist, and above all state-capitalist regimes taking the pattern of the USSR.

Our subject immediately presents a second difficulty. Marx and Engels's way of thinking is not easy to comprehend, for it evolved significantly in the course of a half-century of observation as they tried to make it reflect the living reality of their times.

Besides they did not always succeed in choosing between the two contradictory trends of their thought: authoritarian and libertarian. (I have already drawn attention to a major inconsistency in Engels's thought.) We have hence to free ourselves from all kinds of dogmatization of Marxism, either by some French Catholic commentator or by Stalinist perverters.

Let us consider several instances.

The young Marx, a disciple of the philosopher Ludwig Feuerbach and a humanist, is very different from the Marx of riper years who, having broken with Feuerbach, retreats into a fairly rigid scientific determinism.

The Marx of the *Neue Rheinische Zeitung* (1848–9), whose sole desire is to be regarded as a democrat, and who sought an alliance with the progressive German bourgeoisie, bears little resemblance to the Marx of 1850, Communist and even Blanquist, the spokesman of permanent revolution, of independent Communist political action and the so-called dictatorship of the proletariat.

The Marx of the following years, postponing till much later the international revolution and shutting himself away in the library of the British Museum, devoting himself there to extensive and peaceful scientific research, is again completely different from the insurrectionary Marx of 1850, who believed in an imminent general uprising.

The Marx of 1864–9, playing the role at first of disinterested and discreet counsellor (behind the scenes) of the assembled workers in the First International, suddenly becomes, from 1870 onwards, an ultra-authoritarian Marx who rules from London over the General Council of the International.

The Marx who, at the start of 1871, issued severe warnings against a Parisian insurrection is not the same as the one who, only shortly after, in the famous address, published under the title of *The Civil War in France*, praises the Paris Commune to the skies (certain aspects of which, be it said in passing, he idealizes).[5]

The Marx who, in the same work, asserts that the Commune had the merit of destroying the machinery of the state and replacing it with communal power is not the same one who, in the *Critique of the Gotha Programme*, endeavoured to convince the reader that the state must survive for quite a long period after the proletarian revolution.[6]

Thus, then, there is no question of considering the original Marxism, that of Marx and Engels, as a homogeneous bloc.

Let us examine Marx and Engels in action, fitting into the movement of the labouring masses, in first the episode of the *Neue Rheinische Zeitung* and later the impulse given by them to the International during the years 1864–72.

The early episode reveals, at the same time, the undeniable value of the two precocious founders of scientific socialism, and their weak points: authoritarianism, sectarianism, lack of understanding of and feeling for libertarian perspectives.

It was two young men of 30 and 28 who set up the Rhineland newspaper in 1848. Their talent as journalists equalled their courage. They ran the risk of all kinds of harassments and legal repression, by both police and judiciary. They were resolutely internationalist and supported all the revolutionary movements of the various countries seized by the fever of 1848. They struggled alongside the workers of their own native land, and Engels was justified in maintaining, much later, in 1884, that 'no newspaper was so successful in rousing the proletarian masses'.[7]

Both devoted really wonderful pages to what they called the Paris workers' insurrection of June 1848, which was to be crushed bloodily. Marx was not boasting when he asserted afterwards: 'We alone understood the June revolution.' The two friends apprehended the dramatic divorce between, on one side, the Parisian workers, forced into the most violent of riots, and, on the other side, the mass of small peasantry, excited against the *partageux* (whose who wanted to share out the land).

Marx and Engels, in addition, saw clearly the European repercussions of the workers' defeat in June 1848. From that point the revolution was forced to beat a retreat throughout the continent. The courageous attitude of the two young journalists was to be no less prejudicial to them; and their stand in favour of the Parisian insurgents put to flight their last shareholders.

But beneath this extremism appear the already authoritarian traits of early Marxism. Engels, recalling the Rhineland newspaper in 1884, acknowledged that Marx exercised his 'dictatorship' over the editorial staff. All his collaborators, recognizing his intellectual superiority, submitted to the authority of their chief editor. He abused that power, just as, we will see later, he was to abuse it in the General Council of the First International. He displayed authoritarianism and also excess of pride. Thus, brought before a tribunal in Cologne, he cried, with complete disdain, 'As far as I'm concerned, I assure you that I prefer following great world events, analysing the march of history, to wrestling with local idols.'

The two cronies lost no opportunity to pitch into Proudhon and Bakunin. The brave speech given by the former at the 31 July 1848 session of the National Assembly, to the jeers of his furious colleagues, aroused the mockery of the German journalists. Yet in this speech the anarchist deputy dared to show solidarity with the June insurgents and to fling a socialist challenge to the bourgeois order. But for the merciless Marx and Engels it could be nothing but a clever ruse. To carry off his *petit-bourgeois* Utopias successfully, the father of anarchism was, they contended, 'obliged to hold a democratic attitude in the face of this whole bourgeois chamber'.

For the *Appeal to the Slavs* published in 1848 by Bakunin, Marx and Engels had the same sarcasms. For this Russian patriot, the word 'liberty' replaces everything. This is not a word of reality. All you find in the *Appeal* are more or less moral categories, '*which prove absolutely nothing*'. Only 'Bakunin's imagination' was unaware of geographical and commercial necessities which 'are vital questions for Germany'. The northern parts of Germany, are they not 'completely Germanized'? Are these good Germans to be forced to speak dead Slavonic languages? The political centralization imposed by the German conqueror, and which only 'the most resolute terrorism' can safeguard, is the expression of a 'pressing need' of an economic character. It is too bad if it involves 'brutally crushing a few tender little national flowers', exclaims Engels.

Let us now consider Marx and Engels's activities inside the First International from 1864 to 1872.

At the time of the birth of the First International on 28 September 1864, Marx had had to content himself, as he later related to Engels, with playing 'a silent role' on the platform at

St Martin's Hall. However, he received his compensation a few weeks later by writing the Inaugural Address of the new Association. None the less, he was to remain touchingly unselfish and modest for a long time. When the chairmanship of the General Council was offered to him, he humbly declined, regarding himself as 'unqualified, as he was an intellectual worker, not a manual worker'.

On the eve of the Lausanne Congress in 1867, he stated that he was in no fit state to go, and stood down as a delegate. Moreover, he was to remain absent from all the annual conferences until the fateful one of 1872. He even professed a faith in spontaneism. Writing the fourth annual report of the General Council for the Brussels Congress of 1868, he proclaimed that: 'The International Working Men's Association is the daughter neither of a sect nor a theory. It is the spontaneous [in German *naturwüchsig*, begotten by nature] product of the proletarian movement, which itself springs from the normal and irrepressible tendencies of modern society.'

But quite soon Marx was to take an authoritarian turn. This was for several reasons. To begin with, in September 1867 he had published the first volume of his *Capital*, which had brought him speedy fame and the congratulations of the Internationalists, the Germans being the first. Second, under the banner of Wilhelm Liebknecht and August Bebel, Germany Social Democracy had rapidly flourished and had succeeded, in spite of government restrictions, in getting about a hundred unions to affiliate to the International. Bebel boasted of this affiliation in the Reichstag in 1869. Marx, who was Secretary of the Regional Council for Germany, swelled with pride. He was no longer alone. At last he had a great political party to protect him from the rear.

Marx was quite attached to his title and function. At the General Council session of 11 May 1868, he snapped at the secretary, his countryman J. G. Eccarius, for having omitted his name at the bottom of an address that the habitual spokesman of the International had drawn up. He was most indignant: 'Mr Eccarius must not be allowed to make use of Council members' names as he pleases.' Personally, he was quite indifferent, he said, as to whether his name was mentioned, but 'the Secretary for Germany is an entity, not a fiction'.

And then, in September 1868, Bakunin founded an International Social Democratic Alliance and aimed to enter *en bloc* into the International Working Men's Association. Scared not without reason, Marx managed to get the General Council to refuse this admission. But, in March 1869, a shaky compromise was made:

only the national sections of Bakunin's libertarian organization were accepted into the International. With bad grace, Marx had dissected the programme and statutes of the Alliance, in the margin of which he had scrawled a reference to Bakunin as *asinus asinorum* ('the ass of asses'). Weary of this internal struggle, so wounding to his pride, Marx called on Engels for help, had him admitted as a member of the General Council, and entrusted him with the job of undermining Bakunin and his partisans, including the non-anarchist British, in all the countries concerned. Landed in the saddle in this way, Engels proved himself more aggressive and more sectarian than even Marx himself.

Finally, Marx and Engels made use of the growth in prestige and power of the International Association, originally created by the workers themselves, but soon monopolized by the two brain-workers, to plot the expulsion of the anarchists, treated as spoil-sports, declared enemies of the state, opponents of electoral compromises of the kind practised by the German Social Democrats.

The expulsion was organized in two stages: first, at a so-called conference (non-statutory) held in London in September 1871, then at the Congress held at The Hague in 1872. Two main spokesmen for libertarian socialism, Bakunin and the French-Swiss James Guillaume, were expelled by a fake majority. Nearly all of the British made common cause with the penalized.

The perpetrators of this baneful trick managed to get the General Council relegated from London to New York, care of their friend Friedrich Albert Sorge. The International, at least in its previous form, was dead.

Nevertheless, it was able to survive, up to 1877, as a 'federalist' or 'anti-authoritarian' International Association. Jacques Freymond, in his work *La Première Internationale*, devotes two of his four volumes to the very rich and thrilling continuation of the International. It was mainly led by French-Swiss, Italian, and Spanish anarchists, but also by non-anarchists: Belgian and British Internationalists.

After the final divorce, at the Congress of Verviers (Belgium), in 1877, between anarchists and the non-authoritarian socialists, the remaining International Association died, this time, in earnest.

Henceforth the links were broken between anarchism and socialism, a disastrous event for the working class, since each movement needed the theoretical and practical contribution of the other.

During the 1880s, an attempt to create a skeletal anarchist International failed. The purpose was deserving, but its initiators were largely isolated from the labour movement, whereas, at the same time, a stunted Marxism was developing rapidly in Germany with the growth of Social Democracy and in France with the founding of the Parti Ouvrier of Jules Guesde.

Later on, the various Social Democratic parties united to create the Second International. At its successive congresses, there were lively confrontations with the anarchists who had succeeded in participating in these sittings, using trade unionist credentials. In Zurich, in 1893, the Dutch libertarian socialist Domela Nieuwenhuis attacked the German Social Democrats vehemently and was greeted with boos.

In London, in 1896, Marx's daughter, Eleanor Aveling, and the French socialist Jean Jaurès insulted and flung out the few anarchists who had penetrated the precincts of the congress. To be sure, the anarchist terrorism which raged in France between 1890 and 1895 had contributed not a little to the hysterical repudiation of them. Anarchists were regarded from then on as 'bandits'. But these cowardly and legalistic reformists were not capable of understanding the revolutionary motives of the terrorists, judging irrelevant their recourse to violence as a form of resounding protest against an abhorrent society.

Up to 1914 German Social Democracy and (even more so) the heavy machinery of the German trade unions spewed anarchism out. Even Kautsky, for a time, soon forgotten, when he declared himself in favour of mass strikes was suspected by the bureaucrats of being an 'anarchist'!

In France, the opposite took place. Jaurès's electoralist and parliamentary reformism made the progressive workers so ill-disposed that they took part in the founding of a very militant revolutionary and federalist organization, the memorable CGT (General Confederation of Labour) of the years prior to 1914. Its pioneers, Fernand Pelloutier, Emile Pouget, Pierre Monatte, etc., came from the anarchist movement.

The Russian Revolution, and, later on, the Spanish Revolution, finished deepening a gulf between degenerate Marxism and anarchism, a gulf which was to become not only theoretical but also bloody.

Anarchists and Marxists, as early as their political birth, had come into ideological conflict with one another.

The first skirmish was started by Marx and Engels against Max Stirner in their nasty book *The German Ideology*.[8] It rested on a reciprocal misunderstanding. Stirner does not underline clearly enough that beyond his exaltation of the Ego, of the individual considered as a 'Unique One', he advocates in fact the voluntary association of that 'Unique One' with others, that is to say, a new type of society founded on federative free choice and the right of secession – an idea to be taken up later by Bakunin and finally by Lenin himself when discussing the national question. On their side, Marx and Engels misinterpreted Stirner's diatribes against communism, the regimented 'crude' state communism of the utopian communists of his time, such as Weitling in Germany and Cabet in France, for Stirner estimated, rightly, that that kind of communism endangered individual liberty.

Next occurred Marx's furious assault on Proudhon, in part for the same reasons. Proudhon extolled limited personal property in as far as he saw in it a measure of personal independence. What Marx failed to grasp was that for major industry, in other words for the capitalist sector, Proudhon came down fair and square on the side of collective ownership. Did he not remark in his *Carnets* that 'small-scale industry is as stupid a thing as small-scale culture'? For large-scale modern industry he is resolutely collectivist. What he calls the 'workers' companies' would play, in his eyes, a considerable role, that of managing the major employers of labour, such as the railways and the large manufacturing, extractive, metallurgic, and maritime industries.

On the other hand, Proudhon, at the end of his life, in *De la capacité politique des classes ouvrières*, opted for the total separation of the working class from bourgeois society, that is, for class struggle. This did not stop Marx from having the unfairness to reduce Proudhonism to *petit-bourgeois* socialism.

Returning to the violent and despicable quarrel between Marx and Bakunin inside the First International, Bakunin attributed dangerous authoritarian designs to Marx, a thirst to dominate the working-class movement, whose features he exaggerated some-what and shared himself. But by doing so, the Russian anarchist showed himself to be a prophet. With wonderful acumen, he predicted that Marx's dictatorial propensities would spread out among his successors at some future and remote date, into what Bakunin called a *red bureaucracy*. He foresaw the kind of tyranny which the leaders of the Third International would exercise over the world labour movement.

However, were genuine Marxism and anarchism so remote from each other? If we look a little closer, it is not hard to realize that they had mutually influenced each other.

Errico Malatesta, the great Italian anarchist, wrote: 'Almost all the anarchist literature of the nineteenth century was impregnated with Marxism.'

We know that Bakunin bowed respectfully before Marx's scientific abilities, to the extent of having started to translate into Russian the first volume of *Capital*. For his part, the Italian anarchist, his friend Carlo Cafiero, published a summary of the same work.

Going the other way, Proudhon's first book, *What Is Property?* (1840), and particularly his great book, *The System of Economic Contradictions: or, The Philosophy of Poverty* (1846), deeply influenced the young Marx, even though shortly afterwards the ungrateful economist was to mock his teacher and write against him the venomous *The Poverty of Philosophy*.

In spite of their quarrels, Marx owed a lot to the views expressed by Bakunin. The address Marx composed on the Paris Commune is largely of Bakuninist inspiration, as Arthur Lehning, the editor of the *Archives Bakounine*, has pointed out. It was thanks to Bakunin, as has been already said, that Marx saw himself obliged to condemn the slogan of his Social Democrat associates' *Volkstaat*.

We are therefore confronted with a new difficulty concerning the definition of a system of political thought. For even less than Marxism does anarchism form a coherent body of doctrine. The denial of authority, the emphasis placed on the priority of individual judgement, particularly incites anarchists, as Proudhon wrote in a letter to Marx, to 'profess anti-dogmatism'. Thus their views are more diverse, more fluid, more difficult to apprehend than those of the socialists who are regarded as authoritarian. Countless are the various currents of anarchism. It would be vain to enumerate them here.

My conclusion is that the kind of anarchism least distanced from authentic Marxism is collectivist anarchism (and what I shall later be calling libertarian communism). It is not at all by chance that it is this variety of anarchism, and it alone, which I have attempted to delineate in my *Anarchism: From Theory to Practice*. So what we have to attempt here is the comparison of collectivist anarchism (or libertarian communism) and authentic Marxism.

Marxism and anarchism are not only influenced by one another. They have a common origin. They belong to the same family. As materialists we do not believe that ideas are born purely and simply in the brains of human beings. They merely reflect the experience gained by the mass movements through class struggle. The first socialist writers, as much anarchists as Marxists, together drew their inspiration first of all from the great French Revolution of the end of the eighteenth century, then from the efforts undertaken by the French workers, starting in 1840, to organize themselves and struggle against capitalist exploitation.

Very few people know that there was a general strike of building trades in Paris in 1840. (And during the following years there was a flourishing of workers' newspapers, such as *L'Atelier*.) Now it was the same year 1840 – the coincidence is remarkable – that Proudhon published his *What Is Property?*, and four years later, in 1844, the young Marx recorded, in his for long unedited *Manuscripts*, the tale of his visit to the Paris workers and the vivid impression that these manual labourers had made on him. The year before, in 1843, an exceptional woman, Flora Tristan, had preached the Workers' Union to the labourers and undertaken a *tour de France* to make contact with the workers in the cities.

Thus anarchism and Marxism, at the start, drank at the same proletarian spring. And under the pressure of the newly born working class they assigned to themselves the same final aim, i.e. to overthrow the capitalist state and to entrust society's wealth, the means of production, to the workers themselves. Such was subsequently the basis of the collectivist agreement concluded between Marxists and Bakuninists at the 1869 Congress of the First International, before the Franco-Prussian War of 1870. Moreover, this agreement was directed against the last disciples, turned reactionaries, of Proudhon (who had died in 1865). One of these was Henri Tolain, who clung to the concept of private ownership of the means of production.

It seems to me noteworthy that the Martyrs of Chicago, sentenced to death in 1887, claimed themselves to be, at the same time, anarchists and socialists. Parsons, Fischer, and Engels asserted together that 'anarchism and socialism are as much alike as one egg is to another', differing 'only in their tactics', and that 'it is wrong to claim that these two doctrines have nothing in common with each other'. The Chicago Martyrs called themselves 'politically anarchists, and economically communists or socialists'. This was surely their originality and one of their merits.

I have mentioned that the first spokespeople of the French workers' movement were inspired by the great French Revolution. Let us come back to this point in a little more detail.

At the heart of the French Revolution there were in fact two very different sorts of revolution, or, if you prefer, two contradictory varieties of power, one formed by the left wing of the bourgeoisie, the other by a pre-proletariat (small artisans and waged workers).

The first was authoritarian, nay dictatorial, oppressive to the unprivileged. The second was democratic, federalist, composed of what today we would call workers' councils, that is to say, the forty-eight districts of the city of Paris associated within the framework of the Paris Commune and the people's societies in the provincial cities.[9] I dare to say that this second power was essentially *libertarian*, as it were the precursor of the 1871 Paris Commune and the Russian soviets of 1917, whereas the first kind was christened (although only after the event in the course of the nineteenth century) *Jacobin*. What is more, the word 'Jacobin' is incorrect, ambiguous, and artificial. It was taken from the name of a popular Paris club, the Society of Jacobins, which itself came from the abbey of a monastic order in whose building the club was set up. In fact, the demarcatory line of the class struggle between bourgeois revolutionaries on one side and unprivileged on the other passed inside and right through the Society of Jacobins. Put more plainly, at its meetings those of its members who extolled one or other of the two revolutions came into conflict.

However, in the later political literature, 'Jacobin' was commonly used to describe a revolutionary bourgeois tradition, directing the country and the revolution from the top by authoritarian means, and the word was used in this sense as much by the anarchists as by the Marxists. For example, Charles Delescluze, the leader of the majority right wing of the Paris Commune Council of 1871, regarded himself as a Jacobin, a Robespierrist.

Proudhon and Bakunin, in their writings, denounced the 'Jacobin spirit', rightly considered by them as a political legacy of the bourgeois revolutionaries. On the other hand, Marx and Engels had some trouble in freeing themselves from this Jacobin myth, made glorious by the 'heroes' of the bourgeois revolution, among them Danton (who in actual fact was a corrupt politician and a double agent) and Robespierre (who ended up as an apprentice dictator). The libertarians, thanks to the keenness of their anti-authoritarian vision, were not duped by Jacobinism. They understood quite clearly that the French Revolution was not only a civil war between absolute monarchy and the bourgeois revolutionaries, but also, a little later, a civil war between 'Jacobinism' and what we will call, for convenience's sake, *communalism*. This was a civil war whose outcome, in March 1794, was the defeat of the Paris Commune and the beheading of its two municipal magistrates, Chaumette and Hébert, that is to say, the overthrow of the people's power – just as the October Revolution in Russia ended in the liquidation of the factory councils.

Marx and Engels swung perpetually between Jacobinism and communalism. Right at the beginning they praised the 'example of rigorous centralization in France in 1793'. But much later, much too late, in 1885, Engels realized that they had been misled and that the said centralization had laid the way open to the dictatorship of Napoleon the First. Marx wrote that the Enragés, the supporters of the left-wing ex-priest Jacques Roux, spokesman of the working-class population of the suburbs, had been the 'principal representatives of the revolutionary movement'. But, conversely, Engels claimed elsewhere that to the 'proletariat' of 1793 'could at the very least be brought assistance from above'.

Lenin, later on, showed himself to be much more of a Jacobin than his teachers, Marx and Engels. According to him, Jacobinism was 'one of the culminating points that the oppressed class reaches in the struggle for its emancipation'. And he liked to call himself a Jacobin, adding always: 'a Jacobin linked with the working class'.

My conclusion on this point is that the anarchists suspect the Marxists with good reason for not having purged themselves completely of any Jacobin inclination.

Now let us state the principal points of divergence between anarchism and Marxism.

First of all, although they agree on the ultimate abolition of the state, the Marxists, and even more the Leninists, believe it necessary, after a victorious proletarian revolution, to create a new state, which they call a 'workers' state', for an indefinite period – after which they promise that such a state, sometimes labelled 'semi-state', would finally wither away. On the contrary, the anarchists object that the new state would be much more omnipotent and oppressive than the bourgeois state, due to the whole economy being the property of the state, and that its ever-growing bureaucracy would refuse to 'wither away'.

However, there is an important difference between classical anarchists and what are called in France libertarian communists. We, the latter, do not believe that in a trice we could jump from the present capitalist state to a total non-state society. We regret that we are obliged to admit that a transitional space of time would probably temporarily exist. But, unlike the authoritarian socialists, we want to act in such a manner that the features of the libertarian society to come – workers' councils, federalist structure, self-management, and so on – would already be present and developed during the transitional period, instead of reinforcing the centralized and dictatorial state, as do the Marxist-Leninists.

We are suspicious as regards the mission assigned by Marx and

Engels to the Communist minority of the population. If we were to consult their Holy Scriptures, we would have too good reason to harbour doubts on the subject. Certainly, in the *Communist Manifesto*, you can read that 'the Communists do not have separate interests from the rest of the proletariat' and that 'they consistently represent the interest of the whole movement'. Their 'theoretical concepts', swear the authors of the *Manifesto*,

> are not in the least based on the ideas or principles invented or discovered by some world reformer or other. They are only the general expression of the effective conditions of an existing class struggle, of a historic movement operating before our eyes.

Yes, here we are in agreement. But the sentence I shall now quote is somewhat ambiguous and alarming: 'Theoretically they [the Communists] have the advantage over the rest of the proletarian mass of understanding clearly the conditions, the progress and the ultimate general results of the proletarian movement.'

This trenchant affirmation could well mean that, because of such an 'advantage', the Communists reckon to have a historic right to appropriate the leadership of the proletariat. If such is their claim, imbued with the spirit of Jacobinism, we libertarians would no longer approve. We disagree that there can be a vanguard *outside* of the workers themselves, and we believe that we should limit ourselves to playing the role, at the side of or among the proletariat, or disinterested advisers, so as to aid the workers in their own efforts with a view to their reaching a higher degree of consciousness.

Thus we are brought to the question of the revolutionary spontaneity of the masses, a specifically libertarian notion. In fact, we very often find the words 'spontaneous' and 'spontaneity' flowing from the pens of Proudhon and Bakunin. But we never do, which is rather strange, in writings of Marx and Engels, at least not in the original German. In translations, the words in question appear from time to time, but they are inexact approximations. In reality, Marx and Engels refer only to the 'self-activity' (*Selbsttätigkeit*) of the masses, a more restrained notion than spontaneity.

Indeed, a revolutionary party, in addition to its more important undertakings, may take credit to itself for admitting a certain dose of mass 'self-activity', but spontaneity would risk damaging its pretensions to a leading role.

Rosa Luxemburg was the first Marxist to use, in German, the word *spontan* ('spontaneous') in her writings, after having borrowed it from the anarchists, and to accent the predominant role of spontaneity in the mass movement. She did it alone, and one could suspect that the other Marxists harbour a secret distrust of a social phenomenon which does not leave sufficient room for the intervention of their would-be leaders.

Then the anarchists observe severely that the Marxists are quite willing to use to their advantage the means and artifices of bourgeois democracy. Not only do they readily make use of the vote, which they regard as one of the best ways of taking power, but it happens that they delight in concluding sordid electoral pacts with bourgeois liberal or radical parties, when they think they will not succeed in winning parliamentary seats without such alliances. Certainly anarchists do not have, as people are too ready to imagine, a metaphysical horror of the ballot box. Proudhon was once elected to the 1848 National Assembly; another time he supported the candidature of Raspail, a progressive doctor, for the presidency of the Republic. However, later on, under the Second Empire, he dissuaded the workers from presenting candidates at the elections. But for him it was a simple question of opportunity – and his disapproval of any oath of allegiance to the imperial regime. On one occasion, the Spanish anarchists avoided taking a rigid position against participation in the *Frente Popular* elections in February 1936. But apart from these rare exceptions, the anarchists recommend quite different ways to vanquish the capitalist adversary: direct action, trade-union action, workers' autonomy, the general strike.

Now we come to the dilemma: nationalization of the means of production or self-management? Here again Marx and Engels evade the issue. In the *Communist Manifesto* of 1848, which was directly inspired by the French state socialist Louis Blanc, they announced their intention of 'centralizing all the means of production into the hands of the state'. But by the word 'state' they meant the 'proletariat organized into a leading class'. Then why on earth call that kind of proletarian organization a *state*? And why, too, do they repent much later on and add, in June 1872, a preface to a German edition of the *Manifesto* in which they revise their summary statism of 1848, referring to *The Civil War in France* where the phrase is henceforward 'self-government of the producers'? Doubtless they felt the need to make this concession to the anarchist wing of the International.

But it must be pointed out that Marx never examined in detail the ways in which self-management could function, whereas Proudhon devoted pages and pages to it. The latter, who began life as a worker, knew what he was talking about: he had observed attentively the 'workers' associations' born during the course of the 1848 revolution. The reason for Marx's attitude is probably that it was inspired by disdain or that he considered the question to be 'utopian'. Today anarchists have been the first to put self-management back on the agenda,[10] whence it has become so in vogue that it has been confiscated, recuperated, altered by anyone and everyone.

And, finally, what of the present?

Without a doubt a renewal of libertarian socialism is taking place today. It is hardly necessary to remind ourselves how the renaissance occurred in France in May 1968. It was the most spontaneous, the most unexpected, the least prepared of uprisings. A strong wind of freedom blew across my country, so devastating and at the same time so creative that nothing could remain exactly the same as it had existed before. Life changed, or, if you like, we changed life. But a similar renaissance also took place in the general context of a renaissance of the whole of the revolutionary movement, notably among the student population. Due to this, there are hardly any watertight barriers any longer between the libertarian movements and those who claim to be 'Marxist-Leninists'. There even is a certain non-sectarian permeability between these different movements. Young comrades in France pass from 'authoritarian' Marxist groups to libertarian groups and vice versa. Entire groups of Maoists have split up under the libertarian influence, or been attracted by the libertarian contagion. Even the small Trotskyist groups are developing certain of their views and abandoning several of their prejudices under the influence of libertarian writings and theories. People like Jean-Paul Sartre and his friends in their monthly review expounded anarchist views, and one of their articles was entitled 'Goodbye to Lenin'. Of course there are still some authoritarian Marxist groups who are particularly anti-anarchist, just as you can still find anarchist groups who remain violently anti-Marxist.

In France the Libertarian Communist Organization (OCL) to which I belong finds itself positioned on the borders of anarchism and Marxism. It has in common with classical anarchism affiliation with the anti-authoritarian current which dates back to the First International. But it also has in common with the Marxists the fact that they both take their stand resolutely on the field of proletarian class struggle and of the fight to overthrow bourgeois capitalist power. On one hand, the libertarian communists endeavour to revive all that has been constructive in the anarchist contribution to the past.[11] On the other, they do not reject those things in the heritage of Marx and Engels which seem to them still valid and fruitful and, in particular, relevant to the need of the present day.

An example is the notion of alienation contained in the young Marx's 1844 *Manuscripts*, which fits in well with the anarchists' concept of individual liberty. Similarly with the affirmation that the emancipation of the proletariat ought to be the work of the proletariat itself and not that of substitutes, an idea which is found as much in the *Communist Manifesto* as in its later commentaries and in the resolutions of the congresses of the First International. The same applies to the revelatory theory of capitalism, which remains even today one of the keys to understanding the workings of the capitalist machinery. So it is, too, with the famous method of the materialist and historical dialectic which is still one of the threads connecting the understanding of past and present events. There is one necessary condition, however: do not apply this method rigidly, mechanically, or as an excuse not to fight under the false pretext that the material bases for a revolution might be absent, as the Stalinists pretended three times in France in 1936, 1945, and 1968. Besides, historical materialism should not be reduced to a simple determinism; the door must stay wide open to individual free will and the revolutionary spontaneity of the masses.

As the libertarian historian H. E. Kaminski wrote in his excellent book on Bakunin, a synthesis of anarchism and Marxism is not only necessary but inevitable. 'History', he adds, 'makes her compromises herself.'

I should like to add, as my own conclusion, that a libertarian communism, the fruit of such a synthesis, would without a doubt express the deepest wishes (even if sometimes not yet wholly conscious) of progressive workers, of what is nowadays called 'the labour left', much better than degenerate authoritarian Marxism or the dated and fossilized old-style anarchism. In spite of some negative and discouraging appearances, the remote future seems to me, beyond the double bankruptcy of private and state capitalism, to belong to libertarian and self-management communism.

Notes and references

1 Cf. my *Rosa Luxemburg et la spontanéité révolutionnaire* (Paris, 1971).
2 Cf. Elzbieta Ettinger (ed.), *Comrade and Lover: Rosa Luxemburg's Letters to Leo Jogiches* (Cambridge, Mass., 1979).
3 Cf., in my *Pour un marxisme libertaire* (Paris, 1969), the essay 'La Révolution déjacobinisée'.

4 Ibid., the essay 'Lenine ou le socialisme par en haut'.

5 Cf., in my *La Révolution française et nous* (Paris, 1976), the essay 'Gare aux nouveaux Versaillais!'.

6 It is true that the piece on the Commune was really an address to the First International. Marx, holding the pen, had to take into account the various currents of that working-class organization where statist authoritarians rubbed shoulders with libertarians and was obliged to make them concessions, disclaimed later on.

7 Engels, 'Marx und die *Neue Rheinische Zeitung*', *Sozialdemocrat* (Zurich), 13 March 1884.

8 In fact this vituperative attack remained in manuscript form and was not published until 1932 (in French 1937–47), bringing into conflict with Stirner a number of Marxists of this century, such as Pierre Naville.

9 Cf. my *La Lutte de classes sous la Première République (1793–1797)*, 2 vols (Paris, 1968, 2nd edn); and the digest *Class Struggle in the First French Republic* (London, 1977; this is the English translation of *Bourgeois et bras nus* (Paris, 1973)); also *La Révolution française et nous*, op. cit.

10 The essential framework of my *Anarchism: From Theory to Practice* (Paris, 1965; English trans. New York, 1970) is self-management, the dynamics of which were accentuated by the May 1968 upsurge.

11 I must mention that that was my aim in publishing *Anarchism: From Theory to Practice* and the anarchist anthology *Ni Dieu ni maître* (Paris, 1965).

4

Human nature and anarchism

Peter Marshall

Critics of anarchism, indeed of any attempt to expand freedom, have repeatedly fallen back on the tired argument that it is against 'human nature'. The conventional wisdom amongst historians of political thought is that anarchists have an optimistic view of human beings as being naturally good and that it is only the state that produces evil in people. Abolish the state, they believe anarchists assert, and society will achieve a condition of perfect harmony. Convinced of the need for political authority, they argue that in reality the opposite would occur; without the state, society would collapse into the Hobbesian nightmare of violent disorder and permanent war. To criticize anarchism, it becomes enough to assert that is just a 'puerile Utopia'.[1] 'Human nature' is thus depicted as a nasty fellow blocking our path to a free society and any further improvement.

The concept of human nature is undoubtedly a powerful weapon. It is appealed to as if it has its own invincible weight. On the one hand, it is given the force of logic so that like $2+2=4$ it only has to be asserted to be self-evidently true. On the other, it is presented as an empirical reality. Traditional Christian moralists who asserted that we are irredeemably fallen in original sin with depraved and corrupt natures were given a pseudo-scientific gloss by the Social Darwinists of the last century who maintained that in the struggle for survival only the most powerful and cunning survive. In our own century, psychoanalysts have given their own version of original sin by arguing that we are in the grip of irrational and unconscious forces or driven by the will to power. In their attempt to trace the biological roots of capitalist society, the sociobiologists have argued more recently that human beings are naturally aggressive, genetically selfish, and overwhelmed by a territorial imperative.

The corollary of these arguments is that a society of violent, property-owning egoists seeking power and wealth is natural and that political authority in the shape of the state and law is necessary to curb human excesses. Any alternative model of society which might suggest that human beings are capable of governing themselves and of leading peaceful and productive lives without external coercion is dismissed as hopelessly naïve, implausible, and utopian. The anarchist vision of a free society is therefore said to be not only an impossibility but a self-deluding fantasy.

I would like to argue, however, that while classic anarchist thinkers, such as William Godwin, Max Stirner, and Peter Kropotkin, share common assumptions about the possibility of a free society, they do not have a common view of human nature. I also hope to show that their views of human nature are not so naïve or optimistic as is usually alleged. Finally, I would like to present my criticism of the very notion of human nature and offer a plausible view of the limits and possibilities of human beings which embraces the anarchist ideal of a free society. Libertarians clearly have to explain why the violence, oppression, and exploitation which have characterized so much of the past need not continue in the future. They also have to show how the increasing power of states in modern industrial societies throughout the world can be not only checked but actually dissolved. An account of human behaviour is needed which can explain the horrors of Auschwitz and Hiroshima and which can envisage the reign of peace, justice, and freedom.

Human nature and classical anarchist theory

If we look at the views of human nature put forward by the three nineteenth-century anarchist thinkers, William Godwin, Max Stirner, and Peter Kropotkin, we find some profound and often incompatible differences. Godwin was the most consistent and logical. In his *Enquiry Concerning Political Justice* (1793), Godwin firmly based his ethics and politics on a clear view of human nature. He believed in universal determinism; that is to say, both human nature as well as external nature are governed by necessary and universal laws. Within this broad philosophical framework, Godwin then asserted that the 'characters of men originate in external circumstances'.[2] The effects of heredity are therefore minimal (there are no innate ideas or instincts): we are almost entirely the products of our environment. We are not born either virtuous or vicious, benevolent or selfish, but become so according to our upbringing and education.

But while Godwin argues that human nature is malleable, he

also believes that it possesses certain characteristics. In the first place, we are both unique individuals and social beings. Godwin certainly valued personal autonomy and made the corner-stone of his anarchism the Dissenters' 'right to private judgement'. He insisted that to be truly happy we must not forfeit our individuality by becoming dependent on others or losing ourselves in the mass. But it is wrong to categorize him as an individualist who did not take into account the social dimension of human life. He repeatedly stressed that we are social beings, that we are made for society, and that society brings out our best sympathies and abilities. Indeed, he saw no tension between autonomy and community, since 'the love of liberty obviously leads to a sentiment of union, and a disposition to sympathize in the concerns of others'.[3] In a free and equal society, Godwin believed that we would become both more social and more individual.

Godwin also thought that we are rational beings who can recognize truth and act accordingly. As potentially rational, we are voluntary beings, capable of consciously directing our actions. It is through reason that Godwin reconciled his belief in determinism and in human choice: while every action is determined by a motive, reason enables us to choose what motive to act upon. The will is therefore 'the last act of the understanding'.[4] Since we are both rational and voluntary beings, Godwin inferred that we are also progressive. Godwin's view of the 'perfectibility of man', as he called it, was based on the proposition that our voluntary actions originate in our opinions and that it is the nature of truth to triumph over error. He made his case in the form of a syllogism:

> Sound reasoning and truth, when adequately communicated, must always be victorious over error: Sound reasoning and truth are capable of being so communicated: Truth is omnipotent: The vices and moral weakness of man are not invincible: Man is perfectible, or in other words susceptible of perpetual improvement.[5]

If vice is nothing more than ignorance and our opinions determine our actions, then education and enlightenment will enable us to become virtuous and free. Thus while we may be products of our circumstances, we can think critically about them and are able to change them. We are therefore to a large extent the creators of our own destiny.

Godwin has often been dismissed as a naïve visionary because he believed that human beings are rational and progressive in this way. In fact, his position is far from naïve. As a historian, he was only too well aware that from one point of view history is 'little

else than a record of crimes'.[6] He knew from first hand the power
of evil and the weight of coercive institutions. Yet Godwin
discerned in the past clear signs of social and intellectual progress
and saw no reason why the process should not continue in the
future, although he warned that improvement would be inevitably
gradual and often interrupted.

Again, it is difficult to sustain the charge that Godwin was too
rational. He may have felt with John Stuart Mill that truth should
be left alone to fight its own battles – he based his eloquent
defence of the freedom of thought and expression on the belief –
but he was fully informed of the force of prejudice. The fate of his
own work and the political reaction in Britain after the French
Revolution proved a daily remainder of the fragility of truth.
It is true that Godwin argued that people usually do what they
think is right. But while there is clearly on some occasions a gap
between thought and action, it is quite plausible to say that we
cannot be really convinced of the desirability of an object without
desiring it.

Finally, Godwin cannot be accused of dismissing the power of
the emotions. He maintained that 'passion is inseparable from
reason' and that virtue cannot be 'strenuously espoused' without it
being 'ardently loved'.[7] Indeed, reason is not an independent
principle, and from a practical point of view is 'merely a
comparison and balancing of different feelings'.[8] It is a subtle
position which cannot easily be dismissed. In the final analysis,
however, Godwin held firm to his view that human beings are
potentially rational and that it is to the development of our reason
that we are to look for the improvement in our social condition.

Godwin's view of human nature and social change placed him in
a difficult dilemma. On the one hand, he stressed how opinions are
shaped by economic and political circumstances, especially in the
form of government. On the other, he was committed to education
and enlightenment as the principal means of reform. It followed
for Godwin that, since government is founded in opinion, all that
is necessary to dissolve the foundation of government is to change
public opinion. This meant, however, that he was left with the
contradiction that human beings cannot become wholly rational as
long as governments exist and yet governments will exist as long as
human beings remain irrational.

Although Stirner like Godwin came to similar anarchist conclusions
about the dissolution of the state and political authority, their
views of human nature could not have been more disparate.
Stirner was an out-and-out egoist. Where Godwin thought that

human beings are capable of reason, benevolence, and solidarity, Stirner did not believe that such ideals were possible. Where Godwin claimed that the rational person would be benevolent, Stirner maintained the very opposite and asserted that human beings could only act in a self-interested way. There is no place for Godwin's calm reason and universal benevolence in Stirner's scheme of things: man (the word is appropriate, not sexist in this context) is driven by selfish instincts, and the self is his most valuable possession.

As the title of his principal work *The Ego and Its Own* (1845) implies, Stirner maintains that each individual is unique and the ego the sole arbitrator. His position may best be understood in the context of the left-Hegelian critique of religion that developed in Germany in the 1840s. Opposing Hegel's philosophical idealism which saw history as the unfurling of Spirit, the left-Hegelians argued that religion was a form of alienation in which the believer projected certain of his own desirable qualities on to a transcendent deity. Man is not created in God's image, but God is created in man's ideal image. To overcome this alienation, they argued that it was necessary to 'reappropriate' the human essence and to realize that the ideal qualities attributed to God are human qualities, partially realized at present but capable of being fully realized in a transformed society. The critique of religion thus became a radical call for reform.

Stirner went even further in his critique. Where the left-Hegelian Feuerbach argued that, instead of worshipping God, we should try to realize the human essence, Stirner declared that this kind of humanism was merely religion in disguise. Since the concept of human essence is merely an abstract thought, it cannot be an independent standard by which we measure our actions. It remains, like the concept of the people, nothing more than a 'spook'.[9]

In metaphysical terms, Stirner is not strictly a solipsist in believing that the ego is the only reality, but he does hold that the ego is the highest level of reality.

In his psychology, be believes in psychological egoism. The self is a unity acting from a self-seeking will: '*I* am everything to myself and I do everything *on my account*.'[10] The apparent altruist is an unconconscious, involuntary egoist. Even love is a type of egoism: I love 'because love makes *me* happy, I love because loving is natural to me, because it pleases me'.[11] Stirner thus anticipates Freud in his stress on the force of the desires to influence reason, and Adler in his description of the will as the highest faculty of the ego.

In his ethics, Stirner believes that self-interest is the sole good. There are no eternal moral truths and no values to be discovered in nature. There are no natural rights, no social rights, no historical rights. Right is merely might: 'What you have the *power* to be you have the *right* to.'[12] The dominant morality will therefore be the values of the most powerful. The individual has no obligation to law or morality; his only interest is the free satisfaction of his needs. The conscious egoist is thus beyond all good and evil:

> Away, then, with every concern that is not altogether my concern! You think at least the 'good cause' must be my concern? What's good, what's bad? Why, I myself am my concern, and I am neither good nor bad. Neither has meaning for me.
>
> The divine is God's concern; the human, man's. My concern is neither the divine nor the human, not the true, good, just, free, etc., but solely what is *mine*, and it is not a general one, but is – unique, as I am unique.
>
> Nothing is more to me than myself![13]

Indeed, Stirner goes so far as to place one's 'ownness' above the value of freedom, since it is easier to be oneself than be free:

> one becomes free from much, not from everything. . . . 'Freedom lives only in the realm of dreams!' Ownness, on the contrary, is my whole being and existence, it is I myself. I am free from what I am *rid* of, owner of what I have in my *power* or what I *control*. *My own* I am at all times and under all circumstances, if I know how to have myself and do not throw myself away on others.[14]

With this stress on the primacy of the ego, Stirner goes on to develop a view of freedom which calls not merely for an absence of constraint, but for the ability to act out of a truly free choice of the uncircumscribed individual: 'I am my *own* only when I am master of myself.'[15] On these grounds, he proceeds to demolish all those doctrines which demand the subordination of the interests in the individual to such mental fictions and abstractions as God, Humanity, Law, State, and Church.

Given his account of human nature, Stirner, no less than Hobbes, sees society as a war of all against all. As each individual tries to satisfy his desires he inevitably comes into conflict with others. But while Stirner's view of human nature as selfish, passionate, and power-seeking is close to that of Hobbes, they come to opposite conclusions. Where Hobbes called for an all-powerful state resting on the sword to enforce its laws to curb the unruly passions of humanity, Stirner believed that it is possible and desirable to form a spontaneous union of egoists. Moreover, he did not think that a long period of preparation and enlightenment would be necessary as Godwin suggests. People simply have to recognize what they are: 'Your nature is, once for all, a human one; you are human natures, human beings. But, just because you already are so, you do not still need to become so.'[16]

The reason why the state and even formal institutions of society can be done away with is because we are more or less equal in power and ability. It is enough for people to become fully egoist to end the unequal distribution of power which produced a hierarchical society with servants and masters. In the 'war of each against all', force might be necessary to redistribute wealth, but Stirner goes beyond any revolution which seeks to make new institutions in his final celebration of individual self-assertion and rebellion:

> Now, as my object is not the overthrow of an established order but my elevation above it, my purpose and deed are not a political and social but (as directed toward myself and my ownness alone) an *egoistic* purpose and deed.
>
> The revolution commands one to make *arrangements*, the insurrection demands that he *rise or exalt himself.*[17]

In fact, Stirner celebrates the will to power not over others but rather over oneself. If all withdrew into their own uniqueness social conflict would be diminished and not exacerbated: 'As unique you have nothing in common with the other any longer, and therefore nothing divisive or hostile either.'[18] He therefore believed it was possible to form loose associations or spontaneous unions with other egoists. Human beings might therefore be fundamentally selfish, but it is possible to appeal to their selfishness for them to make contractual agreements among themselves to avoid violence and conflict and to pursue their selfish interests. In the final analysis, it seems little different from Adam Smith's enlightened self-interest.

With Godwin and Stirner we thus have two diametrically opposed views of human nature, but a common faith in the desirability and possibility of a free society without government. They both look to some form of enlightenment to change human conduct. But where Godwin felt human beings are capable of reason and benevolence and looked to education to improve their lot, Stirner felt human beings are irredeemably selfish and merely called on them to follow their interests in a clear-sighted way.

The problem with Stirner's position is that, given his view of
human beings as self-seeking egoists, it is difficult to imagine that
in a free society they would not grasp for power and resort to
violence to settle disputes. Without the sanction of moral
obligation or threat of force, there is no reason to expect that
agreements would be binding. If such agreements were only kept
out of prudence, then it would seem pointless making them in the
first place. Again, to say that, because they have a substantial
equality, a truce would emerge in the struggle for power seems
unlikely. It was precisely because people have roughly equal
talents that Hobbes felt there would be a war of all against all
outside the restriction of the laws.

Like Hobbes's, Stirner's model of human nature would seem to
reflect the alienated subjectivity of capitalist society. He applied
the assumptions of capitalist economics to every aspect of human
existence and reproduced in everyday life what is most vicious in
capitalist institutions. As such his view differs little from that of
Adam Smith (whose *Wealth of Nations* he translated into German)
or the contemporary apologist of *laissez-faire* capitalism, Murray
Rothbard.

In the final analysis, however, Stirner is not entirely consistent
in his doctrine of amoral egoism. The consistent egoist would
presumably keep quiet and pursue his own interest with complete
disregard for others. Yet by recommending that everyone should
become an egoist, he implies a moral ground. Stirner may reject
all objective values, but he celebrates some values, even if they are
only egoistic ones. His aggressive nihilism would therefore seem to
imply a moral position after all.[19]

Kropotkin at the end of the nineteenth century proposed a very
different model of human nature. On the one hand, he rejected
what he called Stirner's 'superficial negation of morality'.[20] On the
other, he echoed Godwin in his scientific view of nature as
governed by necessary laws, his stress on man as a social being,
and his recognition that change will often be gradual. What was
new was his confidence in the creativity and virtue of people living
in simple societies, his desire to give a scientific grounding to his
anarchist conclusions, and his overall evolutionary perspective.

Kropotkin's approach to nature and 'man' (as he called the
human species in the linguistic habit of his day) was rigorously
scientific. As a professional geographer and explorer, the subjective
and windy imaginations of Stirner were anathema to him. He came
to realize, he tells us, that anarchism is

part of a philosophy, natural and social, which must be developed in a quite different way from the metaphysical or dialectical methods which have been employed in sciences dealing with men. I saw it must be treated by the same methods as natural sciences . . . on the solid basis of induction applied to human institutions.[21]

In *Modern Science and Anarchism* (1901), he went further to argue that the movement of both natural and social science was in the direction of the anarchist ideal.

Kropotkin developed his views in the context of Darwin's theory of evolution. The theory had come to be used by Social Darwinists to give pseudo-scientific support to capitalism, racism, and imperialism. Since there is allegedly a struggle for survival in society as well in nature, they argued that it is right and inevitable that the fittest should survive and rule, whether it be a class, a race, or a nation. T. H. Huxley, Darwin's bulldog, presented moreover the animal world as a perpetual 'gladiator's show' and the life of primitive man as a 'continuous free fight'. Kropotkin threw himself into the controversy to offer an alternative interpretation of the evolutionary process.

It was his contention that there is more evidence in nature of co-operation within species than of competition. In his book *Mutual Aid* (1902), he suggested with a rich array of data taken from the life of animals and the development of human society that biological and social progress is best fostered by the practice of mutual aid:

we maintain that under *any* circumstances sociability is the greatest advantage in the struggle for life. Those species which willingly or unwillingly abandon it are doomed to decay; while those animals which know best how to combine have the greatest chance of survival and of further evolution.[22]

Kropotkin made clear that the struggle for survival which takes place is a struggle *against* adverse circumstances rather than *between* individuals of the same species. Where the Social Darwinists argued that the struggle between individuals leads to the survival of the fittest, Kropotkin asserted that the unit of competition is the species as a whole and that the species which has the greatest degree of co-operation and support between its members will be the most likely to flourish. Mutual aid within the species thus represents 'the principal factor, the principal active agency in that which we may call evolution'.[23]

Kropotkin does not hesitate to apply these observations of the animal world to human society. He maintains that society is a natural phenomenon existing anterior to the appearance of humanity, and humanity is naturally adapted to live in society without artificial regulations. Humanity is and always has been a social species. Kropotkin draws on the findings of anthropology to argue that in traditional societies human beings have always lived in clans and tribes in which customs and taboos ensured co-operation and mutual aid. He concludes from his historical studies that mutual aid reached its apogee in the communal life of the medieval cities. Even the appearance of coercive institutions and the state has not eradicated voluntary co-operation. According to Kropotkin, evolutionary theory, if properly understood, will demonstrate the possibility of anarchism rather than justify the capitalist system. Anarchism as a social philosophy is therefore not against but in keeping with evolving human nature.

Kropotkin not only argues that this is an accurate and true description of nature and the human species, but sees it as providing the ground for morality. 'Nature', he writes in his posthumous *Ethics* (1924),

> has thus to be recognized as the *first ethical teacher of man*. The social instinct, innate in men as well as in all the social animals, – this is the origin of all ethical conceptions and all the subsequent development of morality.[24]

Human beings are therefore naturally moral. Moreover, by living in society they develop their inherent sense of justice so that it comes to operate like a habit. As a result, we are morally progressive, and our primitive instinct of solidarity will become more refined and comprehensive as civilization develops.

Kropotkin thus presents man as a social being, and suggests that the most important factor in his development has been voluntary co-operation and mutual aid. But for all his respect for the sociability of traditional societies, Kropotkin does not reject the gains of civilization and culture. Humans like other animals need their basic needs satisfied, but they are also creative and imaginative beings. Indeed, our intellect and moral sense are primarily called forth by society. In *The Conquest of Bread* (1906), Kropotkin's principal criticism of the unequal distribution of property was that it does not give the necessary leisure for all to develop full human personalities:

> Man is not a being whose exclusive purpose in life is eating, drinking, and providing a shelter for himself. As soon as his material wants are satisfied, other needs, which generally

speaking may be described as of an artistic nature, will thrust themselves forward. These needs are of the greatest variety; they vary with each and every individual, and the more society is civilized, the more will individuality be developed, and the more will desires be varied.[25]

In the development of civilization in a free society, human beings would not only be able to evolve the full range of their artistic and intellectual abilities but become more truly social and individual. For this reason work would be made attractive and meaningful, fulfilling and not degrading the workers as at present. The incentive to work would be moral rather than material – the conscious satisfaction of contributing to the general well-being. And once bread was secured, leisure to develop the full human potential would be the supreme aim.

Kropotkin's anarchism is thus, like Godwin's, firmly based on a clear view of human nature. Mutual aid is a principal factor in natural and human evolution. There is a moral principle in nature which ensures that human beings have a sense of justice. We are naturally social, co-operative, and moral. But while society is a natural phenomenon, the state with its coercive institutions is an artificial and malignant growth.

If co-operation is natural, Kropotkin of course is left with the problem of explaining existing inequalities and egoism. To overcome this, he implies that human beings developed a secondary drive of self-assertion which led them to seek power and to dominate and exploit their fellows. Again, while he recognized the influence of economic arrangements on political institutions, his account of the origin of the state by which a minority combined military and judicial privileges suggests that political power was initially more important than economic power.

Nevertheless, Kropotkin remained confident that the dispossessed majority would destroy the new coercive institutions, and develop their natural propensity to help each other. If political authority were removed with all other artificial restrictions, Kropotkin was convinced that human beings would act socially, that is to say, in accordance with their social nature. However distant, he believed that a free society would eventually be realized as the natural outcome of human evolution.

Human nature, philosophy, and history

While I share some of the assumptions of these three classic anarchist thinkers, my own philosophical starting-point is somewhat different. I have little sympathy for Stirner's egoism and consider his account of human motivation to be simply false. Godwin's view of human beings as potentially rational, voluntary, and progressive is attractive, but it is ultimately based on the belief in the omnipotence of universal truth which is difficult to maintain. Kropotkin's evolutionary perspective is important, but his ethical naturalism is untenable. There are no values to be discovered in nature; all values are human creations.

It is my view that we should abandon the use of the term 'human nature' since it implies that there is a fixed essence within us which requires certain conditions to express itself, or some inherent force which directs us outside the influence of history or culture.

Sweeping assertions about human nature are notoriously suspect. They are often disguised definitions – as in the statement 'all men are wild beasts' – and as such cannot be verified, proved, or disproved by appealing to any evidence. In addition, they usually contain a confused mixture of fact and value, a description of how people are and how they should be. The statement that 'human beings are naturally aggressive' is posed as a factual statement – 'all beings are actually aggressive' – but it also implies the value that we should all be aggressive. This becomes even more evident in statements like 'pacifism is unnatural'.

Clearly facts are relevant to values, for to understand what we are helps us to decide what we can and should do. But what counts as a fact invariably depends on a prior theory and value. Ethnologists and psychologists are notorious for projecting human values into nature and then claiming that they have observed them as hard and certain 'facts'. They extend, for instance, ideas of domination and hierarchy into the natural world of non-human biological relationships, but such ideas are the product of the socially conditioned human mind. Thus 'man' is depicted as a 'naked ape' driven by a 'territorial imperative' and prey to geese-like 'aggression'. Science can help us to understand society and culture, but it is well to remember that so-called 'objective' science is also shaped and influenced by them.

In the circumstances, it would perhaps seem a good idea to go beyond the whole 'fact/value', 'is/ought' debate and to recognize that there is no unbridgeable gap between normative and prescriptive statements. Viewed dialectically, 'what could be' and 'what should be' are inseparable parts of 'what is', since the former contain the moral and practical potential of the latter.

The trouble with most views about 'human nature', particularly the ones put forward by psychoanalysts and sociobiologists, are that they have an uncanny similarity with the world view of the class to which the thinkers belong. In the West, the view of the dominant class is that human beings are fundamentally selfish, competitive, and aggressive. Yet this view is historically limited to the rise of capitalism and the nation state, and takes no account of either the organic and co-operative behaviour of traditional societies or even the mutual aid practised in the Middle Ages. The possessive individualism of the West is a comparatively recent development. The ruling class and their ideological apologists try to persuade us that certain human traits like self-interest and possessiveness which are historical and temporary are in fact existential and permanent.

Another difficulty with the concept of human nature is that for an assertion about human nature to be true it has to be true of all those beings classified as human. If counter-examples of human behaviour can be discerned in the findings of anthropology and history, then such statements are not universally valid. They should therefore be qualified by certain conditions; for instance, it can only be said that in certain capitalist societies human beings are possessive. Alternatively, such statements should be interpreted as only carrying the weak sense of meaning that people, or even most people, normally behave in particular ways. If this is the case, then it is easy for libertarians to argue that even if most people have been aggressive in the past, or even if most people are selfish today, it does not follow that they always will be, or that changed conditions will not bring about different behaviour. It then becomes possible to point to different societies in time and place (drawing on anthropology and history as Kropotkin and more recently Murray Bookchin have done) to show that self-interest and hierarchy are not universal and that it is possible to create a society different from the models held up by those in power. Rather than offering a single model of humanity, a knowledge of history and anthropology would suggest that human behaviour is systematically unpredictable.

I would take the argument further, however, and suggest that it is quite misleading to talk of the collective abstraction 'Man'; there are only men and women, human beings. Human beings are social animals but they also have an irreducible uniqueness of their own. The human species is too diffuse to talk about an underlying fixed essence which society and culture are designed to express. Since 'human nature' is such an ambiguous and misleading term it would seem a good idea to abandon its use altogether.

This is not to suggest that there are no characteristics which are peculiarly human. We are a species which has developed during millions of years of biological evolution. With other species, we share the fundamental instincts of hunger and sex. Without the satisfaction of the former, we would not survive as individuals, and without the latter, our species would die out. I would also agree with Marx that we are fundamentally social beings: we are all born into a set of social relationships. But unlike other species we have emerged from the natural world to become thinking beings – *Homo sapiens*. The human mind is uniquely capable of conceptual thought, symbolic communication, and self-consciousness. We are therefore the product of an evolutionary process which has gone in the direction of increasing complexity, consciousness, and individuality.

Beyond biological evolution, we have entered in the last million years a phase of cultural evolution, in which our accumulated experience is handed down from generation to generation. The result is that while we share biological needs with other animals the manner in which they are expressed and satisfied is determined culturally and socially. In addition, human society itself has created new needs, such as the need for productive work, loving relations, and a meaningful relationship with the world.

Although we do not have a 'human nature' as a fixed essence, we are born with a certain evolving range of perceptual, conceptual, and linguistic powers. These innate capacities, which form a central part of human consciousness, enable us to think, to communicate, and to create. In the case of language, for instance, we are born with an ability to understand and use language. It not only enables us to interpret the world we find ourselves in but provides the basis of personal identity and social freedom. The advantage of this position is that it avoids the reductionism both of the rationalist, who maintains that we are born with innate ideas, and of the empiricist, who argues that we are blank sheets at birth.

The innate powers or capacities are not fixed however, but open. They may be innately determined but are also shaped by experience. The tired debate of the relative importance of heredity and environment, nature versus nurture, overlooks that the fact that neither are constant variables. From the moment a human being is conceived, heredity and environment interact on each other, and later experience is always interpreted according to earlier experience. Even varieties in height, for instance, used to depend on environmental factors like diet and health, and only recently have become largely genetically determined.

It follows that the way in which our innate capacities are expressed will depend on the circumstances we are born into. Our circumstances act as a series of limits and pressures upon us. But our circumstances, like everything else in the universe, are in a state of flux. In addition, since we are conscious beings, we are capable not only of adapting to our circumstances but of creating new ones. By changing our circumstances, we change ourselves. We are both the products and agents of history. Human society is thus not built on an unchanging bedrock of 'human nature', or on some fixed biological foundation, but develops dialectically and can be consciously shaped to express and satisfy our needs.

There are of course existential limits to our human condition: we long for immortality, yet we are born to die; we search for absolute knowledge, yet remain in doubt. Again, we do not choose our parents: we are born into a particular body in a particular time and place. But how we respond to our existential predicament is not predetermined or fixed.

It is our consciousness which sets us free. Because consciousness is intentional, we can become aware of and understand the influences at work on us. We can then choose which influences we want to check or develop, which motives we wish to act upon. Between ourselves and the world, there is a gap in which we can say 'no'. We are not foregone conclusions: we can refuse to be the type that our mentors and leaders would like us to be.

Therein lies our freedom, the area of conscious choice. We are free to come to terms with our existential and social condition and to take up our past and to launch ourselves into a future of our own making. We have all been conditioned into dependence and obedience. We can choose, as Sartre suggests, not to choose and so become like a stone. We can be fearful of freedom and avoid the responsibility it entails. Nevertheless, in the end we are all responsible to a large degree for our individual lives, for our social arrangements and for nature itself.

This position may be called a kind of soft determinism. It recognizes that there are causes which influence us, but it sees all causes as incomplete and open-ended. Such causes dispose but do not determine.[26] It sees knowledge as inseparable from freedom and defines freedom both as the release from external restraint and as the ability to realize one's innate capacities. Like plants, human beings realize their potential according to their environment; but unlike plants, they can change the environment they find themselves in.

It also offers the possibility of elaborating a case for anarchism, as Noam Chomsky has hinted, based on the self-regulation of the innate intellectual and creative abilities of the human mind.[27] It is a kind of self-regulation which does not require coercive institutions or political authority; indeed, it is positively harmed by them. It sees freedom as the unique condition under which human consciousness and happiness can develop and grow. It is a liberty, as Bakunin observed, which implies

> the full development of all the material, intellectual and moral capacities latent in everyone; the liberty which knows no other restrictions but those set by the laws of our own nature, consequently there are, properly speaking, no restrictions, since these laws are not imposed upon us by any legislator from outside, alongside, or above ourselves. These laws are subjective, inherent in ourselves; they constitute the very basis of our being.[28]

Moreover, it is not only the mind but also our emotional and sexual drives which regulate themselves when not interfered with by artificial restrictions imposed by coercive institutions. As Wilhelm Reich argued; 'The vital energies, under natural conditions, regulate themselves spontaneously, without compulsive duty or compulsive morality.'[29] The traditional conflict between reason and desire is not inevitable but a result of our social arrangements. Since the body and mind are two aspects of the whole person, and the whole person is self-regulating, only in a free society of self-governing individuals would people be able realize their full potential as social and creative beings.

To be self-regulating and autonomous individuals does not mean that we are floating atoms unconnected to each other. We are shaped by the whole and can only realize our individuality through others. To become truly individual, we must become fully social. This apparent paradox becomes less problematic when compared to Arthur Koestler's description of biological and social individuals as 'holons' – 'self-regulating systems which display both the autonomous properties of wholes and the dependent properties of parts'.[30] They have a dual tendency to assert their individuality as autonomous wholes and to function as an integrated part of a larger evolving whole.

As for the controversy about whether we are 'naturally' good or bad, selfish or benevolent, gentle or aggressive, I consider the search for one irreducible quality to be as absurd and reductionist as looking for a human essence. We have innate tendencies for both types of behaviour; it is our circumstances which encourage or check them. While our present authoritarian and hierarchical society encourages egoism, competition, and aggression, there is good reason to think that a free society without authority and coercion would encourage our benevolent and sympathetic tendencies. Instead of universalizing what we find in our own society, we should recognize that it is an exception rather than the norm. The present ideology, which identifies progress with growth and competition, defines happiness with consumption, and confuses having with being, is historically unique.

Anthropology shows that there have been many gentle societies where human beings have no wish to kill or dominate each other. The very disparate societies of the Arapesh of New Guinea, the Lepchas of Sikkim in the Himalayas, and the pygmies of the Ituri rain forest in the Congo offer striking examples. There is a wealth of data to demonstrate that for the greater part of history human beings have lived co-operatively and peacefully without rulers. These societies vary from small groups of hunter-gatherers like the Eskimos and Bushmen, to the Tiv gardeners, who number over a million in Nigeria. Even amongst agricultural societies, which can create a surplus for a ruling class and often have governments, there have been a number of highly decentralized federations. The Berbers, throughout the Middle East, and the Kabyles in Algeria, manage themselves through autonomous village councils. Again, the Santals, over three million of whom dwell in eastern India, decided their affairs in free and open meetings with the village headman merely being the voice of the consensus.

The anarchy of these traditional societies without rulers does not necessarily mean that they are free in the modern sense of offering a wide range of choices to the individual. They are often characterized by sexism and ageism, with power conferred on men and elders. In place of laws, there are also strong sanctions to reform the wrongdoer and to make the dissenting individual conform. These can be religious sanctions, such as the threat of supernatural punishment, and social ones, particularly in the form of ostracism, ridicule, and gossip. The force of habit and custom is also very strong, and can perpetuate ignorance, intolerance, and prejudice. Nevertheless, these societies show that human beings have lived and can live without coercive institutions and authoritarian leaders and rulers.[31]

In recent history, there have moreover been several self-conscious attempts to realize on a large scale a commonwealth which contains age-old patterns of co-operation with a modern desire for personal freedom. The self-managing districts in the Paris Commune remain an inspiration. The peasants in the Ukraine during the early days of the Russian Revolution formed anarchist communes. The greatest experiment so far was during the Spanish Revolution, when peasants in Aragon and Valencia and workers in Barcelona organized themselves in communes and councils and fought the civil war against Franco on anarchist lines. The fact that the revolution failed, largely due to external factors, does not alter the case that the anarchist ideal was partially realized and shown to be practicable.

The present direction of history would seem to be towards more centralized, militarized, and authoritarian states, but the dying breed of indigenous anarchies can tell us much about how to organize society without rulers. They show that the nation-state is only a recent cancer on the body politic. Above all they remind us of the important truth that liberty is the mother and not the daughter of order. While no self-conscious anarchist society as yet exists, the great social experiments in the last hundred years show that it is an ever-present possibility and an ineradicable part of human potential. A free society is in the realm of objective possibilities. There is no pre-ordained pattern to history, no iron law of capitalist development, no straight railroad which we have to follow. Although it is always made on prior circumstances, history is what we make it; and the future, as the past, can be either authoritarian or libertarian depending on our choices and actions.

Towards a free and ecological society

Having exposed the myth of human nature as some fixed essence and sketched an alternative view of human limits and possibilities, I would like consider some moral implications. While nature does not preclude the possibility of freedom and autonomy, it is difficult to ground an objective ethics in a philosophy of nature as Kropotkin and now Murray Bookchin have attempted.[32] In the first place, such an attempt overlooks the logical fallacy of maintaining that, because something *is*, it follows that it *ought* to be. A study of aggression in geese may or may not illuminate aggression in men; it does not tell us whether aggression is good or bad. There are no moral values to be discovered or revealed in nature. Stirner is right in stressing that it is human beings that create values. We tend to read into nature what we want to find. Kropotkin's and Bookchin's strategy, like that of the Social Darwinists and their contemporary counterparts, the sociobiologists, makes this fundamental error.

Nevertheless, I would argue that it is important to keep an evolutionary perspective which recognizes that human beings have changed in the past and are likely to continue to do so in the future. It reminds us that we are one species amongst others, and that there is a difference only in degree and not in kind between us and other animals. We are a part not only of human society, but of a wider community of all living beings. We have no God-given prerogative to become managers of the cosmic process or the lords of creation.

More important still, we should develop an ecological perspective which sees humanity as an inseparable part of the living web of nature, recognizes that our survival depends on the survival of our habitat, and sees different species as intrinsically valuable members in a non-hierarchical world. The integrity of the whole and the integrity of the part are mutually dependent. This is not to say that we should appeal to mere expediency to stop humans despoiling the earth. Nor does it imply that all organisms are equal citizens in a biospheric democracy.[33]

Contrary to biocentric ethics, I would argue that all organisms are not of equal worth. They do not possess equal 'rights' which entitle them to identical treatment. Not only are rights purely human conventions, but such reasoning would put human beings and rhinos on the same level as the AIDS virus or smallpox. But while the utilitarian calculus can lead to abhorrent conclusions, and the language of rights is ambiguous and confused, I believe on the ground of the ability to feel – to suffer pain or enjoy happiness – that there should be equal consideration of different species.[34] The degree of consciousness may have a side constraint in our deliberations. While both are capable of suffering, it would be reasonable to conclude that the interests of a child are more important than the interests of a slug, since one is more conscious than the other. But even if we make this decision, we should also bear in mind the wider principles of the sanctity of life and the vitality of evolution and recognize that there is a place in the world for slugs as well as children.

While it is misleading to transpose observations about the natural world to human society, it is nevertheless salutary to be reminded of the ecological principle that the more variety there is in nature the greater the overall vitality. It offers a model of unity in diversity, difference with equality, change and equilibrium in a non-hierarchical framework. Applied to society, the principle suggests that the health of a free society might be measured by the amount of individuality it could tolerate and parasites it could support. Again, ecology presents the earth as a self-regulating and evolving system which reflects the self-regulating and evolving capacity of human beings.

We have evolved to be uniquely conscious and creative beings, and as such we have a responsibility for the world. We are rational and moral agents. We are in a position to participate in natural evolution and help realize the evolutionary trend towards greater complexity, consciousness, and individuality. We should go beyond Kropotkin, who was still committed to the nineteenth-century notion of 'industrial progress' as a 'conquest over nature', and develop Godwin's notion of stewardship of the good things of the world.[35] We should act not as conquerors but as stewards of the planet. It may be too arrogant and ambitious to try to 'free' nature itself by developing its potential, as Bookchin has suggested, but, by our intervention into the natural processes of evolution, we can certainly foster diversity, diminish suffering, and encourage latent life forms.[36] It is worth stressing that this is a moral and social problem, not to be confused with the fashionable misanthropy or vague calls for universal love which permeate sections of the Green movement.

How do we create a free society which is ecologically sound? I believe that such a desirable state of affairs is likely to be brought about gradually and peacefully. I do not agree with Godwin that a period of education and enlightenment must precede the dissolution of government, but share Kropotkin's confidence in the ability of ordinary people to shape their own lives and govern themselves. The resort to violence to transform society, however, which has been a minor but significant trend in the anarchist tradition, is inevitably self-defeating. As the major revolutions this century – the Russian, the Chinese, the Cuban – have only too vividly demonstrated, it is impossible to use authoritarian means to realize libertarian ends. The means have to be the same as the ends, or the ends themselves become distorted. The process and goal must be one. Although there is a possibility, there is no certainty that a free society will ever be achieved. If it is to be realized, then it will only be through our conscious choice and through persuasion and example.

I hope by now that I have persuaded that nasty fellow 'human nature' to step aside and to question his very existence! I have also tried to make clear that anarchism is not a puerile dream based on an unduly optimistic or simple view of what it is to be human. It not only expresses a central part of human experience but reflects the organic processes of nature itself. It offers a plausible ideal for the post-industrial age to come. I therefore see no bar within our make-up to prevent the creation of a society which will free us from psychological dependence and economic want and enable us all to develop in harmony with nature the full potential of our being.

Notes and references

1 For a recent version of this view, see Leszek Kolakowski's review of David Miller, *Anarchism* (London: Dent, 1984), in the *Times Literary*

Supplement, January 4 1985, p. 3. Miller himself is not guilty of such an oversimplification (op. cit., p. 76).

2 William Godwin, *Enquiry Concerning Political Justice*, ed. Isaac Kramnick (Harmondsworth: Pelican, 1976; reprint of 3rd edn, 1798), book I, chapter iv.

3 *The Anarchist Writings of William Godwin*, ed. Peter Marshall (London: Freedom Press, 1986), pp. 172–3. See also my *William Godwin* (New Haven, Conn., and London: Yale University Press, 1984), pp. 112–13, 400.

4 Godwin, *Political Justice*, op. cit., p. 349.

5 *The Anarchist Writings of William Godwin*, op. cit., p. 61.

6 Godwin, *Political Justice*, op. cit., p. 83.

7 *The Anarchist Writings of William Godwin*, op. cit., p. 29.

8 Ibid., p. 51.

9 Max Stirner, *The Ego and Its Own*, trans. Steven T. Byington (London: Rebel Press, 1982; reprint of 1963 edn), pp. 39–43.

10 Ibid., p. 162.

11 Ibid., p. 291.

12 Ibid., p. 189.

13 Ibid., p. 5.

14 Ibid., p. 157.

15 Ibid., p. 169.

16 Ibid., p. 332.

17 Ibid., p. 316.

18 Ibid., p. 209.

19 Cf. John P. Clark, *Max Stirner's Egoism* (London: Freedom Press, 1976), p. 53.

20 Peter Kropotkin, *Ethics: Origin and Development*, ed. N. Lebedev (Dorchester: Prism Press, n.d.; reprint of 1924 edn), p. 338.

21 Quoted by George Woodcock, *Anarchism: A History of Libertarian Ideas and Movements* (Harmondsworth: Penguin, 1983), p. 184.

22 Kropotkin, *Mutual Aid: A Factor of Evolution* (London: Heinemann, 1919; reprint of 1902 edn), pp. 49–50.

23 Kropotkin, *Ethics*, op. cit., p. 45.

24 Ibid., p. 45.

25 Kropotkin, *The Conquest of Bread* (London: Elephant Editions, 1985; reprint of 1913 edn), p. 108.

26 Cf. Mary Midgley, *Beast and Man: The Roots of Human Nature* (London: Methuen, 1980), p. 64.

27 In an interview with Paul Barker published in *New Society*, 2 April 1981, Chomsky argued that the 'libertarian left should have a vested interest in innateness'. I would not, however, go so far as Chomsky, who believes in a well-defined biological concept of human nature which is independent of social and historical conditions. He does not hesitate to consider the faculty of language as part of human nature and maintains that in such domains 'we can begin to formulate a significant concept of "human nature", in its intellectual and cognitive aspects' (*Language and Responsibility* (New York: Pantheon Books,

1979), p. 77). Cf. Carlos P. Otero, 'Introduction to Chomsky's social theory', in Noam Chomsky, *Radical Priorities*, ed. C. P. Otero (Montréal: Black Rose Books, 1981), pp. 26–8. Where Chomsky claims that there is no inconsistency in believing that the 'essential attributes of human nature give man the opportunity to create social conditions and social forms to maximize the possibilities for freedom, diversity, and individual self-realization' (*For Reasons of State* (New York: Pantheon Books 1973), pp. 395–6). His stress on human nature as an underlying innate structure undermines a creative and open-ended view of human intelligence and action.

28 Bakunin, 'The Paris Commune and the idea of the state', in *Bakunin on Anarchy*, ed. Sam Dolgoff (London: Allen & Unwin, 1973), pp. 261–2, and cited by Noam Chomsky in the *New York Review of Books*, 21 May 1970. Chomsky compares in his note 11 Bakunin's remark on the laws of individual natue with the approach to creative thought in his own works *Cartesian Linguistics* (New York: Harper & Row, 1966) and *Language and Mind* (New York: Harcourt, 1968). In an interview with Graham Baugh, a version of which appeared in *Open Road* (Summer, 1984), Chomsky acknowledges, however, that 'one cannot simply deduce social or political consequences from any insights into language'. He adds that while one may hope to be able 'to show that structures of authority and control limit and distort intrinsic human capacities and needs, and to lay a theoretical basis for a social theory that eventuates in practical ideas as to how to overcome them', there are 'huge gaps' in any such argument.

29 Wilhelm Reich, *The Function of the Orgasm* (New York: Noonday Press, 1942), p. xix, quoted by Charles Rycroft, *Reich* (London: Fontana, 1971), p. 40.

30 Arthur Koestler, *The Ghost in the Machine* (Chicago: Regnery, 1967), p. 341. Cf. Clark, *Egoism*, op. cit., p. 98.

31 See Harold Barclay, *People without Government: An Anthropology of Anarchism* (London: Kahn & Averill with Cienfuegos Press, 1982), especially chapter 8.

32 See Kropotkin, *Mutual Aid*, op. cit.; and *Ethics*, op. cit.; Bookchin, *The Ecology of Freedom: The Emergence and Dissolution of Hierarchy* (Palo Alto, Calif.: Cheshire Books, 1982); and 'Thinking ecologically: a dialectical approach', *Our Generation*, 18, 2 (Spring/Summer 1987). While Bookchin's contribution to social ecology has been profound and stimulating, his attempt to ground an 'objective ethics' in nature not only assumes a rational pattern and order in nature but tends to undermine the moral spontaneity and creativity of human beings. Again, his view that human society is a 'second nature' derived from 'first nature' made self-conscious, and his dialectic in which 'what could be' is contained in 'what is' seems unduly deterministic and Hegelian. Finally, he argues that 'human nature' does exist, even though he suggests that it consists of 'proclivities and potentialities that become increasingly defined by the instillation of social needs' (*Ecology of Freedom*, op. cit., p. 114). Such a loose definition hardly

adds up to the notion of a 'human nature' as usually defined.

33 For this view, see Bill Devall and George Sessions, *Deep Ecology* (Salt Lake City: Peregrine Smith Books, 1985), p. 67.

34 Cf. Peter Singer, *Animal Liberation: Towards an End to Man's Inhumanity to Animals* (London: Paladin, 1977), p. 22.

35 Kropotkin, *Mutual Aid*, op. cit., p. 221; *The Anarchist Writings of William Godwin*, op. cit., pp. 130, 133.

36 Bookchin, 'Thinking ecologically', op. cit., p. 36. See also his article 'Social ecology versus "deep ecology"', *Green Perspectives*, 4–5 (Summer 1987), p. 21.

5

The role of contract in anarchist ideology

Robert Graham

Pierre-Joseph Proudhon, the first self-proclaimed anarchist, once wrote that in anarchism 'the notion of Government is succeeded by that of Contract'.[1] When this claim is juxtaposed with Sir Henry Maine's famous dictum that the development of modern liberal society constitutes above all a 'movement from status to contract', anarchism can then be seen either as the apotheosis of the liberal conception of society, in which contractual relationships finally replace all coercive ties, or as its unintentional *reductio ad absurdum*. Indeed, Murray Bookchin has recently argued that contractual notions of freedom constitute no advance over bourgeois conceptions of justice, but rather a capitulation to them, since the notion of contract is irredeemably tied to bourgeois notions of equivalent exchange.[2]

It is my argument that the notion of contract originally played a dual role in anarchist ideology. First, it was through means of contract that economic justice was to be achieved. The equivalent exchange of products between free and equal producers was meant to ensure the elimination of economic exploitation. Second, it was by means of contract that individual liberty was to be guaranteed. In place of the economic coercion exercised by the capitalist over the worker, and the political and legal coercion imposed on the citizen by the state, all economic and political relationships were to be transformed by means of contract into completely voluntary relationships free from all coercion. As anarchists began to embrace communist economic views, the notion of contract as equivalent exchange came to be replaced by distribution according to individual need. However, the notion of contract as free agreement continued to play an important role in anarchist ideology.

It is with Proudhon that the notion of contract assumed a role of fundamental importance in anarchist ideology. He envisaged a society in which all social relationships, save those within the family, were to be based on voluntary contracts between free and equal individuals. He criticized both capitalism and the state on the basis of this contractarian ideal.

Proudhon regarded contract as necessary to ensure liberty and equality. In turn, he regarded liberty and equality as necessary to each other.

Proudhon argued that only equals can form a free association. The capitalist is not the worker's associate, but an enemy who exploits him. Through his labour the worker provides his employer with the means of 'independence and security for the future', while obtaining for himself only daily subsistence.[3] The worker is in a precarious position, with no guarantee of wages for the morrow, holding 'his labour by the condescension and necessities of the master and proprietor'.[4] Any contract between such unequal parties is necessarily null and void.

Capitalist property relationships destroy equality by promoting the accumulation of wealth unconnected with individual labour. Through rent and interest the capitalist is able to live off the labour of others. Economic necessity forces the worker to sell his labour to the capitalist at a price which does not reflect its real value. The workers, then, according to Proudhon, are both unequal and unfree.

Proudhon regarded not only the instruments of labour, but also the capacity for labour itself, as forms of collective property. 'The smallest fortune, the most insignificant establishment, the setting in motion of the lowest industry', Proudhon wrote, 'demand the concurrence of so many different kinds of labour and skill, that one man could not possibly execute the whole of them'.[5] By associating together, the workers create a 'collective force' greater than the sum of their individual productive capacities, but it is the capitalist who reaps the benefit.

Only when the worker becomes entitled to the full product of his labour will economic freedom and justice be achieved. The worker will then be free to exchange what he has produced for something of equivalent value, value being determined by cost of production and labour time. In place of private property, Proudhon advocated individual possession, or the right of usufruct. By this he meant a right of access to the means of subsistence and production for personal use and exchange with others. In his later works, Proudhon saw private property as a necessary counterweight to the power of the state.[6] Rent was to be abolished and interest reduced to a minimum.

Proudhon argued that contract, conceived as an agreement for equal exchange between free and equal producers, necessarily excludes the idea of government. In a truly voluntary contract, the parties 'obligate themselves to each other, and reciprocally guarantee' that they will perform their respective duties under contract, 'recognizing that they are otherwise perfectly independent, whether for consumption or production'.[7] Each party enters the contract on the basis of 'a real personal interest . . . with the aim of securing his liberty and his revenue at the same time, without any possible loss'.[8]

In contrast, Proudhon argued, between the governing and the governed, 'no matter how the system of representation or of delegation of the governmental function is arranged, there is *necessarily* alienation of a part of the liberty and of the means of the citizen'.[9] Proudhon's notion of contract is therefore tied to a notion of self-assumed obligation. The only obligations binding on the individual are those resulting from promises, oaths, and contracts expressly and freely entered into by the individual himself. 'In so far as I have not wanted the law,' Proudhon stated, 'in so far as I have not consented to it, voted for it, signed it, I am under no obligation to it; it has no existence.'[10] In the place of hierarchy of political powers, he advocated the organization of economic forces on the basis of individual contracts of equivalent exchange.

It is from this perspective that Proudhon criticized the social contract of Rousseau, whom he denounced as a charlatan and a sophist. Proudhon interpreted Rousseau's social contract as a narrowly political contract limited to providing security of the person and of private property.[11] But to secure the current unequal distribution of wealth, which has arisen from the exploitation of labour, is to sanctify injustice by giving it the force of law. Rousseau's social contract is nothing more than an enormous swindle, a 'coalition of the barons of property, commerce and industry against the disinherited lower class'.[12] By ignoring the multitude of economic relationships in which people are constantly engaged in their daily lives, Rousseau tacitly condoned existing inequality and economic servitude.

Rousseau, Proudhon claimed, sought to render tyranny respectable by making it appear to 'proceed from the people', but instead of genuine self-government the citizen is left with nothing 'but the power of choosing his rulers by a plurality vote'.[13] Proudhon interpreted Rousseau's social contract as a contract between the individual and the state rather than as a contract between individuals themselves. The state enjoys the power of deciding the content of the law, and hence each citizen's political obligations, rather than the citizens themselves, who are then subject to laws to which they have never agreed and punished for the violation of them. In place of the reciprocal obligations freely undertaken by the individual himself in his personal transactions, there is the general obligation to obey whatever the government commands.

For Proudhon, a contract which results in the subordination and exploitation of one part of the citizenry by another is not a contract at all, but a fraud 'against which annulment might at any time be invoked justly'.[14] For a contract to be valid and binding, it must not only leave each party as free as before, it must add to his liberty; it must not only protect his property, it must add to his prosperity. Proudhon's notion of contract can be described as a self-interested bargain or exchange between free and equal individuals imposing reciprocal obligations on each party to their mutual benefit or advantage.

Proudhon conceived of society as being composed of a variety of groups. There are individual peasant smallholders, artisans, and proprietors, workers' associations in the larger enterprises, such as railways and factories, and geographical units, such as districts and municipalities, which are to administer public works. Each individual, each association, each locality 'should act directly and by itself in administering the interests which it includes, and should exercise full sovereignty in relation to them'.[15] Society itself will then become an 'organic union of wills that are individually free', based on 'the harmony of their interest, not in artificial centralization, which, far from expressing the collective, expresses only the antagonisms of individual wills'.[16]

Proudhon emphasized that the constitutive units of society are themselves to be democratically organized, whether those units are a workers' association, a people's bank, or a municipal administration, the one important exception being the family, which Proudhon believed should be organized along patriarchal lines. The management of large-scale enterprises is to be elected by the workers themselves, who are to own these enterprises collectively and share in the profits, or losses, in proportion to their individual labour. Each enterprise will be in competition with other worker collectives, but all will have access to credit at negligible interest rates. Only if capital is made freely available, Proudhon thought, can there be true competition, which he regarded as necessary for determining economic value and appropriate wage rates. Competition, by instilling a sense of responsibility in the worker, and by providing 'the hope of profit and of the social distinction which results from it', also acts as a spur to economic growth.[17]

This system of market socialism without the state was to be

based ultimately on an oath of fidelity made by all the members of society to uphold the rules of equivalent exchange, to respect the liberty and property of others, and 'never to lie or deceive in commerce or any transaction'.[18] While Proudhon at one time thought that people would embrace his 'mutualist' system, as he described it, out of rational self-interest, he later came to emphasize the role of the family in socializing the individual, and in providing the proper moral sentiment necessary to sustain a market socialist society.

Proudhon denied that the family could be conceived in contractual terms. The love and affection found in the family cannot be measured according to any notion of equivalent exchange. Familial relations, unlike contractual ones, are based on devotion and self-sacrifice.

Through interaction in the family, man develops feelings of self-respect and respect for others which provide the basis for his relationships in society as a whole. The moral education acquired in the family encourages man to rise above the debit/credit morality of the market-place and to adhere to the principles of justice in his daily transactions. For Proudhon, it is not so much rational self-interest but moral conscience, developed within the family, which will ensure that man will act in good faith, keep his obligations, and follow the rules of fair bargaining.

Proudhon's conception of the family is completely patriarchal in character. The family is to provide a moral education primarily for the male worker engaged in economic transactions in the market-place. The father-worker is the sole representative of the family in civil society, and later, after Proudhon came to the conclusion that politics cannot be dissolved in the economic organization of society, in political life as well.[19] Women are to stay at home, where their love and nurturance will provide the necessary moral sustenance for the male members of the family.

Proudhon's writings on the family are more than the expression of a conservative moral sensibility. They constitute an implicit recognition of an important limitation to the Proudhonian project of basing all social relationships on voluntary, contractual obligations. By emphasizing the important socializing influence of the family, Proudhon was tacitly admitting that contractual relationships are based on and presuppose a sphere of non-contractual relationships. It is within this underlying non-contractual sphere that the individual develops the moral and social capacities necessary to engage in the social practice of contracting. The family provides the foundation for Proudhon's entire contractarian edifice.

With his vision of a society where political rule has been replaced by industrial rule, Proudhon can be seen as one of the originators of syndicalist doctrine. Yet he himself later came to reject such views as utopian. In *The Principle of Federation*, Proudhon put forward the view that authority and liberty necessarily presuppose each other. Every society has authoritarian and libertarian tendencies, but no society can exist without both. Even in a society purportedly based on free contract, Proudhon argued, in order to resolve disputes the parties would have to submit themselves to the authority of an independent arbitrator.[20] Anarchy, a society in which 'political functions have been reduced to industrial functions, and . . . social order arises from nothing but transactions and exchanges', is fated to remain a perpetual desideratum.[21]

Proudhon thought that the conflict between authority and liberty could be resolved in favour of the latter by means of his theory of federation. He transposed his earlier views on free economic contract into the sphere of politics. He still conceived of society as being composed of a variety of contracting groups, from the patriarchal family to townships, districts, and provinces, but saw the necessity of these groups entering agreements for political purposes, such as national security and the arbitration of disputes, distinct from daily economic transactions.

Proudhon's political contract has the same structure as his economic contract. It imposes reciprocal obligations on the parties, with each undertaking to exchange with the other something of equal value. The political contract is confined to particular objects expressly stipulated by the parties upon entering the contract, so that everyone knows the nature and extent of the obligations he has assumed.

For the political contract to be binding, each citizen must have as much to gain as he sacrifices, and he must 'retain all his liberty, sovereignty, and initiative, except that which he must abandon in order to attain that special object for which the contract is made'.[22] By means of such contracts citizens associate together into a state, which provides the guarantee that the objects of the contract will be fulfilled. Unlike the fictive contract of Rousseau, in Proudhon's theory of federation

> the social contract is more than a fiction; it is a positive and effective compact, which has actually been proposed, discussed, voted upon, and adopted, and which can properly be amended at the contracting parties' will. Between the federal contract and that of Rousseau . . . there is all the difference between a reality and a hypothesis.[23]

The essential characteristic of the federal contract is that in entering it the contracting parties 'reserve for themselves more rights, more liberty, more authority, more property than they abandon'.[24]

The federal contract is the model for all contracts of association between the various units of society. In the political sphere the base unit is the family, whereas in the economic sphere it is the workshop.[25] Each group retains its autonomy so that the 'governing hierarchy is no longer imposed from the top down but rests securely on its base'.[26] By associating together by means of the political contract the contracting parties create a federal authority above them strictly confined to the limited purposes set out in the contract of association. Proudhon argued that such an authority is not really a government, properly so-called, but merely the agent of the contracting parties. It remains under their strict control, and its 'power varies at their pleasure'.[27]

The parties can revise the terms of the federal contract at any time. The federal authority is comprised of delegates from the base units, 'who therefore keep an especially sharp and jealous eye upon the acts of the federal assembly'.[28] The officers of the federal authority may also be removed at the request of the parties. No one party is charged 'with the administration and government of the rest', since this would soon lead to its domination of all the other groups in the federation.[29] Once the federal authority has accomplished its specified task, it withdraws. Its role is reduced 'to that of general initiation, of providing guarantees and supervising', while the actual 'execution of its orders [is] subject to the approval of the federated governments and their responsible agents'.[30] In the federal system, Proudhon argued, unlike traditional systems of centralized government, the powers of the central authority 'diminish in number, in directness, and in . . . intensity as the confederation grows'.[31]

Proudhon again emphasized that each member of the federation, with the exception of the family, is to have a directly democratic structure based on the federal contract. Between centralized, unitary governments there can be no federation, but at the most '*coalitions*'. Such governments would never agree to 'abandon some part of their sovereignty and recognize an arbiter set above them'.[32] Moreover, the political or economic enslavement 'of part of a nation denies the federal principle itself'.[33] Proudhon argued that in a society divided into antagonistic classes of capitalists and workers, federation would soon degenerate into either a unitary democracy, if the people are stronger, or a constitutional monarchy, if the bourgeoisie are victorious. He therefore insisted that political federation requires, as its corollary, 'agro-industrial federation', by which he meant the mutualist economic system he developed in his earlier works.[34] Public services will be run by the workers themselves, the tax burden equalized, the right to work and to education guaranteed, mutualism in credit and insurance established, and work organized so as to allow 'each labourer [not only] to become a skilled worker and an artist' but also 'to become his own master'.[35]

Federation, as Proudhon conceived it, necessarily implies the right of secession. When the federal authority oversteps its bounds by attempting to do something unauthorized by the federal contract, thereby infringing the autonomy of its members, they are entitled not only to resist such an invasion of their rights but also to withdraw completely from the federal compact. However, Proudhon seriously, if not fatally, qualified this right of secession by arguing that, in matters involving disputes over the interpretation or better application of the terms of the federal contract, the majority has a right to compel minority compliance where the majority would suffer the greater loss. This qualification renders the right of secession essentially nugatory.

To deprive the minority of the right to construe the terms of the federal contract according to its own understanding constitutes a serious infringement of the minority's autonomy, something the federal contract is supposed to guarantee. Although the problem of ensuring that contracting parties fulfil their obligations is a real one, Proudhon's 'solution' is completely inadequate. Ultimately his argument is based on his notion of 'the right of war', a notion more fully developed in his book, *La Guerre et la paix*, which some of his critics have interpreted as a proto-fascist document.[36]

There is more truth in the remark that Proudhon was a liberal in proletarian clothing than in the claim that he was a harbinger of fascism. With the liberals, Proudhon shared the ideal of a society based on contractual relationships between free and equal individuals. He also shared with them the view that society is essentially a conglomeration of individuals. Proudhon, in opposition to some of his socialist contemporaries, argued that society comes after the individual; the individual does not come into existence after society.[37] But unlike his liberal contemporaries, Proudhon denied that either capitalism or the state is compatible with a consistently contractarian view of society.

Between the worker and the capitalist there can be no free contract, because the unequal bargaining power enjoyed by the capitalist enables him to extort concessions from the worker in exchange for which the worker receives the bare necessities of life.

By virtue of this unequal relationship the capitalist is able to obtain a greater share of the worker's product than he is really entitled to. This latter claim of Proudhon's was based on his moral interpretation of the labour theory of value. As with many socialists of his era, from the idea that labour is the ultimate source of economic value Proudhon inferred that each worker was morally entitled to the full product of his labour, which he should then be free to exchange with others according to his own needs and desires. Later anarchist communist thinkers would argue that this was a complete *non sequitur*. Proudhon's mistake was to confuse economic value with moral desert.

Proudhon never satisfactorily dealt with his notion of 'collective force'. If, as Proudhon argued, both the instruments of labour and the capacity to labour itself are collective products of society, how is it possible to determine the actual moral worth of any particular individual's contribution to the economy? The idea that the individual worker should be entitled to the full product of his labour is based on the moral notion of just desert. To be faithful to the idea of desert, Proudhon should have opposed the right of inheritance, which enables one person to confer unearned benefits on someone else. Bakunin, who at one time also argued that the individual worker should be entitled to the full product of his labour, was more consistent in this regard, demanding the complete abolition of the right of inheritance, so that all benefits received by an individual would be earned by the individual himself.[38]

Having rejected the state, and therefore any system of central economic planning, Proudhon had to search for alternative methods for ensuring social order and economic justice. This helps to explain Proudhon's reliance on market mechanisms, such as competition, and his free credit schemes. The idea was to achieve exchange without exploitation. Proudhon thought individual exchange was necessary to safeguard individual autonomy, but for such exchange to be non-exploitative it had to be made on the basis of equivalent values. Equivalent exchange in the market was meant to ensure that each worker would be fairly compensated, without having to rely on any regulatory agency or political authority. Proudhon's economic ideas are therefore not peripheral to his general social theory, but central to it. The success of Proudhon's doctrine is ultimately tied to the viability of some form of market socialism, although not necessarily in the form conceived by Proudhon himself. Ironically, the most interesting work in this area is now being done by economists coming out of the Marxist tradition, as they try to grapple with the economic and political problems confronting state socialist societies.[39]

Proudhon never seriously considered communism as an alternative. He thought that communism would require a strong state for its effective implementation, and that it would restrict spontaneity and freedom of thought and of action. With his views on moral desert, he thought it unfair that a lazy person could obtain as much if not more than a hard-working person when distribution is based on need rather than on individual contribution. Communism, by relieving the worker of individual responsibility, would encourage shirking and lead to inefficiency and general economic decline. Proudhon believed that man only rouses himself from idleness 'when want fills him with anxiety'.[40] Later anarchist communist thinkers responded to such objections by arguing that the reliance on the threat of economic destitution as a spur to productivity would force people as a matter of economic necessity to engage in work for which they had neither the temperament nor the aptitude, and that it was this misapplication of individual talent in unfulfilling and onerous toil which was the real cause of laziness. Work itself was for them an intrinsic human need. They would argue that Proudhon's mutualist system merely replaces the economic power of the capitalist with generalized want.

Proudhon's contractual model of society can be seen as an attempt to ensure that individuals would only be subject to duties and obligations to which they had expressly and freely agreed. But Proudhon's notion of self-assumed obligation was tied to his notion of contract as equivalent exchange. He failed to distinguish contracting from other social practices by which people can freely assume their obligations, such as promising, which are not necessarily tied to any notion of equivalent exchange. His model of social relationships in both economic and political life was the self-interested bargain.

Proudhon's attempt to base social relationships and obligations on self-interested exchange raises some serious problems. Each party to a contract will always be tempted to get more out of the exchange than he bargained for, and to renege on his own obligations upon receiving the benefits offered by the other party. Individualist anarchists would further argue that any obligation requiring certain future conduct constitutes a constraint on individual liberty, so Proudhon's contractual model of society provides no great advance beyond traditional conceptions of political authority.

For Proudhon, the assurance that people would keep their

bargains would be provided by the moral influence of the family and by an express oath of fidelity to the rules of contracting. The problem with the latter device is that it assumes the very practice of self-assumed obligation which it is to provide the basis for. As for the family, although it certainly provides an important environment for individual moral development, whether it provides for the proper development of the autonomous individual necessary for a contractual society is another matter. Both radical and feminist psychoanalysis suggest that in fact the patriarchal nuclear family encourages submission to authority and an authoritarian sensibility, both of which ill-equip someone for the role of the autonomous contracting agent.[41] Furthermore, by relegating women to the home, Proudhon imposed on them a subordinate status and denied their freedom and equality with male workers. One can agree with Proudhon that the family should not be conceived in contractual terms without accepting his patriarchal conclusions.[42]

In *The Principle of Federation*, Proudhon hints at a third solution to the problem of ensuring that people fulfil their obligations. Perhaps people could rely on the federal authority created by their express agreement to ensure that people will adhere to their commitments. This appeal to a higher authority is the traditional response of orthodox political theory. Proudhon sought to avoid this alternative with his theory of federalism, but given his support of majority rule in case of disagreement, it is difficult to say that he was successful. The appeal to authority is itself problematic. As people come to rely on the federal authority to ensure that others keep their agreements, they will become even less inclined to do this themselves. A relationship of hierarchical authority between the individual and the state will soon replace the mutual ties of obligation between the citizens themselves. Far from ensuring that people will keep their bargains, penalties imposed by the federal authority will merely become one further factor to be considered when deciding whether it is worthwhile to renege on a commitment.

In capitalist society the breaching of contracts is a common occurrence, despite an elaborate court system, particularly when the benefits obtained by the breach outweigh any probable award of damages. To ensure the proper enforcement of contracts would require the reconstruction of virtually the entire coercive state apparatus – courts, policing agencies, prisons, and the like. But the problem of ensuring that people fulfil their obligations would remain, because the problem arises not so much from a lack of authority but from the nature of relationships based on competition and self-interest.

Instead of regarding other members of society as associates, the individual contractor will regard them as competitors for economic resources and benefits. He may only keep his bargains so long as it is to his advantage, and break them whenever it is not. Sanctions external to the relationship (of contracting) imposed by a hierarchical authority exacerbate this competitive mentality by encouraging moral evaluation based on the likelihood of sanction rather that on the intrinsic merits of a particular course of action (e.g. keeping faith). It is difficult not to conclude that Proudhon's contractarian society would be inherently unstable, and that such instability would soon encourage the development of more traditional forms of hierarchical political authority, and ultimately the reconstitution of the state. The idea that the family alone could provide sufficient glue to keep such a society together is implausible. Indeed, Proudhon himself suggested as much when he advocated that when disputes arise the majority has a right to compel minority compliance.

After Proudhon, the role of contract in anarchist ideology became much less pronounced. Bakunin developed a critique of contract theory, ostensibly aimed at Rousseau and Kantian liberals, which in many respects was equally applicable to Proudhon, as Bakunin himself sometimes acknowledged.

Bakunin denounced as ridiculous the idea of the Proudhonian mutualists that society is the 'result of the free contract of individuals absolutely independent of one another . . . entering into mutual relations only because of the convention drawn up among them'.[43] Bakunin thought this idea ridiculous because the act of contracting presupposes a number of abilities which can only be acquired within society. These abilities include the ability to speak a common language, the ability to make critical judgements and informed choices, and, most importantly, the ability to understand what it means to make a contract and to assume an obligation.

Bakunin's analysis of society, individuality, and freedom was very different from that of Proudhon. Working out of a framework of general determinism, Bakunin's focus was not on the abstract, 'free individual', but on the social conditions which make the emergence of such a person possible. Bakunin saw the free individual as the culmination of a long process of historical and social development. Society, far from being the denial of individual liberty, created the very basis for it. From this perspective, freedom is conceived as a 'feature not of isolation but of interaction, not of exclusion but rather of connection', for it is dependent on three eminently social phenomena: material emancipation from want and toil through collective labour, rational upbringing and education, and the reciprocal awareness and recognition of one's humanity and rights in the consciousness of equally free human beings.[44]

Bakunin's critique of the social contract theory of the state shares some similarities with Proudhon's, but it is based on fundamentally different premises. Proudhon criticized existing political relationships and institutions for not being based on express and truly voluntary contractual ties between individuals. The social contract was seen by him as an historical fiction which, suitably modified, ought to be made real. While Bakunin agreed that the social contract was an historical fiction, he went one step further and argued that it was also a conceptual impossibility. The ability to enter contractual relations with others presupposes a level of individual development and self-awareness which can only be achieved within society. By emphasizing that society must precede contract Bakunin was able to undercut one of the central ideological justifications of social contract theory in a way in which Proudhon was not.

According to social contract theory, society and the state are created by a contractual agreement between naturally free individuals constrained by no law or authority. To escape this 'state of nature' these individuals agree to subordinate themselves to a higher authority, exchanging their natural liberty for the protection of the state. But if society must precede contract, as Bakunin held, this presupposes 'natural contact among individuals and consequently *reciprocal limitations of their liberties*', amounting to the social contract itself existing as a natural fact prior to any agreement to constitute the state.[45]

Bakunin adopted Proudhon's theory of federation with only minor variations. Gone is the family as a political unit headed by the husband/father, but the workers' association, the co-operative, and the commune remain. Each organization is to be completely autonomous, freely federating with other organizations, from the bottom upward, into a complex network of interlocking associations developed for the purpose of satisfying the multifarious needs, interests, and aspirations of the people. As with Proudhon, Bakunin defended the absolute right of each group to secede from the federation, but unlike Proudhon he did not vitiate this right by allowing for majority rule over a recalcitrant minority. For Bakunin, no 'obligation in perpetuity is acceptable to human justice'.[46] The sole penalty reserved for the allegedly disobedient group is expulsion from the federation.

The movement in anarchist ideology away from Proudhon's contractarianism became virtually complete with the advent of anarchist communism. The anarchist communists attacked Proudhon's views, although not always by name, on primarily two grounds. First, they argued that it is impossible to determine the *moral* worth of any particular individual's contribution to the economy. In place of equivalent exchange they advocated distribution according to need. Second, they began to question the moral basis of contractarian ideology, which they regarded as evincing a 'shopkeeper's mentality'.

Kropotkin, the best-known exponent of anarchist communism, hit at the very heart of Proudhon's position by denying the validity of the labour theory of value. Merely because the 'exchange-value of commodities "generally" increases when a greater expenditure of labor is required' does not entail that the 'two quantities are proportional to each other'.[47] Kropotkin regarded the claim that labour and exchange value are proportional as a mere hypothesis unproven by scientific evidence. He insisted that a correlation between labour and price does not establish that *the one is the measure of the other*.[48] In a modern capitalist economy many other factors enter into the determination of price, 'so as to alter the simple relation that may have existed once between labour and exchange value'.[49] Today 'the scale of remuneration is a complex result of taxes, of governmental tutelage, of capitalist monopoly'.[50]

Kropotkin had as little use for the Marxist theory of 'surplus value', which he regarded as a pretentious way of stating the obvious fact that workers who have nothing to sell but their own labour will be exploited by capitalists to the latter's advantage. The workers are forced by economic necessity to sell 'their labour-power at a price which makes profits and the creation of "surplus values" possible'.[51] It is the unequal relationship between capitalist and worker, protected and maintained by the state, and not some 'natural law' of economics, which is the real cause of exploitation.

What the anarchist communists denied is that there is any necessary connection between economic price or value and moral worth or desert. Price is determined by a number of factors, such as costs of production and supply and demand. Moral value or worth is subjective and unascertainable. As Alexander Berkman put it, the 'same thing may be worth a lot to one person while it is worth nothing or very little to another'.[52] When labour itself is treated as a commodity, as a basis of exchange, as it is in Proudhon's mutualist system, its market price, even if uniform, will not necessarily reflect either the moral worth of the individual worker's exertions or the social utility of the product itself.

The anarchist communists accepted Proudhon's argument that there can be no freedom of contract between worker and capitalist, but they extended this critique to economic necessity as such and advocated the complete abolition of wage labour. In a communist economic system the notion of equivalent exchange simply has no role to play, although Kropotkin did suggest that 'in exchange for a half-day's, or five-hours' work' a large city organized along anarchist communist lines could guarantee 'to every inhabitant dwelling, food and clothing'.[53] But this kind of exchange is not based on any notion of equivalence, for Kropotkin denied that there is any just standard by which the value of individual labour can be measured. The individual worker is to be guaranteed the means to satisfy his needs regardless of the value of his own daily contribution, so long as he contributes something. Kropotkin's proposal can be regarded in part as a device for ensuring individual recognition of one's social responsibilities through an explicit act of commitment to the community. While rejecting the notion of equivalent exchange, Kropotkin did agree with Proudhon that the only actions one can require of an individual are 'those which receive his free acceptance'.[54]

Despite the rejection of contract conceived as equivalent exchange, the anarchist communists continued to espouse free agreement and voluntary association. Anarchist communism, Kropotkin wrote, shall 'cover society with a network of thousands of associations to satisfy its thousand needs', united by free agreement, with each association organized on a strictly voluntary basis.[55] Malatesta advocated the organization of 'social life by means of free associations and federations of producers and consumers, created and modified according to the wishes of their members'.[56] Kropotkin foresaw 'a society in which all the mutual relations of its members are regulated . . . by mutual agreements between the members of that society and by a sum of social customs and habits . . . continually developing and continually readjusted in accordance with the ever-growing requirements of a free life'.[57] In such a society, government would constitute an unnecessary imposition.

As for the problem of ensuring that people will abide by their agreements, Kropotkin thought that the 'simple habit of keeping one's word, the desire of not losing confidence, are quite sufficient in an overwhelming majority of cases to enforce the keeping of agreements'.[58] In a capitalist society, where the capitalist can impose terms on the worker who must accept them 'from sheer necessity', there can be no free agreement.[59] In such conditions 'force is of course necessary, both to enforce the supposed agreements and to maintain such a state of things'.[60] But in an anarchist communist society, where agreements will be 'entered upon by free consent, as a free choice between different courses equally open to each of the agreeing parties', the enforcement of agreements will no longer be necessary.[61]

Implicit in the idea of free agreement is some notion of self-assumed obligation, but it is a concept of obligation which is not connected to any concept of equivalent exchange. Through the process of free agreement individuals publicly commit themselves to future courses of conduct voluntarily chosen by them. The underlying model of obligation then is no longer contract, but promising. A promise is an act by which people assume an obligation to do some future act, but this obligation need not be tied to the receipt of some benefit. Promises can be unconditional in this sense, whereas contracts are a conditional form of exchange. One is only obligated under a contract upon the condition that the other party perform its side of the bargain.

This helps to explain why in contractual relationships problems of enforcement are more likely to arise. Where neither party can be sure that the other will perform its obligations under the contract, both parties will seek to obtain the greatest benefit with the least amount of risk to themselves. Often, it will be more advantageous to a party which has already received some benefit under the contract to refuse to complete it rather than to fulfil its own obligations at the risk that the other party will likewise breach the contract. Kropotkin could argue that the free agreements in an anarchist communist society would not have to be enforced because these agreements would not be contracts of equivalent exchange. Rather, they would be the public expression of free choice between persons whose relationships are characterized by co-operation and mutual aid instead of the manoeuvring for competitive advantage found in capitalist society.

One criticism that individualist anarchists would level at both Proudhon and the anarchist communists is that any sort of future obligation infringes individual liberty. On this view, contracts, promises, and free agreements are all equally unacceptable because they constrain future liberty of action and initiative by requiring someone to act according to prior commitments rather than according to his or her own present understanding or choice. The most forceful exponent of this view was the rationalist utilitarian anarchist, William Godwin. Godwin developed a critique of social contract theory similar in some respects to the critiques of Proudhon and Bakunin, but unlike them he went on to attack the very notion of obligation itself.

Godwin criticized social contract theory on a number of by now familiar grounds. Assuming that the social contract must be entered into by each citizen, since it would be absurd to base political obligation on agreements entered into by one's ancestors, what sort of consent is necessary for one to be bound by the contract? Godwin ruled out mere acquiescence, because this would justify even the most tyrannical of governments. Furthermore, people may acquiesce to the rule of a particular government for a number of reasons, none of which implies support for the government. They may feel intimidated, they may regard the government as the least evil of the available alternatives, or they may be financially unable to leave its jurisdiction. Godwin mocked Locke's doctrine of tacit consent, according to which acquiescence 'is sufficient to render a man amenable to the penal regulations of society', while 'his own consent is necessary to entitle him to the privileges of a citizen'.[62]

Further problems arise when considering the extent of political obligation based on actual consent. If consent is irrevocable, the citizen may later be compelled to obey a government or laws which he or she no longer supports. The citizen must not only consent to the content of all existing laws, but also 'to all the laws that shall hereafter be made'.[63] Godwin regarded this as self-evidently absurd. The opportunity to vote on the acceptance of future laws is insufficient, for the more important power of determining the content of the laws offered for public approval is left to someone else. Lastly, Godwin rejected the view that a minority can be bound by a majority vote. It is impossible to construe 'unremitting opposition in the first instance, and compulsory subjection in the second', as consent.[64]

Godwin saw the force of social contract arguments as resting upon the presumption that we are positively obligated to fulfil our voluntary commitments. He attacked this presumption on utilitarian grounds. Godwin believed that all moral agents have an overriding duty always to do that which will yield the greatest happiness. In any given situation there will be only one available course of action which will accomplish this objective. It is this course of action which the moral agent is obligated to undertake, regardless of any prior promise or agreement. The 'obligations' created by express agreements are either superfluous or positively evil, for they will either require conduct conforming to that required independently on utilitarian grounds, or they will require conduct which in the particular circumstances will not create the greatest pleasure or happiness.

Godwin also thought that self-assumed obligations are incompatible with individual autonomy, which requires that each individual independently evaluate all possible courses of action open to him or her according to utilitarian principles. To bind one's future conduct, even voluntarily, prevents one from properly exercising one's private judgement, besides sometimes causing one to do things which are not most conducive to happiness. Promising, at best, is but a temporary expedient, a necessary evil.

None of the later anarchist thinkers responded directly to these arguments, being for the most part unfamiliar with Godwin's work, but they did have to deal with other individualist anarchists who put forward similar views. To the claim that 'an obligation to co-ordinate one's own activities with those of others . . . violates liberty and fetters initiative', Malatesta replied that, to the contrary, it is only by 'co-operation with his fellows that man finds the means to express his activity and his power of initiative'.[65] Godwin, on the other hand, regarded co-operation as, 'in some degree, an evil', for it requires the individual to conform his or her actions to the needs and expectations of others, so that they may work in concert.[66]

Underlying these disagreements are differing conceptions of individuality and community. For Bakunin and the anarchist communists, individual autonomy presupposes certain levels of moral, social, and cultural development. They conceived of liberty in more positive terms, as a kind of social relationship, rather than merely as the absence of constraint. To attempt to escape natural social influence was, according to Bakunin, to condemn oneself to nothingness. Godwin's free individuals, indulging in society as a 'luxury', are nothing more than intellectual abstractions.

Godwin could deny the need for co-operation and community only because he assumed that in any given situation there will be one correct course of action which will be equally apparent to all rational agents. Free agreement is unnecessary because all will do what is right solely as a result of their own deliberations, which will independently yield essentially the same conclusions. Underlying Godwin's account of utilitarian moral calculation is a reified view of Reason as something timeless and abstract, existing independently of social relationships, and equally accessible to all thinking persons.[67] Not only is this concept of reason implausible, it is extremely alienating. Instead of dealing directly with each other as autonomous, emotional human beings, Godwin's moral agents will regard each other as so much data for their utilitarian calculations. Ironically, instead of safeguarding autonomy, Godwin's utilitarianism threatens it by encouraging the objectification of other persons.

One can also challenge Godwin's claim that self-assumed obligation infringes individual autonomy. Carole Pateman has recently argued that, far from conflicting with individual autonomy, self-assumed obligation, as exemplified by promising, presupposes it. To assume freely an obligation one must be able to make reasoned choices and to evaluate critically various courses of action. The person assuming the obligation defines the content of it, and in this sense is self-legislating or autonomous. Although self-assumed obligations bind future conduct, it is always open to the individual to re-evaluate his or her commitments. Situations may arise where conflicting moral demands require one to break a promise, but this does not imply that the promise was never binding. To the contrary, if promises were not considered as creating future obligations there would be nothing 'binding' to be broken.

Perhaps Godwin would respond that, although the act of promising requires the exercise of certain critical faculties, the result of that exercise, namely a binding obligation, nevertheless constrains individual autonomy. But this is to misunderstand the 'binding' nature of self-assumed obligations. That someone is bound by an obligation simply means that it is publicly understood that that person has undertaken to perform a particular future act. This gives rise to a public expectation that the act will indeed be performed, such that if it is not, some sort of explanation will normally be expected or required. But none of this prevents the individual from continuing to exercise his or her critical judgement after assuming the obligation, or from later deciding that, all things considered, it ought not to be performed.

Self-assumed obligations are not 'binding' in the same sense that laws or commands are. A law or command is binding in the sense that failure to comply with it will normally attract the application of some sort of coercive sanction by the authority promulgating the law or making the command. The binding character of law is not internal to the concept of law itself but dependent on external factors, such as the legitimacy of the authority implementing and enforcing it. A promise, unlike a law, is not enforced by the person making it. The content of the obligation is defined by the person assuming it, not by an external authority. The failure to keep a promise does not necessarily incur some sort of punishment. The 'rule' that promises oblige has not been implemented and enforced by any political authority, nor is the validity of that rule tied to the legitimacy of such an authority. That promises oblige, and that obligations are binding, in the sense explained above, is simply part of the meaning of these concepts, a conceptual fact existing independently of any political authority, forming part of a coherent social practice comprised of publicly understood and accepted conventions and rules.

Suppose that Godwin would be willing to grant that promising, as a social practice, does not necessarily infringe individual autonomy. It would still be open to him to argue that the *content* of self-assumed obligations may clearly conflict with individual autonomy, as when someone makes a promise to obey. He could then argue that this potential threat to individual autonomy, sometimes realized, is sufficient to justify completely expunging the concept of obligation from our moral vocabulary.

Proudhon, Bakunin, and the anarchist communists would have been unwilling to accept this alternative. They conceived of obligation, freely assumed, more as an extension of agency than as a limitation to it. Through co-operation with others on the basis of free agreement and association, individuals expand their scope of action and initiative. Free association is seen as a form of collective self-empowerment, as a way of uniting various individuals on a strictly voluntary basis for the mutually beneficial satisfaction of their many needs and interests. Through the creation of social relationships of reciprocal obligation, free association gives expression to and reaffirms human solidarity and community. In contrast, as Carole Pateman has noted, by opposing co-operation Godwin deprives his individuals of the social means of acting on their judgements and of 'transcending their own subjectivity'.[68]

This is not to say that the anarchists who favoured free agreement believed that one must always fulfil one's obligations. Their ideal of free agreement was based on underlying notions of individuality, freedom, and community. In so far as the process by which an agreement is reached, or the content of the agreement itself, is incompatible with these underlying ideals, then no binding obligation can arise from it. Between worker and capitalist there can be no free agreement, because of the inequalities of power existing between them. Particular social preconditions must exist before it can be said that agreements genuinely have been freely entered into. The anarchist proponents of free agreement were explicit as to what these social preconditions are, namely equal well-being for all and the abolition of all hierarchical social relationships. What they strove for was to create a society in which, to use Malatesta's words, 'everybody has the means to live and to act without being subjected to the wishes of others'.[69]

Promises to obey, contracts of (wage) slavery, agreements requiring the acceptance of a subordinate status, are all illegitimate and unenforceable, as they do constrict and restrain individual autonomy. But far from justifying the complete rejection of the notion of self-assumed obligation, this merely emphasizes the continuing need for people to exercise their critical judgement and choice when deciding whether an obligation ought to be assumed or performed.

Godwin originally isolated obligation as the underlying concept which gave social contract theory its particular force as a justification of political authority. By accepting the concept of self-assumed obligation, there is a risk that the other anarchist thinkers left open the possibility of the legitimacy of some forms of political authority, thereby seriously compromising their anarchism. In fact, Carole Pateman has argued that the notion of self-assumed obligation provides a conceptual basis for a theory of direct, or participatory, democracy.

Direct democratic voting is seen as the political counterpart of promising or free agreement. By directly voting in favour of a particular law or proposal, the individual citizen assumes an obligation to abide by it. The citizen, in concert with others, defines the content of his or her political obligations, and in so doing must exercise critical judgement and choice. Political obligation is not owed to a separate entity above society, such as the state, but to one's fellow citizens. Although the assembled citizens collectively legislate the rules governing their association, and are bound by them as individuals, they are also superior to them in the sense that these rules can always be modified or repealed. Collectively the associated citizens constitute a political authority, but their authority is based on horizontal relationships of obligation between themselves, rather than on the vertical relationship existing between the individual and the state. The citizens do not exchange their obedience for the protection of the state, as in the social contract, but create reciprocal relationships of obligation in their collective undertakings and social life, from the workplace to the community, on the basis of their own voluntary choice. Each vote constitutes an express renewal of the social compact, which may be dissolved at the will of the parties. Society is conceived as a complex web of directly democratic associations. Pateman's scheme remains anarchist in the sense that there is no central authority, or state, claiming sovereignty over the various associations. Rather there is an association of associations, each having a directly democratic structure, freely federated with one another.

If this scheme looks familiar, it should, for it closely resembles Proudhon's theory of federation, and Bakunin's subsequently modified conception of federalism. The relationship between anarchism and democratic theory has always been ambiguous. Both Proudhon and Bakunin adopted as the base unit of their federalist scheme the directly democratic association (with the exception, in Proudhon's case, of the family). Kropotkin cited the directly democratic sections of the Paris Commune in the French Revolution as the first historical expression of the anarchist idea.[70] More recently, Murray Bookchin has championed an ecological conception of direct democracy.[71] Yet anarchists have claimed to reject all political authority, denouncing the tyranny of the majority and the fraud of universal suffrage.

Critics of anarchism would claim that this merely demonstrates the conceptual incoherence of anarchism. But if one conceives of direct democratic voting as an expression and extension of self-assumed obligation, as Pateman does, then this supposed incoherence disappears. It is perfectly consistent for the anarchist proponents of free agreement to support direct democracy when it is conceived as giving political expression to the ideals of self-assumed obligation and individual autonomy which they support. While this may commit the anarchists to some sort of political authority, it is not the same kind of authority as that claimed by the state.

The political authority claimed by the state is hierarchical, coercive, and monopolistic. The state is necessarily authoritarian. It is not a voluntary association created by free agreement, but a compulsory body exercising authority over all those it claims fall within its jurisdiction, regardless of their individual consent. The most it offers its subjects is the opportunity to elect their rulers during periodic elections. The content of the law, and hence of the citizen's political obligations, is decided by someone else. The political obligation owed by the citizen to the state is not and cannot be self-assumed.

When Proudhon denounced universal suffrage as the counter-revolution he was not thereby denouncing democracy as a whole. In fact, he sometimes described what he was advocating in its place as 'industrial democracy'.[72] Similarly, when Bakunin denounced democracy it was always parliamentary democracy that he had in mind. For Bakunin, parliamentary forms of democracy scored no great advance beyond aristocratic forms of government, because the essentially hierarchical structure of political authority remained unchanged. It was for this reason that he denounced the socialist 'people's state' as a dangerous illusion, because it still retained the distinction between the ruler and the ruled, a distinction which Bakunin felt could only lead to the domination of the governed masses. Attempts to portray the anarchists, who rejected parliamentary democracy on libertarian grounds, as 'secret friends of the right', 'closet authoritarians', and 'crypto-fascists' are disingenuous, to say the least.[73] Such charges betray a confusion between parliamentary democracy and direct democracy, between obligations which are imposed and those which are self-assumed.

Some confusion regarding the anarchist response to democracy results from the anarchists' own concern that democracy, no matter how direct, may constitute a new form of domination by the majority over the minority, and is therefore unacceptable. The question which then arises is whether the idea of direct democracy is necessarily tied to the concept of majority rule. Carole Pateman suggests it is not, that is, if we conceive of direct democracy as a form of self-assumed obligation.[74] She argues that someone who finds him- or herself in a minority on a particular vote, or who abstains completely, is confronted with the choice either of consenting to the majority decision or of refusing to recognize it as binding. To deny the minority the opportunity to exercise its independent judgement and choice is to infringe its autonomy and to impose obligations upon it which it has not freely accepted. The coercive imposition of the majority will is contrary to the ideal of self-assumed obligation.

The minority may find the decision of the majority so contrary to the ideals of the association that it has no choice but to disobey. In opposition to majority rule, Malatesta wrote that

> one cannot expect, or even wish, that someone who is firmly convinced that the course taken by the majority leads to disaster, should sacrifice his own convictions and passively look on, or even worse, support a policy he considers wrong.[75]

The anarchists would side with Pateman against Rousseau in the defence of the right of minority dissent. By insisting on the right of dissent, both Pateman and the anarchists rebut the charge that associational, direct democracy is but a new form of tyranny in disguise.

Pateman's recent arguments about democracy constitute an important contribution not only to contemporary democratic theory, but to anarchist theory as well. The notion of self-assumed obligation and the political implications of that notion help to clarify a number of issues confronting anarchist theory and practice. Self-assumed obligation is the underlying idea uniting ideas of contract and free agreement, giving them their peculiar attraction and force, as Godwin recognized. By recognizing the implicit role of self-assumed obligation in anarchist theory it is possible to make sense of the anarchists' ambivalent response to democracy. As the role of contract has receded in anarchist ideology, notions of free agreement and self-assumed obligation have come to the fore, pointing the way to a new conception of direct democracy which is both radical and anti-authoritarian.

Notes and references

1 Stewart Edwards (ed.), *Selected Writings of Pierre-Joseph Proudhon* (New York: Doubleday, 1969), p. 98.
2 Murray Bookchin, *The Ecology of Freedom* (Palo Alto, Calif.: Cheshire Books, 1982), p. 320.
3 Pierre-Joseph Proudhon, *What Is Property? An Inquiry into the Principle of Right and Government* (New York: Dover, 1970; first published 1840), p. 118.
4 Ibid., pp. 117–18.
5 Ibid., p. 117.
6 Edwards, *Selected Writings*, op. cit., pp. 131–43.
7 Pierre-Joseph Proudhon, *General Idea of the Revolution in the Nineteenth Century* (London: Freedom Press, 1923; first published 1851), p. 113.
8 Ibid., p. 113.
9 Ibid., p. 113.
10 Ibid., p. 258.
11 Whether Proudhon characterized fairly the views of Rousseau is open to question. For an interpretation of Rousseau as the great defender of direct democracy and critic of liberal parliamentarism, see Carole Pateman, *The Problem of Political Obligation* (Oxford: Polity Press, 1985).
12 Proudhon, *General Idea*, op. cit., p. 118.
13 Ibid., p. 118.
14 Ibid., p. 114.
15 Ibid., p. 270.
16 Ibid., p. 276.
17 Pierre-Joseph Proudhon, *System of Economic Contradictions: or, The Philosophy of Misery*, Vol. I (Boston: Benj. R. Tucker, 1888; first published 1846), p. 234.
18 Proudhon, *General Idea*, op. cit., p. 295.
19 Pierre-Joseph Proudhon, *The Principle of Federation* (Toronto: University of Toronto Press, 1979; first published 1863).
20 Ibid., p. 20.
21 Ibid., p. 12.

22 Ibid., p. 38.
23 Ibid., p. 39.
24 Ibid., p. 39.
25 Proudhon, *Economic Contradictions*, op. cit., p. 259.
26 Proudhon, *Federation*, op. cit., pp. 48–9.
27 Ibid., p. 41.
28 Ibid., p. 61.
29 Ibid., p. 40.
30 Ibid., p. 49.
31 Ibid., p. 41.
32 Ibid., p. 41.
33 Ibid., p. 42.
34 Ibid., p. 70.
35 Ibid., p. 71.
36 See, in particular, J. Salwyn Schapiro, 'Pierre-Joseph Proudhon, harbinger of fascism', *American Historical Review*, L (1945), pp. 714–37; and his book *Liberalism and the Challenge of Fascism* (New York: McGraw-Hill, 1949). In fairness to Proudhon, he corrected himself in the posthumously published *De la capacité politique des classes ouvrières* (1865), where he argued that the 'right of war' is contrary to the federalist ideal and defended the right of secession as necessary to any valid federal scheme; see the Rivière edition (Paris, 1924), with introduction and notes by Maxime Leroy, pp. 207–8.
37 Proudhon, *Economic Contradictions*, op. cit.
38 Robert M. Cutler (ed.), *From Out of the Dustbin: Bakunin's Basic Writings, 1869–1871* (Ann Arbor, Mich.: Ardis Publishers, 1985).
39 See, for example, Branko Horvat, *The Political Economy of Socialism: A Marxist Social Theory* (Armonk, NY: Sharpe, 1982); and Alec Nove, *The Economics of Feasible Socialism* (London: Allen & Unwin, 1983).
40 Proudhon, *Economic Contradictions*, op. cit., p. 234.
41 See, for example, Bruce Brown, *Marx, Freud and the Critique of Everyday Life: Toward a Permanent Cultural Revolution* (New York: Monthly Review Press, 1973); and Nancy Chodorow, *The Reproduction of Mothering: Psychoanalysis and the Sociology of Gender* (Berkeley: University of California Press, 1978).
42 See Carole Pateman, 'The shame of the marriage contract', in J. Stiehm (ed.), *Women's Views of the Political World of Men*, (New York: Transnational Publishers, 1984).
43 G. P. Maximoff (ed.), *The Political Philosophy of Bakunin: Scientific Anarchism* (New York: Free Press, 1964), p. 167.
44 Arthur Lehning (ed.), *Michael Bakunin: Selected Writings* (New York: Grove Press, 1974), p. 147.
45 Ibid., p. 138.
46 Ibid., p. 96.
47 Roger N. Baldwin (ed.), *Kropotkin's Revolutionary Pamphlets* (New York: Dover, 1970), pp. 177–8.

48 Peter Kropotkin, *Modern Science and Anarchism* (London: Freedom Press, 1923; first published 1912), p. 76.
49 Ibid., p. 77.
50 Peter Kropotkin, *The Conquest of Bread* (New York: New York University Press, 1972; first published 1913), p. 182.
51 Baldwin, *Revolutionary Pamphlets*, op. cit., p. 193.
52 Alexander Berkman, *ABC of Anarchism* (London: Freedom Press, 1977; first published 1929), p. 19.
53 Baldwin, *Revolutionary Pamphlets*, op. cit., p. 298.
54 Ibid., p. 157.
55 Ibid., p. 140.
56 Vernon Richards (ed.), *Errico Malatesta: His Life and Ideas* (London: Freedom Press, 1977), p. 184.
57 Baldwin, *Revolutionary Pamphlets*, op. cit., p. 157.
58 Ibid., p. 64.
59 Ibid., p. 69.
60 Ibid., p. 69.
61 Ibid., p. 69.
62 William Godwin, *Enquiry Concerning Political Justice and Its Influence on Morals and Happiness* (Harmondsworth: Penguin, 1976, 3rd edn; first published 1798), p. 214.
63 Ibid., p. 215.
64 Ibid., p. 216.
65 Richards, *Malatesta*, op. cit., pp. 86–7.
66 Godwin, *Political Justice*, op. cit., p. 758.
67 Pateman, *Political Obligation*, op. cit., pp. 138–40.
68 Ibid., p. 140.
69 Richards, *Malatesta*, op. cit., p. 49.
70 Peter Kropotkin, *The Great French Revolution* (New York: Schocken Books, 1971; first published 1909).
71 Murray Bookchin, *Toward an Ecological Society* (Montréal: Black Rose Books, 1980).
72 Edwards, *Selected Writings*, op. cit., p. 167.
73 For a recent example, see Paul Thomas, *Karl Marx and the Anarchists* (London: RKP, 1980). For a critical response, see the reviews of Thomas's book by Graham Baugh in *Our Generation*, 16 (Spring 1984); and *Telos*, 59 (Spring 1984).
74 Pateman, *Political Obligation*, op. cit., pp. 159–62.
75 Richards, *Malatesta*, op. cit., p. 132.

6

Outline of an anarchist theory of history

Alan Carter

I

Anarchism and Marxism have, since the middle of the nineteenth century, strenuously competed for the minds of the Left. The major strength of anarchist theory has corresponded with the most obvious weakness of Marxism, namely the prediction (successful in the case of anarchism, unsuccessful in the case of Marxism) of the nature of a post-capitalist society brought into being by a revolutionary party seizing control of the state. Anarchists, such as Bakunin, have argued that the state cannot be used by revolutionaries in order to bring about a classless or non-oppressive society. They have argued that any attempt to use the state will inevitably frustrate such a goal. And the experience of 'actually existing socialism' would certainly seem to support the anarchist claim. It is somewhat ironic, therefore, that it is Marxist theory which has come to dominate left-wing thought.

One reason for this is the apparently ahistorical nature of much of anarchist thinking. It is here that the major strength of Marxism and the apparent weakness of anarchism correspond. Whereas anarchists have often been content to confine their attention to the state, Marx was able to develop a theory that seems to account for the major economic transformations which have been evident as societies have moved from one historical epoch to another. But is it the case that anarchism is unable to offer an equally informative theory of historical transition? It is my contention that a theory of historical transition can be developed which not only underpins the anarchist critique of the state (thus successfully supporting Bakunin in his controversy with Marx, and accurately predicting the nature of 'actually existing socialism'), but also manages to explain the changes in the economic relations that Marxist theory so impressively explains.

In this chapter I outline such an alternative theory to Marxism, and I do so by contrasting it with what is undoubtedly the most highly acclaimed, recent attempt to defend Marx's theory of history, an attempt which is unusual in having been presented in a manner acceptable to the rigorous requirements of contemporary analytical philosophy – I refer to the recent work of G. A. Cohen.

II

The 'guiding thread' of Marx's theory of history is presented in his Preface to 'A contribution to *The Critique of Political Economy*'. This crucial text distinguishes between the economic base and the 'ideological' superstructure. According to Cohen, the *superstructure* is 'a set of non-economic institutions, notably the legal system and the state',[1] whereas the *base* is the economic structure and is composed of production relations.[2] By *relations of production* Cohen means relations of, or relations presupposing, effective control of the productive forces.[3] And by *forces of production* Cohen means labour power (that is, strength, skill, knowledge, etc., of the producing agents) and means of production (that is, tools, machines, premises, raw materials, etc.). These clarifications enable us to make sense of the following seminal passage from the Preface:

> At a certain stage of development, the material productive forces of society come in conflict with the existing relations of production, or – what is but a legal expression for the same thing – with the property relations within which they have been at work hitherto. From forms of development of the productive forces these relations turn into their fetters. Then begins an epoch of social revolution. With the change of the economic foundation the entire immense superstructure is more or less rapidly transformed.[4]

Cohen's clarifications thus suggest a three-tiered architectural model where the superstructure is explained by the relations of production situated 'below' it, and the relations of production are explained by the forces of production situated 'below' them. The productive forces are 'material', and they explain the relations of production, which are 'social'. Consequently, Marx presents a 'materialist conception of history' where the 'material' has explanatory primacy. Marx's theory thus appears at first glance to be a kind of technological determinism.

Yet, in the 'Communist Manifesto', Marx writes: 'The bourgeoisie cannot exist without constantly revolutionizing the instruments of production . . .'[5] The reason why the bourgeoisie must revolutionize the forces of production is that competition, which is entailed by market relations, ensures that a producer will go out of business if he or she does not keep up with the latest technological developments. Moreover, a producer will get ahead of his or her competitors if he or she is the first to modernize the productive forces. Capitalist relations of production, therefore, seem to be responsible for the development of the productive forces. And this contradicts 'vulgar' technological determinism, which holds the view that it is the forces of production which influence the relations of production and not vice versa.

The problem is, therefore, how to accommodate two of Marx's premises:

(i) the productive forces have explanatory primacy; and
(ii) the relations of production significantly affect the development of the productive forces.

There are two common 'Marxist' responses to this problem. The first, following from Engels's later letters, is to attenuate the explanatory primacy of the productive forces so that they are claimed to be determinant only 'in the last instance'. Not only is this a later weakening of the theory on Engels's part, but it is far from clear what 'in the last instance' is supposed to mean. Theories of history are not improved by reducing their clarity or their strength.

This criticism is even more applicable to the second common 'Marxist' response, which describes the relationship between the forces and relations of production, or between the base and superstructure, as 'dialectical'. What the term 'dialectical' tends to cover for in such a response is a vague notion of interaction. And if Marxist theory reduces itself to the claim that there is an interaction between forces and relations of production, or between base and superstructure, then it is difficult to see what is distinctly 'Marxist' about it. All the term 'dialectical' does in this case is hide confused and trite claims under the mask of mystification – a mystification which suggests to the uncomprehending some deeper, more profound meaning.

In the light of all this, Cohen's interpretation of Marx has two obvious advantages. First, it is not 'vulgar' technological determinism. Second, it provides an admirably clear account of a strong theory which is free of mystification. How does it do so?

III

Cohen persuasively argues that premises (i) and (ii) can only be reconciled (and reconciled in a manner compatible with the majority of Marx's pronouncements) by invoking 'functional explanation'. Functional explanations are a sub-set of consequence explanations, and consequence explanations relate to consequence laws.[6] Consequence laws take the form:

(1) If (if Y at t_1, then X at t_2), then Y at t_3,

where 'X' and 'Y' are types of events, and where 't_1' is some time not later than t_2, and where 't_2' is some time not later than t_3. For a functional explanation to relate to (1), then Y would have to be functional for X. As an example of a relevant consequence law:

(2) If it is the case that if birds were to develop hollower bones then they would be able to fly better, then they would come to develop hollower bones.

According to Cohen, consequence laws do not commit the apparent fallacy of preceding the cause by the effect, because the actual cause is not the later effect, but a prior disposition. For example, (2) does not claim that being able to fly better is what caused the development of hollower bones. That would be a case of the effect preceding the cause. On the contrary, it claims that birds develop hollower bones in a situation where birds which have developed hollower bones have their flight facilitated.

One problem with such functional explanations is that they are clearly incomplete. To be fully convincing they require 'elaborating'.[7] (2) could be elaborated by means of a theory of genetics which accounted for variation within the species and the development of hollower bones by particular birds, and by means of a Darwinian account of the survival of the fittest whereby only those birds which developed hollower bones (and thus flew better) survived being caught by predators. Nevertheless, Cohen controversially maintains that 'a consequence explanation may be well confirmed in the absence of a theory of *how* the dispositional property figures in the explanation of what it explains',[8] and, *a fortiori*, 'Marxian functional-explanatory claims . . . may be rationally tenable before suitable elaborations are available.'[9]

The problem with this is that it is always possible that the disposition and its apparent effect are jointly explained by an independent cause. In which case, the consequence explanation would be false because it would not be the disposition which explained its apparent effect, but the third feature which explained *both* the disposition *and* its apparent effect. What is more, even if the disposition did have an influence, that influence might only hold under certain conditions – conditions which would not be evident until a full elaboration was provided. Consequently, there should be an onus on anyone offering functional explanations to attempt to provide adequate elaborations.

And even if one does provide an elaboration, it might, of course, be wrong. (2) might have been provided with an erroneous Lamarckian, rather than a Darwinian, elaboration. It would seem likely that the least problematic kind of elaboration is a *purposive* one – in other words, when it can be claimed that an actor's intention to introduce a state of affairs (which he or she rightly believed to be in his or her own interest) led to the introduction of such a state of affairs. Not only is a purposive elaboration usually a complete account, it is also the case that people often *know* (Freud notwithstanding) why they have acted. In addition, with a purposive elaboration there is clearly no problem about causes being preceded by their effects. It is not the future state of affairs which is the cause of an action; it is the actor's present belief about the desirability of the future state of affairs which is the cause. Furthermore, purposive elaborations which identify people as the cause of social transformation avoid a highly questionable acceptance of 'free-floating intentions, purposes that can be held by no specific actor',[10] and which is characteristic of functionalism.

If all this is so, how does Cohen reconcile (i) and (ii)? He holds that 'the character of the forces [of production] *functionally* explains the character of the relations'.[11] Thus,

(3) the bare fact that economic structures develop the productive forces does not prejudice their primacy, for forces select structures according to their capacity to promote development.[12]

In other words, specific economic relations are 'selected' because they are functional for the development of the productive forces. Similarly, Cohen's account of the relationship between the base and superstructure involves functional explanation. Specific legal and political institutions are 'selected' because they stabilize the relations of production. Just as the effect of the relations of production on the development of the forces of production is acknowledged in Cohen's account, so is the effect of the superstructure on the economic base.

But what is to stop us entertaining an alternative account: namely, the superstructure selects specific relations of production because they are functional for the superstructure? An authoritarian post-capitalist state might, for example, choose managerial relations, rather than support factory committees, because the former enable a surplus to be extracted, which the state requires to enforce its rule (as opposed to allowing the proletariat to consume its own produce – a likely outcome if the proletariat or its committees were in control of production and distribution). Another possibility would be that the superstructure selects specific relations of production which develop the productive forces, because the development of the productive forces is functional for the superstructure. Why, therefore, accord explanatory primacy to the forces over the relations and the superstructure when functional explanations which accord primacy to the superstructure over the relations and the forces can just as easily be forwarded?

Furthermore, Cohen writes of the forces of production 'selecting' specific relations of production because the latter are functional for the development of the forces. But 'select' must, in (3), be metaphorical. Productive forces neither act nor have intentions. Cohen leaves himself open to the charge that he is relying on the 'free-floating intentions' associated with functionalism. One considerable advantage of according explanatory primacy to the superstructure, i.e. the state,[13] is that state personnel, unlike productive forces or relations of production, *do* act and *do have* intentions – thus allowing a purposive elaboration. What elaboration can Cohen provide which supports his functional explanations?

IV

Cohen argues that there is a tendency for the forces of production to develop through history (the development thesis). This is due to two main factors:

(a) rationality; and
(b) scarcity.

It is assumed that human beings are rational and that they face a situation of scarcity. It is also assumed, and this is uncontroversial, that it is within the capability of some human beings to develop the forces of production. Since it appears that it is rational for individuals in a situation of scarcity to develop the productive forces, then it can be assumed that the productive forces will tend to develop. If, in order to develop the forces of production further or faster, it is necessary to select relations of production (e.g. capitalist relations) which would be functional for that development, then it would, prima facie, appear rational for such relations to be selected. And if it is rational for the superstructure to change in order that the required relations of production be stabilized, it is rational to select a new, more appropriate superstructure. Thus, if the people are aware of the need for economic relations which are functional for production, and if they are aware of the need for a superstructure which is functional for such economic relations, and if, in consequence, they select appropriate bases and super-structures, then Cohen can present a purposive elaboration of his functional explanations.

But this would only contend with the alternative purposive elaboration (which supports political, rather than technological, primacy) if the mass of people actually *are* in a position where they are free to choose relations of production and superstructures that accord with their rationality. If the mass of people are neither free to reject their state nor free to reject their relations of production, then their intentions, behaviour, and interests are all irrelevant. And Cohen's apparently purposive elaboration would be unconvincing.

Yet we all know that many suffer malnutrition while the rich hoard grain till prices rise. This hardly fits in with the rational choice of the exploited majority, but the economic relations which account for this persist. Again, it is specific relations of production which force producers to build in obsolescence, and thus preserve their markets. This widespread practice hardly provides a solution to scarcity. The persistence of these irrational relations of production surely indicates that the mass of rational people who face a situation of scarcity are not in fact free to reject the economic relations at will, and therefore Cohen's purposive elaboration fails to convince. Competitive relations of production are thus not shown to be explained by a need to develop the forces of production which is grounded in human rationality and scarcity.

In addition, Cohen acknowledges the possibility of an authoritarian socialist state, for its own political reasons, being responsible for increasing production well above meeting scarcity.[14] What Cohen fails to notice is that this fits in with an alternative functional explanation – namely, that the state backs economic relations which facilitate increased production because the latter furthers the state's interests. Whereas Cohen's elaboration does not succeed in linking the interests and actions with the relations of production, the alternative functional explanation can be satisfactorily elaborated: the interests of the state personnel motivate them to stabilize specific relations of production which they believe to be in their interests. And it is, of course, state personnel who *do* stabilize the relations of production (something which Cohen must accept, given that, in his account, the state is 'selected' in order to stabilize the relations of production). The elaboration of this alternative approach (stressing political, not technological, primacy) succeeds in linking the effective actors with the relations of production, i.e. the *explanandum* with the *explanans*.

In summary, the needy do not have control over the relations of production. And the owners of the means of production do not develop them in order to meet scarcity, but instead, in order to remain competitive. Moreover, in authoritarian socialism the state clearly has explanatory primacy when it stabilizes managerial relations in order to increase production so as to protect its own interests. The state would, in such cases, be increasing production because increased production would be functional for its rule. In such cases, it is the state, not the productive forces, which has explanatory primacy.

V

This last point brings me to an interesting issue. Does the state in actual fact have its own interests? Marxists have usually considered the state to be merely an instrument of the dominant economic class (though Engels admitted that in certain circumstances – for example, when there are two equally strong economic classes contesting for power – the state might act as if it were free from either of them). Marx, however, insisted that even the exceptional Bonapartist state acted so as to protect the long-term interests of the bourgeoisie.

Why, then, does Marx hold to an instrumentalist theory of the state? One simple answer is that such an approach follows from his stress on the economy. And given that the modern state does tend to protect bourgeois interests, then it is not surprising that Marx should assume that 'the executive of the modern State is but a committee for managing the common affairs of the whole bourgeoisie'.[15] But does the fact that the modern state tends to protect bourgeois interests provide adequate justification for an instrumentalist theory of the state? No, because the modern state may well protect the interests of the bourgeoisie for some other reason than that it is an instrument of that class. What might this other reason be?

In order to preserve the integrity of its territory, the state must have an army, a police force, etc. – in short, it must have *forces of coercion*. And if it is to finance their development, then it requires a healthy economy which can be taxed. If it were the case that the state had its own distinct interests, then this would give a simple explanation for why it is that the state provides welfare services, etc. – services which force Marxists to accord, inelegantly, a 'relative autonomy' to the state. If the state has its own interests, which include an interest in preserving order and in maintaining a healthy labour force (that it does not directly exploit), then it is not surprising that the state may, at times, increase taxes levied on the bourgeoisie in order to improve the condition of the workers. A mere instrument of the bourgeoisie would be unlikely to do this in so far as the bourgeoisie is preoccupied with maximizing direct exploitation in the short term.

However, such actions as lead to an improvement in the condition of the working class would stabilize the political order, and would ensure a constant supply of labour. Such actions are, therefore, in the long-term interest of the bourgeoisie. But this fact does not mean that *that* is why the state carries out such actions. The bourgeoisie need the subordinate classes to be kept at work so as to produce profit. *The state needs the subordinate classes to be kept at work so as to create the wealth which it must tax in order to pay its personnel.*[16] But this latter fact is sufficient to account for the state's behaviour; and, in so far as it is the state which acts to stabilize the relations of production, then the principle of parsimony suggests that the needs and interests of the bourgeoisie be omitted from the explanation of why it is that the relations of production are preserved. The state will continue to behave in a manner which, as a matter of fact, protects the interests of the bourgeoisie, but only so long as this manner of behaving facilitates the production of the wealth the state requires. So, when the state does act in a manner which protects the interests of the bourgeoisie, it does so when and because bourgeois and state interests happen to coincide, as is usually the case. (And this is not surprising, given that both the state and the bourgeoisie require that the production of wealth be maximized, and given that the bourgeoisie is highly efficient at maximizing it.) In other words, Marxists have mistaken a contingent correspondence between state and bourgeois interests for an instrumental relationship. The modern state does not, as Marxists have thought, act as the instrument of the bourgeoisie; instead, it carries out its own interests – interests which just happen usually to correspond to those of the bourgeoisie.

Now, one possible objection must be dealt with. It might be argued that different elected governments carry out different programmes. Some governments carry out programmes which clearly protect bourgeois interests, while other governments carry out programmes which better protect the interests of the workers. Does this not demonstrate that these governments reflect their (economic) class bases, and are, therefore, to some extent at least, the instrument of their respective economic classes? The short answer is: No. Evidently, some elected governments side more with the capitalists than others do, and some may even side slightly more with the workers than with the capitalists. But even both extremes of government share a common interest in the preservation of the state. The different programmes may actually serve different economic classes to different extents, but *all the programmes chosen serve the state*, as well as a particular economic class. In other words, though certain policies may change from one government to the next (one policy aiding one group in society, another aiding a different group), there is, nevertheless, an overlapping area which is consistent. And that overlapping area concerns the state's interests.

Even if at different times different economic classes manage to get their representatives elected, and even if the representatives remain on the side of their electors, on assuming state power the elected also have an interest in protecting state power, and consequently act so as to protect it. (Though it is no doubt true that representatives from different economic classes may have different visions of how best to do so.) Moreover, the elected usually have limited scope for changing policy, which is more often than not determined by those state personnel who are career civil servants. And the latter have a very good reason for ensuring that state interests are continually protected.

Marxists, therefore, have failed to realize that the state *always* acts to protect its own interests. This is why they have failed to see that a vanguard which seized control of the state could not be trusted to ensure that the state would 'wither away'. What the state might do, instead, is back different relations of production to those which serve the present dominant economic class if it believed that such new economic relations could be used to extract from the workers an even greater surplus – a surplus which would then be available to the state. In other words, the state might transform the mode of production because it is in its interests to do so. But new relations of production which promised a greater surplus to the state would not be egalitarian ones, nor would they allow a libertarian social order. The state is not, therefore, an appropriate tool for bringing about a classless post-capitalist society.

VI

Marx claims that certain relations of production are, for a while, functional for the development of the productive forces. At a certain point in time, however, they become dysfunctional for their further development (or, perhaps in the case of a transition to post-capitalism, their optimal use). A revolution then occurs whereby the superstructure is transformed and then stabilizes new relations of production which *are* functional for the development beyond the present level (or, perhaps, which are functional for the optimal use) of the productive forces.

However, one feature of the development of the productive forces has been the generation of a surplus which has allowed the development of the forces of coercion – armies, police, their weapons, and so on. And their development, along with the growth of nationalistic sentiments, has led to the formation of antagonistic nation states. Marxist theory, because of its stress on the economic, has been quite inadequate when it comes to analysing the nation state.

By doubting the ability of traditional Marxism to account for all interesting and important social features (nationalism, ethnicity, gender relations, and so on), Cohen has been led to mention a third important factor:

> Marxist philosophical anthropology is one-sided. Its conception of human nature and human good overlooks the need for self-definition, than which nothing is more essentially human. And that need is part of the explanation of the peculiar strength of national and other self-identifications, which Marxists tend to undervalue.[17]

Perhaps by taking this third factor into account, along with (a) rationality and (b) scarcity, Marxists might be in a position to explain the features of society which otherwise appear to fall outside the ambit of historical materialism (e.g. nationalism). This third important factor can be characterized as:

(c) self-identification within a community.

What is questionable about the introduction of this third factor into Marxist theory is that once it is introduced we no longer know that the theory can still be constructed in a convincing manner. The theory has been constructed on the basis of factors (a) and (b) only. Factor (c) was not mentioned in the formation of the theory. It would have to be established that factor (c) did not interfere with the construction of the Marxist model.

Let us return to Cohen's elaboration of the functional explanations lying at the heart of Marx's theory of history. According to Cohen, individuals face a situation of scarcity, and they are rational. If only these factors are in play, then clearly it is rational for individuals facing a situation of scarcity to develop the forces of production and thereby increase production, assuming it is in their power to do so. If specific relations of production are required to encourage the development of the forces of production, then it is rational for such relations of production to be selected. If the old relations of production come to fetter the development of the productive forces, then it is rational that new relations of production which would be able to encourage their development be selected. If specific legal and political institutions are needed to stabilize the new relations of production, then it is rational for them to be selected in preference to those which stabilized the 'fettering' relations of production. However, in this account factor (c) is ignored (see Figure 6.1).

Let us, therefore, begin again – this time with factor (c), as well as factors (a) and (b), in play. The significance of factor (c) is that different individuals identify with different groups. And it is within different groups that rational individuals face scarcity. The problem is: Is it always rational for these groups to develop the productive forces and increase their production? Interestingly, it is not always rational for them to do so. First, one's group might reduce undesirable toil with less effort by plundering the produce of another group. In which case, if it is easier to take others' products than it is to produce, then it is rational to be a bandit, rather than a peasant, say. Second, if for some reason one does not wish to be part of a group of bandits or if one is unable to be part of such a group (some do have to produce for the bandits to have something to plunder), then an increase in one's production capability might make one more likely to be plundered by a group of bandits. In a situation where some have chosen or have been able to take the bandit option, it might be extremely unwise to make oneself a more attractive target by increasing production. When factor (c) is in play it cannot be assumed that it is rational to develop the productive forces merely to increase what one *might hopefully* be able to consume. Factor (c) therefore interferes with the construction of the Marxist model.

Now, those who wish systematically to consume the surplus produced by others require the development of the forces of coercion.[18] And the forces of coercion can only be developed if the productive forces have reached a level of development which allows of a surplus. Once such a level has been attained, then one group can systematically force another group to produce more and consume less than they might otherwise. The resulting surplus can then be continually extracted from the subordinate group. This is exemplified in class-divided societies. But such a society can consider itself to be a nation, and wish to oppress another nation.

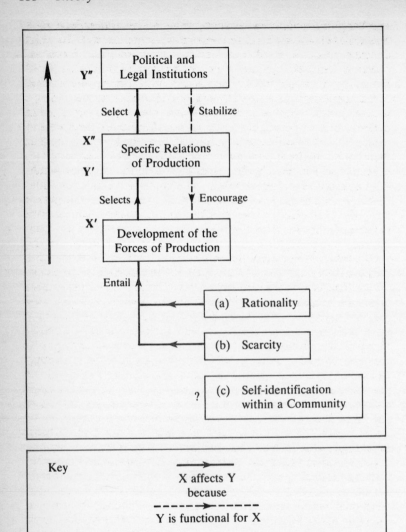

Figure 6.1 Marxist model of historical transition

As it is rational for such groups to form so as to meet scarcity, all
three factors taken together explain the formation of class-divided,
imperialist nations.

But this leads to the formation of an alternative to the Marxist
model, as we shall now see. It is rational not only to oppress

another group and impose upon it greater toil so as to reduce one's own toil, but also to resist the imposition of greater toil. To resist another group it is also necessary to develop the forces of coercion. And this requires the production of a surplus. Consequently, we would not be surprised to find nations where some of the population were expertly engaged in producing the society's wealth, part of which went to others who were expertly engaged in defence and, in consequence, were not themselves employed in production. We would not be surprised if the workers, fearing that their nation might be subjugated by another nation, supported an executive which was charged with their defence. And we would not be surprised to find that those who controlled production (the dominant economic class) supported an executive of the nation state that stabilized those relations of production which both developed the forces of production and increased their own private wealth. Moreover, we would not be surprised to find the state backing those relations of production which developed the productive forces that created the very surplus which it consumes.

The development of the productive forces creates the surplus which is needed to finance a standing army and a police force, for weapons research, etc. – and these forces of coercion are precisely what enables the executive to enforce the relations of production that lead to the creation of the surplus which the state requires. But with such forces of coercion at its disposal, and being a group which, unlike other groups, is not primarily engaged in direct production, the state, not surprisingly, has its own interests *vis-à-vis* the rest of society. And being in control of the instruments of coercion, the state is in a position to protect its own interests.

Thus, an alternative theory of history can be propounded which, in contraposition to the Marxist model (Figure 6.1), claims that the executive of the nation state selects specific relations of production because they encourage the development of the productive forces, which, by allowing the development of the forces of coercion, is functional for the state (see Figure 6.2). Whereas the principal direction of explanation is, in the Marxist model (Figure 6.1), from the bottom to the top, the alternative model (Figure 6.2) reverses the direction of the functional (or, perhaps, consequence) explanations. The alternative model can be summarized as follows: the executive of the nation state, in order to oppress another national group and meet scarcity, or in order to resist another national group threatening to impose greater scarcity, stabilizes specific relations of production which encourage the development of the productive forces and thus allow a surplus to be extracted which finances the development of the forces of coercion necessary for the state to protect its interests. In this alternative model, the 'superstructure' selects relations of production so as to develop the productive forces, and does so for its own politically motivated reasons.

However, Figure 6.2 might be thought to presuppose that state

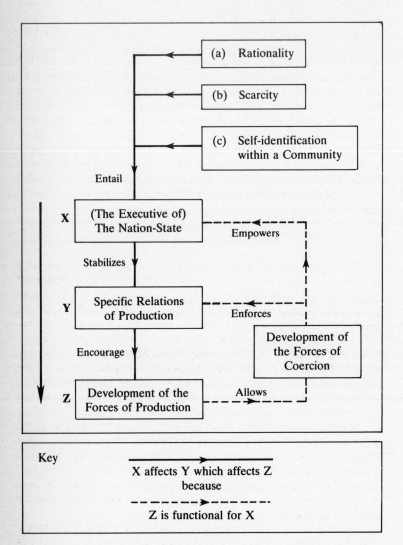

Figure 6.2   Anarchist model of long-term historical transition

personnel *know* which relations of production will encourage the development of the forces of production. This is a questionable assumption. What is likely is that in a revolutionary period state personnel (perhaps the most significant being new personnel coming to importance as a result of the overthrow of the previous government) will back the relations of production which they *believe* would be most conducive to serving their interests (see Figure 6.3). But if these new relations of production are stabilized and then fail to serve the interests of the state satisfactorily, new relations of production might then be tried (also Figure 6.3).[19] The relations of production which, in the long term, would come to be stabilized would be those which, at that level of development of the productive forces, prove in fact to serve the interests of the state (Figure 6.2). In which case, the long-term process schematically represented in Figure 6.2 would be elaborated by reference to the short-term process schematically represented in Figure 6.3 – the short-term process being motivated by the beliefs of the state personnel. Thus, the long-term process is grounded (via the short-term process) in the beliefs and actions of relevant rational actors.[20]

VII

The main significance of the alternative model is that the state cannot be regarded as a mere instrument of the dominant economic class. It is quite possible that if a new set of relations of production which become viable are better suited than the old relations to the development of the productive forces (for example, managerial relations), then the state might cease backing the old relations and start backing the new ones. This possibility is inconceivable if one is restricted to an instrumentalist theory of the state. And by regarding the state as a major actor – one which acts in order to safeguard its own interests – an instrumentalist theory of the state is rejected.

Clearly, the alternative model (Figure 6.2) is the inverse of the Marxist model (Figure 6.1) in so far as it considers to be determining what the Marxist model considers to be determined. Consequently, if it is instantiated, it falsifies Marx's theory of history. But the alternative model would not necessarily be a better one unless it was able to explain as much as the Marxist model. Can it do so?

Consider an account (informed by the Marxist model) of the transition from feudalism to capitalism. In feudalism, the surplus product of the serf had to be extracted by the constant threat of

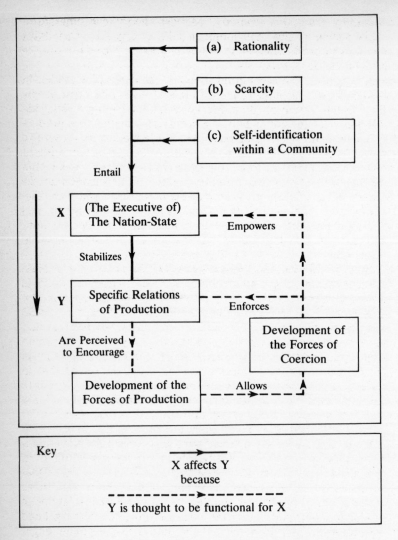

Figure 6.3　Anarchist model of short-term historical transition

force. Market relations emerged alongside technological developments. These relations, being more productive, became dominant, and they allowed a surplus to be extracted without the constant threat of force. All the state was then required to do was protect property rights. This meant that *the state was allowed a measure of autonomy from the economy*. Marxist theory can, therefore, explain technological developments, the emergence of capitalist relations of production, and the liberal appearance of the state in capitalist social formations.

Now consider an account informed by the alternative model. In feudalism, the surplus product of the serf had to be extracted by the constant threat of force. Market relations emerged alongside technological developments. These relations, being more productive, eventually came to be backed by those who exerted coercive power. As they allowed a surplus to be extracted without the constant threat of force, the state restricted its actions within the nation to protecting property rights.[21] This meant that *the economy was allowed a measure of autonomy from the state*. The alternative theory can, therefore, also explain technological developments, the emergence of capitalist relations of production, and the liberal appearance of the state in capitalist social formations.

Both the Marxist model and the alternative model can explain the same historical events. However, in order to oppose Marx it is not even necessary to claim that the alternative model correctly applies to the transition from pre-capitalist to capitalist social formations (though it may well do so).[22] It might be the case that the Marxist model (Figure 6.1) accurately depicts the transition from feudalism to capitalism. But it might also be the case that in the capitalist epoch the state grows to such importance that in order to understand and predict the transition to post-capitalism we would need the alternative model (Figure 6.2). This possibility is sufficient to cast in serious doubt the Marxist model as a tool for analysing the transition from capitalism to post-capitalism.

What, then, is the significant difference between the two models when they are employed to cast light on the transition from capitalism to post-capitalism? The Marxist model, in claiming that superstructures are 'selected' according to their ability to stabilize the relations of production, implies that if egalitarian relations of production arise and, therefore, do not require coercive legal and political institutions to stabilize them, then the state will no longer be required, and will wither away. The alternative model, on the other hand, in claiming that the state selects relations of production according to their ability to serve the state's interests, implies that if egalitarian relations of production arise and do not offer an adequate surplus to the state, then the state will impose new relations of production more to its liking.

In short, the crucial difference between the two models consists in their predictions about the potential power and subsequent behaviour of the post-capitalist state. Since the Bolshevik state did not wither away and, instead, imposed one-man management on industries which had created their own proletarian factory committees, it is the alternative theory which is corroborated. How did Lenin justify the suppression of egalitarian economic relations? By citing the need to increase production. As he declared within a year of coming to power: 'All our efforts must be exerted to the very utmost to . . . bring about an economic revival, without which a real increase in our country's defence potential is inconceivable.'[23] This choice by the state of inegalitarian economic relations in order to increase production for military purposes fits the alternative model *exactly*. And in doing so, the apparently 'Marxist' revolution in Russia in fact *contradicts* the Marxist model!

If a choice is to be made between the Marxist model and the alternative one, with the suppression of direct workers' control and the growth of state power in post-capitalist societies, it is not the Marxist model which ought to be chosen – especially when the alternative model is as capable as the Marxist one of explaining those historically significant changes in the relations of production which Marxist theory has successfully drawn attention towards.

VIII

The consequence of accepting the alternative model in preference to the Marxist one is that any claim about the 'transitional' state withering away must be rejected. State personnel, as the alternative model highlights, back inegalitarian relations of production because it is in their interest to do so. Thus, neither a vanguard seizing state power (and becoming new state personnel) nor setting up a new so-called transitional state will lead to an egalitarian society. And it is precisely this issue of the so-called transitional state which has traditionally distinguished anarchist and Marxist political theory.

This leaves us with a problem. Given the alternative model, how are the workers to gain meaningful control of production and of society as a whole? One thing is clear. A necessary (though not necessarily a sufficient) condition of human emancipation and equality must be the abolition, by the workers themselves, of the state. It is the only way that the process involving the perpetuation of inegalitarian relationships which is represented in Figure 6.2 can be terminated. Marxists, by considering the use of state power as an acceptable means towards equality and freedom, advocate a course of action which perpetuates this very process. Marxists are led by their theory – a theory which overlooks the fundamental importance of the state – to promote a strategy which perpetuates inequality and unfreedom.

So, an anarchist theory of historical transition can be developed which is at least as effective as Marxist theory in explaining technological, economic, and political developments, but which has the added advantage of drawing attention to the tremendous power which the state can exert. And it is by underemphasizing the power of the state that Marxist theory, with its unbalanced stress on the economic, has created such a dangerous pitfall for the Left. By stressing the technological and the economic, Marxists have distracted attention from the state. This proved disastrous in the Russian Revolution, and will do so time and time again if Marx's theory of history is not decisively rejected by the Left.[24]

Notes and references

Extracts of this chapter were presented in papers delivered to political theorists at the 1989 Political Studies Association Conference at Warwick University, to historians at Sussex University on 28 November 1986 and in Leeds at History Workshop 19. For an analysis of some of the vital issues related to those discussed in this essay, see my *Marx: A Radical Critique* (Brighton: Wheatsheaf, 1988).

1 G. A. Cohen, *Karl Marx's Theory of History: A Defence* (Oxford: Clarendon Press, 1978), p. 216.
2 See ibid., pp. 28–9. Here I refrain from taking issue with Cohen's arguments for excluding the productive forces from the economic base.
3 See ibid., pp. 34–5.
4 Karl Marx, Preface to 'A contribution to *The Critique of Political Economy*', in Karl Marx and Frederick Engels, *Selected Works in One Volume* (London: Lawrence & Wishart, 1970), pp. 181–2.
5 Karl Marx and Frederick Engels, 'Manifesto of the Communist Party', in *Selected Works in One Volume*, op. cit., p. 38.
6 Cohen, however, has recently expressed doubts that his analysis of functional explanation in general is correct, and he now wonders whether just 'consequence explanation' would be preferable. Nevertheless, the kinds of explanation which he takes Marx to employ are explanations of the kind described here as 'functional explanations', whether or not they should in fact just be called 'consequence explanations'. 'Functional explanation' in what follows is used to refer to the kind of arguments employed by Marx, whether or not they are just consequence explanations. See G. A. Cohen, 'Functional explanation, consequence explanation, and Marxism', *Inquiry*, 25 (1982).

7 'A satisfactory elaboration provides a further explanation and locates the functional fact within a longer story which specifies its explanatory role more precisely' – Cohen, *Karl Marx's Theory of History*, op. cit., p. 286.

8 Ibid., p. 266.

9 Ibid., p. 271.

10 Jon Elster, *Making Sense of Marx* (Cambridge: Cambridge University Press, 1985), p. 17.

11 Cohen, *Karl Marx's Theory of History*, op. cit., p. 160.

12 Ibid., p. 162.

13 By 'the state' I mean a structure of institutions which comprise (and here I follow Miliband): the government, the administration, the military and the police, the judicial branch, sub-central government, parliamentary assemblies, etc. See Ralph Miliband, *The State in Capitalist Society* (London: Quartet, 1973).

14 See Cohen, *Karl Marx's Theory of History*, op. cit., p. 315.

15 Marx and Engels, 'Manifesto of the Communist Party', op. cit., p. 37.

16 See Theda Skocpol, *States and Social Revolutions: A Comparative Analysis of France, Russia and China* (Cambridge: Cambridge University Press, 1979), p. 30.

17 G. A. Cohen, 'Restrictive and inclusive historical materialism', *Irish Philosophical Journal* 1, 1 (1984), p. 25.

18 Robert Brenner writes: 'In view of the difficulty, in the presence of pre-capitalist relations, of raising returns from investment in the means of production (via increases in productive efficiency), the lords found that if they wished to increase their income, they had . . . to deploy their resources towards building up their *means of coercion* by investing in military men and equipment. . . . Indeed, we can say the drive to *political accumulation*, to *state building*, is the *pre-capitalist* analogue to the capitalist drive to *accumulate capital*' – Robert Brenner, 'The social basis of economic development', in John Roemer (ed.), *Analytical Marxism* (Cambridge: Cambridge University Press, 1986), pp. 31–2.

19 The fact that socialist states have begun to allow market relations might suggest that planning has not served the state as well as it was formerly believed it would do.

20 Consequently, the alternative theory of history is a rational-choice explanation. See Elster, *Making Sense of Marx*, op. cit., p. 9. It is also 'Darwinian': variations in the economic relations are explained by state beliefs about their efficacy; and the relations of production that tend to prevail are those which in fact are most suited to survive in an environment determined by the state.

21 There are, of course, many who believe that the best way for the economy to produce wealth is for the state to leave it alone (as far as is practicable).

22 For example, various monarchies in the European feudal mode of production backed the cities (where capitalist relations were developing) in order to subvert the power of feudal lords. In other

words, they backed a change in the relations of production because it was in their interests to do so.

23 V. I. Lenin, *The Immediate Tasks of the Soviet Government* (Moscow: Progress Publishers, 1970), p. 6.

24 The alternative model is the opposite of the Marxist model. Consequently, if the alternative model is taken to underpin anarchist political theory, then current talk of a synthesis between anarchist and Marxist theory reveals a profound failure to understand precisely what it is that is problematic about Marxist political theory. Or, perhaps, such a synthesis is supposed to involve the acceptance of Marx's economic theory? But the fact that Bakunin was foolish enough to accept it is no reason why anarchist theory as a whole needs do so. Even Cohen, who has provided such an impressive defence of Marx's theory of history, considers it best to ditch Marx's labour theory of value. See G. A. Cohen, 'The labour theory of value and the concept of exploitation', in Ian Steedman *et al.*, *The Value Controversy* (London: Verso, 1981).

Part III

Practice

7

Indian anarchism:
the curious case of Vinoba Bhave, anarchist 'Saint of the Government'

Geoffrey Ostergaard

By 'Indian anarchism' I mean the movement which was inspired by Mohandas Gandhi and which, after his assassination in 1948, was led by Vinoba Bhave and Jayaprakash Narayan until their own deaths in 1982 and 1979, respectively. Whether this self-styled Sarvodaya ('welfare of all') movement and its ideology should be classified as anarchist is disputable. The issue is usually debated with reference to Gandhi, but in this chapter I focus on his successor. I do so partly because Vinoba's ideas deserve to be better known in the West, partly because his anarchism is in some ways more explicit than Gandhi's, and partly because of an extraordinary incident in his career which calls sharply into question the nature of his anarchism. The incident occurred in 1975 shortly after Mrs Indira Gandhi, the Indian Prime Minister, imposed on the country emergency rule which amounted, at best, to a constitutional dictatorship. Asked what he thought of the Emergency, Vinoba, who was in the middle of observing a year of self-imposed silence, made a written comment: 'an era of discipline'. The comment was widely used in the government's propaganda to suggest that Vinoba endorsed the Emergency. Thus, the man who had been hailed as an anarchist saint was projected in the paradoxical role of 'the Saint of the Government' – and a very dubious government at that.

The background to this incident must be briefly sketched. Although Gandhi had led the Indian struggle for national liberation, his objective was the development of India, not as a modern industrial nation state but as a society of self-governing village republics. To this end, he proposed, on the very eve of his assassination, that the Indian National Congress should disband as a political party and be reconstituted as a constructive work organization whose task would be to help the Indian masses, 80 per cent of whom lived in the villages, to achieve 'real independence'. Predictably, Gandhi's 'political heir', Nehru, rejected the proposal; but shortly afterwards Vinoba, Gandhi's 'spiritual heir', emerged to carry forward Gandhi's uncompleted mission. This he did by reorganizing Gandhi's true followers, who were not the politicians but the few thousand workers engaged in Gandhi's Constructive Programme, the best-known item in which was the revival of *khadi* (hand-spun, hand-woven cloth) as a village industry. Through a new organization, the Sarva Seva Sangh (Association for the Service of All), Vinoba launched in 1951 a campaign to achieve a 'land revolution' by means of *bhoodan* – gifts of land to landless labourers – and later, and more radically, by *gramdan* – the voluntary villagization of land. In distributing over one million acres of land to half a million landless labourers, the movement achieved some success at the practical level but rather more at the propaganda level. By 1969 the Sarvodaya movement could claim that 140,000 of India's villages had declared themselves in favour of the *gramdan* idea.

However, when in the early 1970s the movement set about translating the idea into reality, it began to flounder. In the ensuing crisis, Jayaprakash Narayan, the ex-Socialist Party leader who had joined Sarvodaya in 1954, revised Vinoba's strategy of non-violent revolution. In place of peaceful persuasion and the consensual building of an 'alternative society', JP (as he is usually called) emphasized non-violent struggle of the kind used by Gandhi against the British Raj and 'the politicalization of the movement'. Vinoba and some 10 per cent of the workers opposed the new strategy, so a split resulted. Nevertheless, the bulk of the Sarvodaya workers joined JP in an attempt to apply the new strategy. They transformed what otherwise might have been one more ephemeral student agitation in the northern state of Bihar into a 'people's movement' for what JP termed 'Total Revolution'. Through a remarkable campaign directed at mobilizing all the forces opposed to Mrs Gandhi's Congress, JP brought the movement to the centre of India's political stage; and, as a result, the hegemony of Congress rule was seriously challenged for the first time since independence. In a series of mass demonstrations over a period of fifteen months, 'student power' and 'people's power' were pitted against 'state power'. The situation became increasingly revolutionary, and in Bihar attempts were made through the struggle committees to establish a system of parallel 'people's self-government'. Then, in June 1975, the confrontation reached a dramatic climax. A new, more repressive state of emergency, on top of an existing one, was declared; JP and other opposition leaders were gaoled; and the 'people's movement' was suppressed. The Emergency served only to deepen the split in the

Sarvodaya movement. While many of their erstwhile colleagues were in gaol, the minority of workers who looked to Vinoba for guidance rushed to support Mrs Gandhi's twenty-point programme of social reforms – her sweetener to the bitter pill of emergency rule.

The questions that call for an answer are: How and why did Vinoba come to take the position of apparently legitimating the Emergency? And what light does his behaviour throw on the nature of his anarchism and of Indian anarchism generally? But first it is necessary to indicate Vinoba's anarchist credentials.

As evidence of these, what could be clearer than his statement: 'My main idea is that the whole world ought to be set free from the burden of its governments. . . . If there is a disease from which the entire world suffers, it is this disease called government'?[1] Again, referring to the state in the context of the nuclear arms race, he pointed out that the state had now become 'all-powerful with the power of destroying the whole world'. People therefore talked of putting a stop to the production of nuclear weapons and destroying existing ones. But, he went on:

> It is an illusion to hope to limit or restrict or regulate the power of violence of the modern state. The only rational and sensible alternative is to understand that humanity can exist only when it discards violent weapons and accepts the ideal of building up a society in which there is no coercive state.[2]

But anarchism involves more than principled rejection of the institution of government or the state. It implies also distinctive views on matters such as leadership, organization, authority, and politics. On all of these, Vinoba's position was recognizably anarchist. Vinoba inherited, so to speak, Gandhi's mantle, but he was no blind follower of his guru. He advised those constructive workers whose first thought when faced with a problem was what did Gandhi do or say in such a situation to 'forget Gandhi', to think for themselves, and to have the courage to make new experiments on their own account.[3] Practising his own advice, Vinoba was no 'Gandhian' in the sense of someone who invokes the authority of Gandhi to justify his own actions. Like Gandhi, whose concept of *satyagraha* means, literally, 'holding fast to Truth', Vinoba searched for Truth, and it was Truth, not any particular person's relative version of it, which carried the stamp of authority. Vinoba, of course, learned much from Gandhi but he took from him only those ideas that appealed to him, leaving aside those that did not. Those which he took, he imbibed, so that they became in effect his own. Hence, as he put it, 'I am a man of my own ideas.'[4] The clear implication was that others should do likewise, even with regard to Vinoba's ideas. People, he believed, should not accept even a moral authority without thinking out the matter for themselves. 'I don't want you to accept what I say without understanding it. . . . Take my ideas only if you approve of them.'[5]

In common parlance, Vinoba was the undisputed leader of the Sarvodaya movement for over twenty years. But leadership came to him, not he to it. Leadership, so to say, was thrust upon him – as he saw it, by God, who in 1951 had sent a talisman in the shape of the first land gift. But, basically, he rejected the principle of leadership. In a paradoxical but typical expression of this rejection, he said that his kind of leadership could succeed only by demonstrating its failure. Only when he had ceased to be the leader, and his erstwhile followers had become their own leaders, could he be said to have succeeded. 'Not success but failure is my aim', he declared. 'I never had the sense of being a leader of a movement. No leader would desire failure. A leader has hardly any colleagues; he has only followers. I desire failure, and success to my colleagues.'[6] One would have to search hard, I think, to find any other leader of a social movement who was so anxious to eradicate the lust for power, not least that buried in his own breast. In this respect, Vinoba was more anarchistic than either Gandhi before him or JP after him. Thus, when JP accepted the invitation of the Bihar students to lead their agitation, he made clear that he would not agree to be 'a leader in name only': 'I will take the advice of all, of the students, the people, the struggle committees. But the decisions will be mine and you will have to accept them.'[7] This was an attitude reminiscent of Gandhi's occasionally dictatorial stance towards the Congress.

Vinoba's attitude towards leadership was combined with a characteristically anarchist attitude towards organizations. Although anarchists are not opposed to organization as such, only certain types of organization are compatible with anarchism – those that are small-scale, radically decentralized, fluid, and informal. Formal organizations pose problems for anarchists because, analysed sociologically, they are made up not of concrete, whole, and unique individuals but of abstract bits of standardized human beings, namely, roles and statuses. In formal organizations, persons play roles and occupy different (superordinate and subordinate) statuses, to the latter of which authority is attached according to certain norms. Thus, formal organization is the real source of authority – of the type Weber called 'rational-legal', as distinct from 'traditional' and 'charismatic'. So, who says formal organization, says authority. And, as Michels further pointed out, 'Who says organization, says oligarchy.'

Vinoba's suspicion of formal organization was not expressed in these terms, but it was voiced frequently. He was fond of quoting Saint Francis's injunction: 'Do not get yourself entangled in organizations'; and he advised Sarvodaya workers not to get 'imprisoned' in their institutions.[8] A vivid demonstration of Vinoba's attitude occurred in 1956 when, almost overnight, he liquidated the committees that had been formed in the wake of the *bhoodan* campaign.[9] The idea was that the movement should achieve freedom from both organizational control and reliance on financial donations as it developed into the stage of becoming a self-activating 'people's movement', as distinct from a 'movement of workers for the people'. The decision proved premature. The movement did not become a genuine 'people's movement', and in its absence the Sarva Seva Sangh developed its own organization at the provincial and local levels. But the failure of the decision to work in the way intended, and the subsequent compromise, in no way changed Vinoba's basic attitude towards organizations.

The Sarva Seva Sangh, under Vinoba's guidance, adopted the basic rule that all decisions should be taken either unanimously (all members positively agreeing) or by consensus (no member actively disagreeing). Decision-taking by unanimity/consensus is the only mode fully consistent with anarchism. What R. P. Wolff calls 'unanimous direct democracy' is the only solution to the problem of reconciling the conflict between authority – the right to command – and the moral autonomy of the individual.[10] A principle of anarchism, reflecting the latter, is the sovereignty of the individual. Although sovereign individuals may *in fact* conform to, and in that sense obey, the command of others, they do not acknowledge the *right* of others to command obedience – obeying their own consciences is the supreme norm. When sovereign individuals act in concert, formulating rules for themselves or taking decisions, the rules and decisions can be authoritative only if all agree or, at least, none disagrees. What usually passes as self-government is nothing of the kind. As Vinoba put it:

If I am under some other person's command, where is my self-government? Self-government means ruling your own self. It is one mark of *swaraj* [self-rule] not to allow any outside power in the world to exercise control over oneself. And the second mark of *swaraj* is not to exercise power over any others. These two things together make *swaraj*: no submission and no exploitation.[11]

It can be argued that, until his semi-retirement in 1969, Vinoba, the charismatic leader, was in practice the effective decision-maker in the Sarva Seva Sangh – even though he was not a member of it. But the unanimity rule made the Sangh, at least theoretically, an anarchist organization. And the rule also had important consequences when the split occurred in 1974–5. The minority faction prevented the Sangh, as an organization, coming out in favour of the agitation in Bihar. Those workers who joined JP there did so only in their individual capacities. Since 1978 the Sangh has become the exclusive organization of those workers who follow JP's line, and the unanimity rule has been modified to permit decisions if 80 per cent of members are in favour. As a consequence, it has become a *less* anarchistic organization, even if there is also greater emphasis than in the past on 'collective leadership'.

In the anarchist tradition (unlike the Marxist), organizations that carry forward the movement prefigure the desired future society. In insisting that the Sangh should abide by the unanimity/consensus principle, Vinoba was applying to the organization an approach which he saw as applicable to political organization and life generally. In broad terms, Vinoba made two major and related contributions to the theory and practice of non-violence. One was elaboration of the concept of *satyagraha* which, he argued, should be interpreted positively to mean non-violent *assistance* in right thinking, rather than non-violent *resistance* to evil. The other was elaboration of a 'new politics' – the politics of the people, as distinct from the politics of the state.

The hallmark of genuine *satyagraha*, he suggested, is its non-coercive quality, its capacity to convert opponents without arousing their fears. The emphasis on non-coercion and conversion reflects Vinoba's respect for the sovereignty of the individual. To the extent that an individual is coerced and not converted, his or her sovereignty is abrogated. Although he was not always consistent in the matter, and was prepared to compromise, it is clear that Vinoba wished to dispense with *all* coercion, including moral as well as physical coercion. In that sense, he was the 'purest' of anarchists; and, likewise, he favoured the 'purest' form of *satyagraha*. Those who practise *satyagraha*, he believed, should express truth but they should not insist on their own relative truth: they should leave it to truth itself to make its presence felt.

Vinoba's second major contribution is also basically anarchistic, as the term 'politics of the people', contrasted with 'politics of the state', suggests. The politics of the state are defined in terms of power, in the sense of the capacity to get one's way with others despite their resistance, using methods ranging from manipulation through force to naked violence. Such a conception of politics, he argued in effect, can have no place in a society which accords primacy to the values of truth and love (positive non-violence). This kind of politics must, therefore, be transcended. The politics of power must give way to the politics of truth and love. Power in the usual sense – as distinct from the essentially spiritual capacity or strength to express truth and love in one's relations to others – is antithetical to truth and love and must, therefore, be rejected. As Vinoba put it: 'The only way to bring peace is to renounce power. . . . We want to eliminate the craving for power from the minds of men.'[12]

In developing his concept of 'the politics of the people', Vinoba rejected a basic assumption of the old politics, namely, that human beings have different and incompatible interests. On this assumption, conflict and competition are inevitable and become the hallmarks of 'the politics of the state'. In democratic states, conflict and competition are institutionalized in the party system. *Sarvodaya*, however, with its metaphysical belief in the unity of humankind, makes the directly contrary assumption: '*Sarvodaya* means that the good of all resides in the good of one'; hence, it assumes that the interests of human beings are fundamentally harmonious, not antagonistic.[13] It follows that the hallmarks of 'the new politics' are consensus and co-operation. To realize it, party democracy must give way to partyless democracy. And, since all human beings may be deemed to express part of the whole truth, decisions arrived at by consensus and through co-operation provide the surest guarantee that the politics of truth and love, not the politics of power, are being practised.

In seeking to implement 'the new politics', Vinoba chose the path followed by western anarchists, although in his case the signpost was provided by Gandhi's proposal that the Congress be disbanded and by Gandhi's advice to constructive workers to keep out of politics. India's non-violent revolutionaries, Vinoba argued, should not form a party, they should not participate in elections, and they should not seek to capture state power. Instead, the people should be encouraged to take direct action, in the broadest sense of that term. In Vinoba's speeches, Indian echoes of the classical controversy between anarchists and Marxists in the First International can be heard. 'No revolutionary thought', he declared, 'has ever been propagated through the power of the state':[14]

If it was possible to effect a real revolution through the power of the state, would Gautam Buddha have renounced the throne? . . . Buddhism started to lose ground in the country from the time it became associated with state power. The same thing happened when Christianity got the support of the Roman emperors. . . . State power is a conservative force. . . . It may bring about some social reforms, but it cannot radically alter the lives of the people.[15]

Like other anarchists, Vinoba was accused of running away from politics and denying their importance. Not so, he responded. His policy was deliberately chosen and based on 'stark realism'.[16] 'The whole idea of ruling is wrong'; but one could not get rid of ruling by becoming oneself a ruler. If he, Vinoba, were to occupy the seat of power, he would find himself behaving in much the same way as the present incumbents:

Those who get themselves involved in the machinery of power politics, even for the purpose of destroying it, are bound to fail in their purpose. To destroy it, you have to stay out of it. If you want to cut down a tree, it is no use to climb into its branches. The desire to keep contact with something, even to destroy it, is a subtle and insidious illusion.[17]

And Vinoba was as scathing as any western anarchist about the Marxist prediction of the ultimate arrival, via the proletarian state, of a stateless society. The Marxists were 'anarchists in the final stage' but 'totalitarians in the first stage'. Their 'stateless society is only a promissory note but state tyranny is cash down'.[18] *Sarvodaya*, therefore, stood for the immediate reduction in the power of the state.

Like western anarchists, too, Vinoba criticized not only Marxists but democratic socialists who employ the machinery of the state to effect social change. After independence, India had become a representative democracy, but it was not real self-government – that existed nowhere in the world. The representatives were the real masters. The people were masters in name only; they were slaves in reality.[19] Voting is a farce; real power remains in the hands of the few; 'the whole arrangement in fact is sheer bogus'. In some respects, the situation in the new state was worse than in the old. The latter was not a 'welfare state', so there were some sides of life with which it did not interfere. But the new state was a 'welfare state', and the result was 'frightening': 'The government plans for every part of the nation's work. . . . The people are completely passive, they are a mere protectorate – in fact, they are nothing but a flock of sheep.' It all made Vinoba 'wonder whether August 15, 1947, should be called Independence Day or Dependence Day'.

In the light of this evidence of Vinoba's anarchism, how could such a man come to be seen, during the Emergency in 1975, as 'the Saint of the Government'? In answering this question, the first point to note is that the phrase Vinoba actually used in commenting on the Emergency was 'Anushashan parva'. Mrs Gandhi's supporters translated this as 'an era of discipline', implying that Vinoba approved the government's authoritarian measures. But when he broke his year-long silence on Christmas Day 1975, Vinoba explained that 'Anushashan parva' referred to the discipline laid down by *acharyas* (traditional teachers and men of wisdom) in ancient times to guide their pupils.[20] It was to be distinguished from *shashan* or rule enforced by the state. However, in making this belated clarification, Vinoba expressed confidence that the government 'would do nothing to go against the discipline of the *acharyas*'. Hence, there was no need for *satyagraha* in the form of non-violent resistance against the government, and – by implication – the *satyagraha* then being conducted by the opposition in protest at the Emergency was mistaken. It should also be noted that Vinoba then proceeded to convene a conference of *acharyas*, which included vice-chancellors, professors, and retired judges, and which unanimously called for a speedy return to 'normalcy'. When that advice was ignored by Mrs Gandhi, Vinoba himself, shortly afterwards, announced that he would engage in *satyagraha*. But the proposed action – a fast unto death – was over an issue which showed a bizarre sense of priorities. The issue was not the continuance of the Emergency beyond any semblance of justification, not the drastic amendment of the Indian Constitution designed to establish executive autocracy, nor even the plight of the victims of Sanjay Gandhi's ruthless campaign for 'voluntary', but in practice often compulsory, sterilization. The issue, rather, was the legal enforcement of cow protection! The cow, of course, is a sacred animal to Hindus, although Vinoba explained that his motivation was not religious sectarianism; for him the cow symbolized the rural economy and beyond that the unity between human and animal life.

Vinoba's proposed fast was called off when Mrs Gandhi made moves to accommodate his wishes. The incident served to show that he was not quite 'the Saint of the Government' he had been thought to be. But there is no avoiding the conclusion that Vinoba's stance throughout the Emergency was exceedingly dubious and ambiguous, not merely from a revolutionary but also from a liberal-democratic perspective.

Can his stance be explained as a case of an anarchist 'going soft' in his old age? His anarchist statements certainly became fewer as he grew older and as, after 1969, he concentrated more on spiritual matters. But he continued to express anarchist sentiments. In 1980, for example, he expressed more firmly than ever before his opposition to voting in parliamentary elections.[21]

Is the answer to be found, then, in personal relationships? Was he, perhaps, not so much 'the Saint of the Government' as 'the Saint of Mrs Gandhi'? There may be some truth in this suggestion. He certainly had a fondness for the Nehru family. He regarded Nehru as his 'brother' and believed (contrary to much evidence) that Nehru was trying to carry on Gandhi's work. He was also very conscious, so it would seem, that Gandhi had designated Nehru as his 'political heir', leaving the position of 'spiritual heir' open to Vinoba – a decision which suggested a division of labour between the two successors. Vinoba transferred to Nehru's daughter his general attitude towards Nehru, and the politically astute Mrs Gandhi carefully cultivated and exploited the relationship. But, although Vinoba can be criticized for allowing himself, without protest, to be used by Mrs Gandhi, I do not think that his personal regard for her is the really important factor in explaining his stance.

The real clue to the paradoxical – and not entirely accurate – puzzle of Vinoba, the anarchist 'Saint of the Government', is to be found in Vinoba's philosophy, including the anarchistic aspects of it. In a famous speech made in 1916, Gandhi, referring to India's violent revolutionaries, declared that he, too, was an anarchist. He then added, significantly, 'but of another type'.[22] Indian anarchism is not western anarchism in India. It *is* different from mainstream western anarchism, and some of these differences have important consequences.

Leaving aside the more obvious differences, such as Indian anarchism's commitment to principled non-violence and its religious or spiritual basis,[23] three should be noted.

The first is that Indian anarchism is 'gradualist', whereas western anarchism is 'immediatist'. Both assume that it is possible for humans to live an ordered existence without the state, but western anarchists add that it is possible for them to do so *now*. In an extreme form, this addition leads to the Bakuninist theory of spontaneous revolution. To achieve anarchy, all that is really necessary is for the oppressed masses, inspired by heroic revolutionaries, to rise in revolt and throw off the artificial chains of the state. 'Natural society' in the form of free associations and communities will then emerge and be linked in a federal network. In contrast, Indian anarchism believes that anarchy will be realized only when all, or at least the great bulk of, human beings develop the degree of self-discipline that at present only some of them possess. (The 'some' include common-or-garden saints as well as Saints!) Humanity evolves, subduing as it progresses the animal side of its nature until its divine nature is fully revealed. In political terms, this evolution is from a condition of 'no government', where chaos reigns, through 'good government' to, ultimately, 'freedom from government': the situation where people, having internalized moral norms, obey them of their own accord.[24] Referring to modern India, Vinoba distinguished three stages of political development: first, an independent central government; second, the decentralized, increasingly self-governed state; and, third, the stage of pure anarchy. In 1947 India had reached the first stage. The second stage had thus begun and would (or should) be marked by 'the process of dissolving power' (or, to put it in another way, distributing power to the villages and developing the institutions of 'the new politics', such as partyless democracy). This process, he thought, 'may well take us fifty years, but a beginning at least must be made today'.[25] Because they are 'gradualists', Indian anarchists talk, not as western anarchists have usually done about 'abolishing the state' but, like theoretical Marxists do, about 'the withering away of the state'. They also have a different attitude towards government legislation and are prepared to countenance, and even to promote actively, certain laws – for example, those furthering decentralization and those, such as prohibition and banning cow slaughter, which are perceived as expressive of the moral law.

The second difference may be stated thus: whereas western anarchism is 'anti-statist', Indian anarchism might more aptly be characterized as 'non-statist'. As western anarchists see it, the state may have been 'necessary' in the past, but the modern state – each and every state – lacks all legitimacy. Lacking legitimacy, the force that it exercises is perceived as violence, morally indistinguishable from the violence that others may exercise. Violent anarchists simply pit *their* violence against the *state's* violence. But as Indian anarchists see it, the state (not perhaps all states but certainly the Indian state) does possess a certain legitimacy. The state is to be dispensed with, but until that day arrives it retains its legitimacy – *de facto*, of course, but also *de jure*. This implies accepting as valid the conventional distinction between 'violence' and 'force' (the legitimate violence of the state). Vinoba certainly did do. He made a threefold distinction between 'violent power' exercised by unauthorized individuals, the power over violence vested in the state, and 'people's power', which is based on non-violence. Drawing on traditional Indian political thought, he appears to have accepted the typical liberal justification of the state as an institution which was developed to suppress 'naked' or unauthorized violence. State power, he believed, was certainly not non-violence (so a 'peaceful revolution' through the use of state power was not a non-violent revolution); but until society evolved to the stage of freeing itself from violence, authority to use violence had to be delegated by society to its chosen representatives, namely, officers of the state. State power, he added, could be used both for furthering violence or for restricting it and thus progressing towards non-violence.[26]

The third difference to be noted relates to universalism. Western anarchism has been imbued by a universalistic spirit, expressed in its generally cosmopolitan outlook and implacable hostility to nationalism when allied with states or putative states. But its universalism is relatively shallow when compared with that of Indian anarchism, rooted as the latter's is in the postulate of cosmic unity that binds humans to humans, humans to animals (including cows!), both to nature, and all things to God, the Ultimate Reality. At the level of politics, universalism is related to 'populism' in the sense of an ideology centred on 'the people', rather than classes. Some forms of western anarchism, notably anarcho-syndicalism, have accepted much of the Marxian analysis of class in capitalist society. But generally, although western anarchists use the language of class, their appeal is directed towards broad categories of people: the workers, the peasants, the poor, the powerless, the oppressed. Together, these constitute 'the people' who are to be liberated. 'The people' constitute the vast majority, but not everybody – the rich, the idlers, the powerful, the oppressors are excluded. The universalism of western anarchism is consequently limited. As interpreted by Vinoba, however, Indian anarchism is consistently universalistic. *Sarvodaya* means 'The welfare of *all*', not just the majority. 'The people', therefore, includes everybody, the rich and the poor, the powerful and the powerless, the oppressors and the oppressed. *All*, down to or up to the last person, are to be liberated; and *all* are called on to join in the process of collective liberation. Included, of course, are those who presently exercise the power of the state. They, too, are expected to co-operate with others in creating the conditions which will bring about the state's eventual demise! And, further, the social movement which seeks to direct society towards the goal of a stateless society should co-operate with the government, and the government with it – although, naturally, the movement's workers are not expected to co-operate with government plans and projects that militate against the goal.[27]

It is important to appreciate that Vinoba's *anarchism* was involved in his disapproval or, as he might have put it, non-approval of the line taken by JP and the majority of Sarvodaya workers in 1974 and afterwards. This may not be obvious for two reasons. One is that, as JP's movement for 'Total Revolution' developed, public opinion polarized, and Vinoba found himself in a position in which he could be seen as on Mrs Gandhi's side. Polarization has that kind of effect. Willy-nilly people are compelled to take sides; and even if they try not to do so, they cannot, because one side or the other will place them in the opponent's camp – the he-who-is-not-with-us-is-against-us syndrome. The other reason is that JP's movement appeared to be, and in some respects was, more anarchistic – by western standards – than the Sarvodaya movement when guided by Vinoba. For one thing, JP injected into the revised strategy for non-violent revolution the element of active struggle, reverting, so to say, to Gandhi's 'negative' or resistive *satyagraha*. He came to see, as Vinoba never did, that 'consciousness' – that indispensable lever of radical social change – can be generated only by engaging in struggle. For another, JP's movement appeared to be 'anti-statist'. 'People's power' was pitted against 'state power'; and 'people's power', not victory for the opposition parties, was what JP insisted the 'Total Revolution' was all about. Furthermore, JP, perhaps recalling the Marxism of his youth, began to develop more realistic views about the state. Vinoba's theory of the state, like much anarchist theorizing on the subject, is curiously abstract and static – about the state *as such*, and not connected with actual, specific, historical states. If it had been otherwise, how could he so have misread or ignored what was happening to the Indian state led by Mrs Gandhi? JP, in contrast, observing what was happening, came to see that the state in India was not, as Vinoba's theory suggested, some kind of 'neutral' paternal power. It became 'glaringly apparent' to JP that 'the state system was subservient to a variety of forces and interests entrenched in keeping it a closed shop'.[28]

But Vinoba was not convinced. And he was also not impressed by the anarchistic appearance of JP's movement. He suspected that those, like JP's supporters, who ascribed all ills to the government felt that 'the government was everything to them'.[29] And ·he suspected that the movement which placed so much emphasis on the resignation of the Bihar government and the dissolution of the Bihar Assembly would end up by replacing Tweedledum with Tweedledee. He had a shrewd idea of where 'the politicalization of the movement' by JP would lead. And it is significant that what really disturbed him and prompted him to embark on his year of silence, indicative of his non-approval, was JP's decision to take the movement into the electoral arena – a decision which, as it turned out, marked a fatal turning-point in the movement. At the time, Vinoba made clear that he did not believe in democracy (rule by the many – 'demonocracy', he dubbed it) but in consensus, the rule of all by all. The 'People's Front' which JP's supporters were trying to form in order to oppose the Congress and its junior ally, the Communist Party of India, would not, he observed, be a front of *all* the people. At the elections, there would be two groups, one the government and the other the opposition. 'Both', he said, 'will claim that the people are behind them. I don't believe in this system at all.'[30]

The elections did finally come, although not until 1977, after being postponed and after twenty-one months of emergency rule. The electorate was divided into basically two groups, as Vinoba had predicted; and, to the surprise of Mrs Gandhi, the opposition won. It called itself the Janata or People's Party, and it formed a 'people's government'. Referring to it later, Vinoba quipped: it was a party to which people had given their votes and notes, that is, currency notes. 'That party slipped and proved useless.'[31] But he exaggerated. It was not quite 'useless'. It did dismantle the 'Indira Raj': Mrs Gandhi's apparatus of executive autocracy. But in its three years of office, it achieved little that was positive. As far as changing the system is concerned, as distinct from restoring the old system, it did prove 'useless'. In that sense, Vinoba, who had predicted in 1974 that nothing would come out of the agitation started in Bihar and led by JP, was finally proved right.

To say this is not to condone Vinoba's questionable stance either before or, especially, during the Emergency. It is also not to say that JP was wrong to have revised Vinoba's strategy of revolution, although in doing so JP made several huge mistakes which the failure of 'the Janata experiment' served only to highlight. But it is to say that the issues which divided the Sarvodaya movement in 1974 and which are still not finally resolved are more complex than is generally supposed by protagonists on either side. If Indian anarchism as a social movement was to make progress in the early 1970s and not collapse as the campaign to implement *gramdan* began to falter, it had to 'go beyond' Vinoba. JP took it 'beyond', moving it, bewilderingly, in both a *more* and a *less* anarchist direction. But, if after the setbacks and disappointments of recent years, it is to continue to make progress, it will have to 'go beyond JP'. And 'going beyond' may involve going back to *some* of Vinoba's ideas, while retaining *some* of JP's – and, of course, developing new ideas that are relevant to the present difficult situation the movement faces.

One last observation, by way of addendum. Although my own instincts and proclivities led me to side with JP when the differences between the two Sarvodaya factions emerged, I have to admit that Vinoba was probably more of an anarchist, even by western standards, than was JP. It was fitting, therefore, that the anarchist who was dubbed 'the Saint of the Government' was spared the ultimate irony that befell JP – as it had befallen Gandhi before him. He was not accorded the 'honour' of a state funeral![32]

Notes and references

1 Vinoba Bhave, *Democratic Values* (Kashi: Sarva Seva Sangh Prakashan, 1962), p. 64.

2 Viswanath Tandon, *Selections from Vinoba* (Varanasi: Sarva Seva Sangh Prakashan, 1981), p. 162.

3 *Harijan*, 8 January 1950. *Harijan* was a journal founded by Gandhi. In its issue of 29 March 1952, it published an extract from *Freedom*, its editor explaining: '*Freedom* is a London weekly of the Anarchist School and to a certain extent akin to the *Harijan*.'

4 Tandon, *Selections*, op. cit., p. 3.

5 Bhave, *Democratic Values*, op. cit., p. 192.

6 *Bhoodan*, 27 November 1957.

7 *Everyman's Weekly*, 22 June 1974.

8 Vinoba Bhave, *Bhoodan Yajna* (Ahmedabad: Navajivan, 1953), p. 93.

9 See G. Ostergaard and M. Currell, *The Gentle Anarchists* (Oxford: Clarendon Press, 1971), pp. 201–4.

10 R. P. Wolff, *In Defense of Anarchism* (New York: Harper & Row, 1970).

11 Bhave, *Democratic Values*, op. cit., pp. 13–14.

12 *Bhoodan*, 28 November 1956.

13 Vinoba Bhave, *Revolutionary Sarvodaya* (Bombay: Bharatiya Vidya Bhavan, 1964), p. 2.

14 Tandon, *Selections*, op. cit., p. 96.

15 *Bhoodan*, 21 November 1956.

16 *Bhoodan*, 12 December 1956,

17 Bhave, *Democratic Values*, op. cit., p. 226.

18 Ibid., pp. 29, 189.

19 Ibid., pp. 67, 71, 77–8, for this and other references in this paragraph.

20 See G. Ostergaard, *Nonviolent Revolution in India* (New Delhi: Gandhi Peace Foundation, 1985), pp. 232–8.

21 Ibid., p. 325.

22 The speech was made at Benaras Hindu University, 6 February 1916. See M. K. Gandhi, *The Collected Works* (Delhi: Government of India, 1964), Vol. XIII, p. 214. Reading the speech led the young Vinoba to write to Gandhi and, then, join his ashram.

23 On the religious basis, see Dennis Dalton, 'The theory of anarchism in modern India – an analysis of the political thought of Vivekananda, Aurobindo and Gandhi', in R. J. Moore (ed.), *Tradition and Politics in South Asia* (New Delhi: Vikas, 1979).

24 Bhave, *Democratic Values*, op. cit., pp. 29, 189.

25 Ibid., p. 15.

26 *Harijan*, 24 April 1949.

27 The extent of the co-operation between the movement and the government during the *bhoodan–gramdan* phase was quite considerable. It can be argued that, in those years, the movement was largely 'co-opted' by the Congress government and used to facilitate its own programme of land reforms.

28 *Everyman's Weekly*, 27 April 1975.

29 *People's Action*, June 1974.

30 Transcript (in Hindi) of a meeting between Vinoba and some executive members of the Sarva Seva Sangh, 12–13 December, 1974.

31 *Sansthakul*, January 1981.

32 This chapter draws on my contribution to the symposium on Vinoba, *Gandhi Marg*, 56–57 (November–December 1983), subsequently republished in book form: R. R. Diwakar and Mahendra Agrawal (eds), *Vinoba: The Spiritual Revolutionary* (New Delhi: Gandhi Peace Foundation, 1984). For further details of Vinoba's thought in his later years, see my *Nonviolent Revolution in India*, op. cit., which also contains a critical assessment of the rival strategies of Vinoba and JP.

8

Kropotkin and technical education:
an anarchist voice

Michael Smith

There are interesting parallels between the 1880s and the 1980s. Then as now the development of the economy was the subject of much debate, and then as now the explanation for perceived deficiencies was sought in terms of the inadequacies of the educational system. Vocational education was the object of particular attention in the 1880s as in the 1980s, and then as now the debate was conducted in characteristically narrow terms. One sees the same preoccupations and the same – wrong – answers emerging. It is particularly interesting, then, to look back at a contribution to the debate which offered a different perspective: Kropotkin's.

Kropotkin had settled permanently in Britain in 1886 and between 1888 and 1890 he published the series of articles which were much later collected into his book *Fields, Factories and Workshops*.[1] Among these articles was one on education in which Kropotkin addressed himself directly to the educational concerns of the day. What is interesting about his contribution is that in it he sets out for the first time in British educational debate a distinctively anarchist position. Godwin, it may be argued, had put forward years before ideas which later writers were glad to accept as anarchist, but his views were those of an individual. The views that Kropotkin was putting forward were not his own but to a considerable degree the received anarchist position. By this time on the Continent anarchist views on education had begun to crystallize. Education had been the subject of much discussion in anarchist circles and in such journals as *Le Révolté* and *La Révolté*. The ideas that Kropotkin expressed in his article were very much a reflection of that discussion.

What were these ideas? The first was that education should be integral. By this a variety of things was meant. It referred first to the all-round development of the human being. Human nature was many-sided, and traditional education which had hitherto concentrated too much on the cerebral and bookish left many sides undeveloped. Second, it referred to the gap between school and work. An education which was derived too much from the concerns of the grammar school was a wholly inadequate preparation for earning a living in a labour market which was, anarchists were only too well aware, stacked against the ordinary worker. Third, it referred to the connection between educational specialization and the division of labour, from which so many social divisions stemmed. What was wanted was an education which would integrate and not divide.

The concept of integral education has an interesting pedigree in terms of socialist thought.[2] The term is first found in Fourier, who used it to express the notion that education should aim at the enhancement of all aspects of a human being's potential (not just the theoretical or scholarly) and that this would best be done through a carefully designed programme of occupational development. The latter idea especially was taken up by Proudhon, who removed it from Fourier's utopian context and restated it in terms of the labour market. What was required, he argued, was an education which would equip the individual with a range of marketable skills so that he or she would not be totally at the mercy of an industrial system which required specialization of its workers and then discarded them when the specialization was no longer of interest to the firm. The child should serve, he suggested, an apprenticeship which was not monotechnical but 'polytechnical', a concept which, mediated by Marx, had a significant influence on the development of both the Russian and the Chinese educational systems.[3]

It is important, given British habits of thought, not to see 'polytechnical' in too narrow terms. For Proudhon, specialization was not just job-related. Each specialization also corresponded to one side of the individual's potential development. Human nature was many-sided, and each side needed to be developed if the individual was to realize his or her full potential. Occupational specialization was a way of drawing out that potential. It followed that a range of specializations was required. Proudhon's concept was, then, individual-driven, not market-driven. Indeed, he was at pains to insist that control over the training process should be located not in the firm or state but in a workers' collective or similar co-operative agency.

Proudhon's discussion of integral education gave the concept added currency in socialist circles, and the term was picked up by both Marx and Bakunin. In Volume 1 of *Capital*, Marx calls for integral education as 'the only method of producing fully

developed human beings'[4] and in *The General Council* he argues
for 'polytechnical training' as a means of enabling young workers
to have their 'many-sided aptitude developed to the full'.[5] It would
also relieve them from the monotony and dependency which the
division of labour imposes on modern workers. Bakunin, in a
series of articles he wrote for the journal *L'Egalité* in 1869, argued
that differences in education lay behind many other social
differences and in particular the difference between worker and
intellectual. Education should be the same for all: 'par conséquent
elle doit être intégrale'.[6] It should integrate and not divide. He
advocated if not a complete common curriculum at least a
curriculum which had a high degree of commonality and he
wanted the curriculum defined in terms of the needs of the
ordinary young worker. He saw the curriculum as having three
main strands: scientific, industrial, and moral. The role of science
in anarchist thinking about education is something that we shall
turn to in a moment, and we shall find that for anarchists it had
implications in terms of moral teaching. Bakunin's account of the
industrial strand runs along lines which are already becoming
familiar. The learner should be introduced to a variety of trades,
thus developing latent capacity over a range of areas and at the
same time equipping him or her for survival in the labour market.
Bakunin saw integral education as significantly emancipatory:
emancipatory in terms of human potential released and also in
terms of the relationships of capitalist society.

An indication of the extent to which integral education had
become part of anarchist – and socialist – thinking about education
by the late 1860s is the fact that Robin drafted a paper on integral
education for the International's Second Congress at Lausanne in
1867. The paper was not actually considered until the following
year when the Third Congress met in Brussels but then it was
adopted as policy.

When, then, Kropotkin introduced the concept of integral
education into the British debate he was drawing on ideas which
were already well established on the Continent. Integral education
had formed part of the programme of the Paris Commune, and,
although there had hardly been time in 1871 to put the programme
into effect, it was not long before ideas of integral education were
being tried out in practice. The key figure here was the French
anarchist and educationist, Paul Robin, who throughout the 1870s
kept up a stream of publications on integral education and in 1880
was given the chance to try out his ideas at an orphanage in
Cempuis. Over the following decade his work there became well
known, and it was certainly familiar to Kropotkin.

What, ultimately, was distinctive about anarchist concepts of integral education, especially in the British context, was the centrality it ascribed to vocational education. While the development of the individual child was important, it saw that development as occurring through vocational education, and as development was many-sided so vocational preparation should be. It should also be the same for all children. Technical education was not an inferior education, a training, to be given to just one class of society while a more restricted social group received the benefits of classical, grammar-school 'real' education. It was something for all children.

The other two key anarchist ideas on education need not detain us at such length. The first idea was that education should be rational. There were three thrusts to this. In the first place education should be secular and humanist. Anarchist thinking on education had tended to develop in countries like Spain where education was predominantly a religious preserve. All the early practising anarchist educators had trouble with the Church. People like Robin and Sébastien Faure lived with it and fell foul of it. People like Francisco Ferrer in Spain fought it at every turn. For Ferrer this was the *first* requirement of anarchist education: it should be out of the hands of the Church. In the second place education should be practical, not bookish. It should be connected with real life and make use of real tasks in its pedagogy. People like Faure, Robin, and Ferrer drew their mathematical examples from real-life, often political, contexts. Workshops were an important part of the school, *the* most important in Robin's and Faure's case. Children were taken out into the environment of ordinary working people, and ordinary people were encouraged to come into the school. Ferrer attached great significance to the adult education which was associated with his Modern Schools. In the third place, however, education should be scientific. Many of the leading anarchist writers were themselves scientists: Robin was, Faure was, Ferrer was – so, of course, was Kropotkin. Science was seen by anarchists as liberationary, first in terms of emancipation from superstition and non-rational systems (such as religion, in their view), and second in terms of intellectual control. The danger of a vocational education was that it might be tied too much to the here and now (to the 'relevant' as we would say). But this was merely to exchange one mental prison for another. By giving children an education in terms of scientific principles educators would help them to see how their particular specialism or specialisms fitted in. They would understand the rationality which lay behind the processes of the specialism. Their own particular mental constructs would be placed in a wider context of rationality. Science, moreover, was an alternative world view (alternative to that of religion). It carried with it its own morality: honesty of reasoning, the availability of all things, including human relations, to reason, a kind of simplicity and purity. Finally, science was of the future; religion was of the past.

For the anarchists, then, education should be rational, and as the century wore on, and science itself developed, this rationalist strain became more and more pronounced in anarchist thinking. It is interesting, for example, that when Ferrer was obliged to flee Spain in 1886 (about the time that Kropotkin was settling in England) and began to involve himself in French anarchist circles in Paris, he became a member of the League for Human Regeneration, which Robin had founded and whose double motto 'Bonne Naissance. Education Intégrale' reflected both Robin's approach to education and his later obsession with neo-Malthusianism. The very influential league that he himself later founded was called the International League for the Rational Education of Children. In the late 1890s and early years of the next century the word in anarchist circles was not so much 'integral education' as 'rational education'.

The third key educational idea of anarchists was that education should be emancipatory. There were shifts in the notion depending on what currently it was thought most important to be emancipated from: the Church, capitalism, ignorance (including sexual ignorance – that was also a feature of anarchist education), political dependency. At the heart of the emancipatory process was the view that proper vocational preparation would give the ordinary worker a flexibility and independence he or she lacked. It would strengthen their position in the labour market, reducing their dependency on a particular job or firm. Associated with this was intellectual emancipation. All the anarchist educators stressed what we would call raising the consciousness of the young potential worker. They sought to do this through engagement in political activity, through democratic participation in the running of the school, as at Faure's La Ruche, through joining in adult political debate in, for example, the adult educational circles often associated with anarchist schools, and also, perhaps most significantly, through the liberationary ideology which should pervade everything that went on in the school. Some anarchists held the view that every lesson should be a lesson in liberation. Examples, even mathematical or scientific ones, should illustrate that theme. In literature and history and geography it was easy. Ferrer expresses this spirit admirably when he says:

We do not hesitate to say that we want men who will continue unceasingly to develop; men who are capable of constantly destroying and renewing their surroundings and renewing themselves: men whose intellectual independence is their supreme power, which they will yield to none; men always disposed for things that are better, eager for the triumph of new ideas, anxious to crowd many lives into the life they have.[7]

So much, then, for the key background ideas which informed Kropotkin's contribution to the British debate on technical education. How did he interpret them in that new context?

His starting-point was the traditional anarchist one of the division between brain work and manual work. He pointed out that many of the early scientists had also worked with their hands, while ordinary workers in small workshops sometimes had the chance – and he cited several British examples – of creative discussion with educated men. The increasing division of labour had, however, changed all that. Ordinary workers were now even more cut off from scientific education than their grandparents had been and in the new specialized workshops they were denied the stimulus of the older, smaller, unspecialized ones. As for the scientists, they had fallen back so much now on pure theory that they required intermediaries – the engineers – between them and those ultimately carrying out some of the ideas they had given rise to. The effect of this was a general decline in inventiveness, which was causing concern among industrialists, and which was the real thing prompting the whole technical education debate. Kropotkin accepted that there was a decline in the creativity which had originally fuelled the Industrial Revolution, and he argued that the underlying causes were the mental compartmentalism brought about by the division of labour and the general lack of scientific knowledge. He saw the remedy as lying in two things: more extensive education in science, and a better integration of knowledge. Scientific knowledge on its own was not enough. It needed to be combined with craft knowledge:

To the division of society into brain workers and manual workers we oppose the combination of both kinds of activities; and instead of 'technical education' which means the maintenance of the present division between brain work and manual work, we advocate the *education intégrale* or complete education, which means the disappearance of that pernicious distinction.

What would such a system of complete education look like? First, all children 'on leaving school at the age of 18 or 20' (think of that in the context of the 1890s – or the 1990s, for that matter) would possess a good general knowledge of science. Second, this knowledge would be such as to acquaint them with the theoretical bases of technical training. Third, they would have 'a skill in some special trade as would enable each of them to take his or her [this applied to girls as well as boys] place in the grand world of the production of wealth'.[8] The last point to note is that Kropotkin saw this education as applying to *all* children. There should be no separate system for bookish children, or girls, or those identified for the professions. Every human being, without distinction of birth, should receive this broad, common education.

Now there are several things to be said about this account. First, on a technical point, Kropotkin's description of the vocational role of integral education is rather narrower than the usual one. He sees the youngster as being trained in one specialism only, not as being put through a series of them, which would draw out different sides of the youngster and increase his or her flexibility in the labour market. It may be that his phrase 'a general knowledge of what constitutes the basis of technical training' is intended to encompass some occupational sampling as well as knowledge of the scientific principles which lie behind them. Or it may simply be that given the vast proliferation of skill areas in modern times he does not believe it any longer possible to take the youngster meaningfully through a series of very disparate skill areas. The best that might be done is to acquaint learners with the scientific principles which are common to all or most specialisms. He does in fact discuss this later in the article, where he suggests that certain broad scientific principles, such as modification of motion (e.g. transformation of circular motion into rectilinear motion), under-pin most mechanical handicrafts. It is better to make sure that the youngster learns these, so that he or she is later in a position to apply them in a given context, than to teach more narrowly the skills specific to one area. The youngster who possesses the more general knowledge clearly 'knows one good half of all possible trades'.[9]

In a way the issue does not matter, except that it connects with another point which many anarchists would wish to put. That is, there is very little emancipatory thrust to Kropotkin's account. General Science, access to basic occupational skills (shades of YTS schemes!), training in a trade – it could all be taken from the Conservative Manifesto. Indeed, the tone of Kropotkin's remarks suggests consensus rather than revolution. He accepts the going definition of an industrial problem and offers solutions which are acceptable in terms of that definition. There is no hint of education as a means of liberation, whether economic, social, or political liberation. Now of course this is partly a question of the context in which the article originally appeared. However, many anarchists would be disquieted not just by Kropotkin's failure to challenge the existing social system (actually he does but puts it in brackets, as it were, for the duration of the article) but also by his lack of identification with the young worker. There is little feeling that he or she might need emancipation in any terms other than intellectual ones. This is most uncommon among anarchist writers on education, who are normally much more open to the charge of misplaced identification with the learner. There is typically a passion for liberation through education in anarchist educators which one does not find in Kropotkin's article. There is good liberal criticism of pedagogic practice (Kropotkin has some knowledge of contemporary educational thinking on the Continent, not just in anarchist writers) and common sense, informed by genuine knowledge, on the teaching of science. But for many anarchists if education is not defined in emancipatory terms it is nothing.

It is important, however, to remember Kropotkin's starting-point. His purpose was not to set out his radical wares in general but to address the specific issue of the division between brain work and manual work and put forward an educational remedy. Even here he quite reasonably, and explicitly, limits the scope of his discussion. Much of his article is taken up in examining the possible advantages that would accrue if a system of integral education were introduced. He explicitly excludes from his discussion consideration of possible economic advantages, possible benefits in terms of social cohesion, possible benefits to the individual in terms of quality of life, and, in general, 'the great social question'. His focus instead is on what we would call cultural matters, and on this he has some interesting things to say.

His first point is that science itself has suffered from the division of labour. It has become the preserve of an increasingly narrow and increasingly isolated elite. He argues, interestingly, that scientific advance is less the product of individuals than is commonly supposed and much more the product of group work and group debate. Many people other than those currently defined as scientists could contribute to data gathering. However, if they are merely gathering and not contributing to data analysis the resultant outcomes are very likely to be narrow. The generation of hypotheses and their verification or falsification are best done in an atmosphere of open critical debate among informed, involved people. One of the advantages Kropotkin sees for integral education is that it would greatly expand the potential number of such people. Scores of societies would come to life, he argues, reflecting their interests and energies, and out of that would spring a critical debate which would itself stimulate new ideas and new work. The model Kropotkin has in mind is almost certainly the local scientific societies which were so much a feature of Victorian times, but it is also a model which is characteristically anarchist and contrasts sharply with the heavily institutionalized model of science which is dominant today. Organizations which have cultural vigour, according to anarchists, are those which spring up spontaneously to meet people's interests and needs. Kropotkin's argument is that this is actually a better model for the organization of science than a centralized, institutionalized one, since it provides more readily for the shared, critical debate which in his view is what really generates advance in science. Science is the expression of a scientific culture. Widen (and deepen through systematic education) the culture and you strengthen the science.

Kropotkin's second point is related but slightly different. It is that the model of science which sees it as something abstract, pure, and theoretical, which is then applied, is wrong. Practice in some form often comes before theory, he says. Theory arises out of practice, not vice versa. 'It was not the dynamical theory of heat which came before the steam engine – it followed it.' If science is too divorced from practice it is cut off from a vital feed. There is a kind of knowledge, says Kropotkin, which is instinctive among those who work practically with it:

> those men – the Watts and the Stephensons – knew something which the *savants* do not know – they knew the use of their hands; their surroundings stimulated their creative powers; they knew machines, their leading principles, and their work; they had breathed the atmosphere of the workshop and the building yard.[10]

When science is cut off from this kind of knowledge it is diminished.

Kropotkin's overall position, then, appears to be that a too stratified society restricts communication in ways which are ultimately damaging to intellectual debate. Science depends crucially on such debate and advances via a process, dialectical one might almost say, of interaction between theory and practice. Restrict that interaction socially and you restrict scientific development.

Kropotkin's definitions, of science to take just one example, are more elastic than we would allow today, and both science and technology have changed in ways that he did not foresee. Yet his central contention, that social division works against the development of science, retains some validity. The difference in status between scientist and engineer, with all the attendant implications, is an example of Kropotkin's which still has force. Where, perhaps, the real significance of his account lies, however, is in his appreciation of the subtlety of the process by which ideas emerge and are passed on, picked up, developed, and then articulated. For Kropotkin a weakness in a country's scientific effort was not something to be put right by a simple-minded management project coupled with an infusion of money. It was too bound up with the society's whole culture for that. It needed to be tackled in more fundamental ways. One of those ways, in Kropotkin's view, was to change education.

It is important to remember this cultural emphasis in Kropotkin's account when discussing his attitude to the more libertarian aspects of the anarchist view of education. Otherwise one is merely conscious of a major gap. Probably the most debated issue in anarchist educational theory is that of compulsion, and on this, apparently, Kropotkin has not a word to say.

The issue arises first in connection with the system of educational provision. Is the state to be the provider, and is attendance to be compulsory? If so then many anarchists would find it difficult to accept Kropotkin's position as an anarchist one at all. Anarchists, almost by definition, have a deep distrust of the state, and this applies *a fortiori* to the state's role in education. To take just one example: Stirner's account of the relations between the individual and the state lays particular stress on the dangers of state control of education. Stirner, it will be recalled, approached the issue of freedom from the point of view of man's relation to the ideas current in society at that particular time. If people's values, beliefs, and general world outlook are properly their own and not the product of conditioning, then they are free: if not, then they are not. Stirner saw the greatest danger in socially dominant belief systems such as that associated with the Church in the past and with the nation state at the time he wrote. Education he saw as the means by which the state inculcated ideas it favoured. The school had become a prime agent of social control; the schoolteacher, in his view, had replaced the priest. The curriculum reflected the state's interest. Even more significant was what we would call today the hidden curriculum of the school. It was in the school that children learned habits of obedience to authority, there that, in Stirner's famous phrase, the gendarme was installed within the breast. State control of education was, therefore, incompatible with the individual's true freedom.[11]

Not dissimilar views were generally held among anarchists at the time Kropotkin wrote, and Kropotkin's failure even to touch on this issue is puzzling. Technical education raised the issue in particularly acute form. Control of provision by the state would ensure that what was offered would reflect the interests of employers, not workers. Moreover, if attendance and participation were compulsory no one would be able to escape. For anarchists it was almost a matter of definition that if the state was to be the provider then education could not be free, certainly not in the anarchist sense of freedom.

The issue of compulsion also arose in connection with pedagogy, and here, it may be felt, Kropotkin is on stronger ground. An extreme, Tolstoyan definition of freedom with respect to pedagogy implies absolutely no compulsion in the teaching pattern. Such a position was certainly held, and passionately held, by anarchists, but many of the most influential anarchist writers on education shrank from pressing the issue to the extreme. Educators like Robin and Faure, for example, took up a relaxed, liberal position whose characteristic features were absolute avoidance of corporal punishment, the imposition instead of social penalties, often communally arrived at, by other pupils as well as staff, and a general sensitive reluctance to breach the child's self-respect and dignity. Many anarchists would in fact take that line. Other anarchists would, however, insist on the child's absolute freedom to determine the pattern of his or her day, to decide whether to attend and what to attend, to initiate or omit activities in whatever form they chose. There is an interesting pedagogic debate on the degree to which self-motivation is essential to the learning act.

Kropotkin's position is clearly the liberal, possibly less distinctively anarchist, one. He deals with pedagogy at some length, actually, in his article. Again, he does not touch on the issue of compulsion, but he does say enough to enable us to get a picture of his general views. Broadly he is in line with the progressive educational movement on the Continent. There was a general reaction at this time against bookish, grammar-school approaches to teaching and a general interest in starting from the practical and concrete and immediate. To this Kropotkin added some touches characteristic of the anarchists: valuation of *making* things as opposed to writing or talking about them, rejection of 'parrot-like repetition', and an emphasis on independent thinking, a general sense of the intelligence implicit in manual operations. The examples he cites are drawn from his own interest in science and his experience and observation. The whole is a wise blend of common sense and current theory; but it is not distinctively anarchist. The impression one gets is that the innovative scientist, not the committed anarchist, is speaking.

Pedagogy is, however, an area in which anarchists differ, and there is less agreement on the essential features of a libertarian pedagogy than there is over the issue of state provision. It is on that second issue that anarchists would take Kropotkin to task. My own feeling is that Kropotkin had accepted for the purposes of his article the context assumed by the general British debate. There were some points that he thought might be accepted and others that he thought would not be, and for the moment he was concerned to urge the former. It is, however, possible to extract from the article, and especially from his discussion of its cultural aspects of the hand–brain divide, the outline of an answer which he could have made if he had been tackled on the compulsion/state provision issue.

What he could have said was that the issue of compulsion becomes less significant when one is dealing with adults who are essentially free to come and go, and this is likely to be the case where technical education is concerned. True, his article assumes that the bases of technical education would be in school, but developing those bases – essentially, through a wide scientific school culture and through sampling one or more industrial occupations – is merely a preliminary to participating in a wider kind of vocational learning which is not institutionalized and which springs rather from the interests and efforts of spontaneous associations of people. What Kropotkin is passionately committed to is that wider kind of cultural learning. That, he insists, can only exist as a product of free, untrammelled action and debate. Formal instruction is merely a preparation for that participation.

Anarchists have always insisted on the superiority of real life to the school as a means of education. There is a well-known passage in one of Tolstoy's pedagogical essays in which he describes a visit he made to Marseilles. Suppose, he asks, you had to form an opinion of the people of Marseilles based solely on what you saw of their children in school. You would surely conclude that they were rather dull, apathetic, and distinctly limited in mental capacity. In fact, the people of Marseilles are not like that at all. On the contrary, they are lively, intelligent, and resourceful. How is this to be explained? He found the answer, he says, in the streets of Marseilles, in its drinking houses, its cafés, its workshops, and its markets. Marseilles itself presented an unusually stimulating environment. Tolstoy draws the following conclusion:

The greater part of one's education is acquired, not at school, but in life. There, where life is instructive, as in London, Paris, and in general, in all large cities, the masses are educated; there where life is not instructive, as in the country, the people are uneducated in spite of the fact that the schools are the same in both.[12]

Kropotkin's argument is clearly similar to Tolstoy's. It is the culture that is important, not the school.

Yes, one might concede provisionally, but in the specific case of technical education is the argument even plausible? One might even be prepared to accept that at the time of Tolstoy's visit to Marseilles in the 1860s the kind of knowledge that was at issue was still a fairly straightforward kind of craft knowledge. But surely, by the time Kropotkin was writing, manufacturing processes in the industrial cities had become so complex and sophisticated that *some* formal instruction could not be dispensed with no matter how stimulating the environment. It is here, I think, that Kropotkin's account appears to advantage. Whatever may be anarchist theory, Kropotkin was enough of a scientist to believe that some formalized knowledge of scientific principles was a prerequisite for joining in the informal debate that he thought was crucial. At the moment the schools were not even providing that general knowledge. Until they did, ordinary people would be cut off from some of the key issues for living in a modern industrial society. The lack of such knowledge was a crucial restriction of their freedom. We return, thus, to the question of whether scientific knowledge is to be the preserve of an increasingly privileged elite or whether it is to be open to all, part of a culture accessible to everybody. What, Kropotkin might have asked, was the most important restriction on freedom in a modern industrial society? For traditional anarchist educators it was weakness in the market-place for labour caused by, among other things, restriction to one set of craft skills. For Kropotkin, writing later and with a greater understanding of the role of science, it was being denied access to knowledge central to living in modern society. I am not sure that Kropotkin's understanding of freedom will not stand the test of time better than the traditional anarchist one.

A purely historical account of an educational issue always rings a little hollow in anarchist ears since it itself exhibits the divorce between the theoretical and the applied, the bookish and the real, which anarchists reject. I would like to conclude, therefore, by reinterpreting the ideas which Kropotkin put forward in the context of the 1880s into terms applicable to the context of the 1980s. Suppose Kropotkin were writing an article on technical education today for, say, the *Guardian*. What might he have written?

Not technical education, but education

British definitions of vocational education are commonly employers' definitions. They specify training in terms of skills relevant to and specific to one job or set of jobs. This is a conservative basis for definition and allows for neither technological change nor occupational mobility. Educating you to be into a job today by this definition is educating you to be out of a job tomorrow. What is wanted, Kropotkin might say, is an education which is general and not specific, is shared by everybody, woman and boy, and is geared to participation in a knowledge-based culture *either* through work *or* through life outside work.

There should be more of it

Kropotkin would not fail to point out that Britain has probably the least educated population of any developed country. This is especially true of adults, who have grown up in a society in which education was restricted largely to those under 16 (or 15), but it remains true of the young, a smaller proportion of whom continue education after 16 than in any other developed country. Employers register concern about the implications of this for the workforce; Kropotkin's concern would be for its effect on democratic debate. There should be more of it, but how?

Increase participation, not provision

One way *not* to increase it is by extending state provision, as both a state-socialist Labour Party and a dirigistically minded Conservative government might prefer. The problem is not facilities but take-up. The British are so used to not having education that even when it is available they don't want it. Admittedly this is partly a question of cash. Only partly. More fundamentally it is a reflection of educational structures which repel take-up rather than invite it. And here, Kropotkin might say, anarchists have something to offer.

What is required are educational structures which elicit participation. Some suggestions follow.

– Enrol not to faceless institutions but to face-to-face groups

A student is enrolled not to a college but to a group following a course of studies. The group is responsible for co-operatively managing its own programme. Acceptance on the course is conditional on willingness to participate in such self-management.

– Adapt the Open University and the Open College

Make it a requirement, departed from only exceptionally, that only groups can register (i.e. you cannot register as an individual) but that any group can register. It is the group's business to run the course. The prime role of the College and the University is to provide materials. The group provides mutual support and feedback. It can hire support staff (e.g. teachers) if it wishes.

– Tilt the balance towards self-help groups and associations

First, remove the power of examination from qualification-awarding bodies, and, second, give it to local testing agencies whose function is solely to test whether candidates meet specified criteria. Third, have candidates who can only be nominated for testing by small local groups which have acted as support groups for them in their studying. Fourth, use criterion-based assessment, not norm-referenced assessment.

– Recognize the role of work groups and work teams in training

Make training a recognized part of the job of work groups and work teams. Require them to work out a programme with the learner; allow them to nominate the learner, as described above; and give them real responsibility.

Kropotkin may not, of course, have hit upon exactly these ideas, but it would certainly be in the anarchist tradition to try to redefine education in terms of co-operative actions by small face-to-face groups – and that, really, is my point.

Revisit integral education

Introduce overlapping Foundation Courses of the sort currently operating only in the field of Art and Design. At present, all students who go on to take a degree course in Art and Design first have to take a one-year Foundation Course which introduces them (by trying it out) to the design areas they can specialize in for their degree and equips them with basic skills. Introduce similar courses for other occupational areas – these days one Foundation Course couldn't cover all the possibilities in the way that it perhaps could in Robin's day. A Foundation Course for Business, perhaps, and one for Science and Technology? And overlap them so that people could move from one to the other if it suited them better. The government is thinking about abolishing the Art and Design Foundation Course (it is administratively untidy). Do not let it. Abolish the rest of the system instead.

Try libertarian pedagogy

Borrow another practice from Art and Design: task-oriented project work. The whole course typically in the Art and Design areas is taught through a sequence of design projects. Try this in Science and Technology. According to libertarian educationists, people learn best by being confronted with real problems in real contexts in which the initiative is theirs. Projects would enable learners to see operations as a whole (in an integrated way, yes), thus offsetting both the limited focus of much industrial work and the bittiness of much of the present curriculum.

But . . .

(a) *All* of an Art and Design Foundation Course is taught through projects. The same would have to go for other Foundation Courses. None of these tame pseudo-projects which teachers presently set!

(b) Pedagogy cannot be divorced from the social structures in which it is set. If they are hierarchical, it will be too. At the moment there are a lot of good experiments in English Further Education, some of them associated (paradoxically) with the Manpower Services Commission: negotiated curricula, student-centred learning, integrative assignments, etc. Do not jettison these. Remember, though, that teachers can use any potentially liberative device in an unliberating way. Unless libertarian pedagogy is embedded in liberating structures of the co-operative sort outlined above, it will not liberate.

Make the most of the decentralizing possibilities of the new technology

Kropotkin was interested in electricity and its implications and if he were alive today would be similarly interested in computers. What he might have said about their implications for education is this: information technology has enormous potential for decentralizing knowledge. It makes it possible to access knowledge anywhere. Thus in so far as education is to do with resources and materials it makes it possible to study at home or at work, in a public library, or indeed anywhere, and not necessarily in an institution with walls called a college or school or university.

In principle it is possible to develop the interactive possibilities of computers so that they will provide feedback to the learner (and feedback is the basis of all learning). What they will not do, however, is provide the psychological support which comes from people. This is very important to learners. In a learning context, therefore, computers need to be complemented by people. The people do not, however, have to be experts: they can be peers. The computer can provide the expertise. What the people are needed for is support and the shared benefit which comes from co-operative engagement and enquiry. This point is often not understood. It is too readily assumed that computer learning is best associated with individuals. (In the author's experience, certainly in a training context, this is not so.) There will be more need for social forms of learning, not fewer. Relate this, Kropotkin might have said, to what was said about face-to-face groups above and you might just see the outlines of a new approach to education emerge. I'll come back, he might have finished, in 2090 and update you.

Notes and references

1 Peter Kropotkin, *Fields, Factories and Workshops* (London: Hutchinson, 1899). For purposes of convenience all references are to the more accessible edition edited by Colin Ward, *Fields, Factories and Workshops Tomorrow* (London: Allen & Unwin, 1974).

2 See Maurice Dommanget, *Les Grands Educateurs socialistes* (Paris: Sudel, 1951); also Paul Avrich, *The Modern School Movement* (Princeton, NJ: 1980); J. M. Raynaud and G. Ambauves, *L'Education libertaire* (Paris: Spartacus, n.d.); and Michael Smith, *The Libertarians and Education* (London: Allen & Unwin, 1983.

3 Ronald F. Price, *Marx and Education in Russia and China* (London: Croom Helm, 1977).

4 Karl Marx, *Capital*, Vol. 1 (New York: Modern Library, n.d.; reprint of 1906 Kerr edn), pp. 529–30.

5 Karl Marx, *The General Council of the First International 1864–1866* (Moscow: Foreign Languages Publishing House, n.d.), pp. 345 ff.

6 Michael Bakunin, *Oeuvres*, Vol. 5, 'Integral Education' (Paris: P. V. Stock, 1911).

7 Francisco Ferrer y Guardia, *The Origin and Ideals of the Modern School* (London: Watts, 1913), p. 52.

8 Kropotkin, *Fields, Factories and Workshops*, op. cit., pp. 172–3.

9 Ibid., p. 177.

10 Ibid., p. 183.
11 Max Stirner, *The False Principle of Our Education* (Colorado Springs: Ralph Myles, 1967).
12 Leo Tolstoy, *Tolstoy on Education*, trans. Leo Wiener (Chicago: University of Chicago Press, 1967).

Co-operatives and anarchism:
a contemporary perspective

Tom Cahill

In this chapter I argue that there is a strong similarity between the theory and practice of the co-operative movement and anarchism. Indeed, I would argue that the recent upsurge of co-operatives is one part of the 'new social movements', which are themselves anarchism in its latest practical manifestation.[1] This chapter, however, makes the connection only between anarchism and co-operatives, bringing the light of anarchist theory to a subject with which it is not commonly associated.

Much of what I have to say is indicative. For example, I outline an argument that leads up to what has been called 'community economic development', but I do not sketch out precise *details* of a future economic order. The absence of complicated (dogmatic) blueprints is also inherent in anarchist theory, since anarchism tends to resist precise plans laid out by theorists. It is clear that unless the co-operative movement finds a practical way to retain the vision of the idealists who began it, the new co-operatives will be absorbed into the dominant economy as a weak third sector of contemporary capitalist structures. In some sense, I am trying to rescue co-ops from social democracy . . . again. On the other hand, I believe that unless anarchism is able to offer a practical, 'prefigurative', economic alternative, anarchists and anarchist sympathizers will be forced into the dominant economy, with the attendant negative effects on the development of the anarchist movement as a whole. I suggest that mutually beneficial insight, at both practical and theoretical levels, would arise for both co-operators and anarchists from the open-minded examination of their separate but interrelated movements.

The anarchist sees the question of change as an immediate one, not something to be postponed until practical pressing matters are dealt with in an effective, but amoral, way. Some have called this a 'prefigurative' model of revolution, one where the means used must be entirely (or nearly so) consistent with the model of society which *eventually* will emerge. The American anarchist Howard Ehrlich captures the sentiment as follows:

> We must view revolutionary change as a process, not an end.
> We must develop a view of the 'good society'.
> We must act on the principles of the society we would like to see.
> Our means must be consistent with our ends.
> We must act as if the future is today.

When referring to this process, he tells us that

> Our transfer culture, then, will be based on experiments in social arrangements, arrangements in which we will consistently be testing new principles of collective social organization. We are attempting uniquely to build freedom in community.[2]

The making of the co-operative movement

It is difficult to summarize the making of the co-operative movement. However, we can tell some part of the story, and ask a number of unanswered questions that must arise when considering the co-operative movement from an anarchist perspective.

The growth of the co-operative movement in the western world embodies a distinct anarchist flavour. 'Co-operation' (in a wider sense), so crucial to Kropotkin and other anarchists, is seen as a quite normal and exceedingly common aspect of human behaviour.[3] It exists everywhere, at all times. Anarchists have responded to the historically specific development of the co-operative movement. For example, Gustav Landauer was himself heavily involved in co-operatives as part of his larger vision. Furthermore, he recognized the interconnected nature of anarchism and co-operation.[4] Both anarchism and co-operation are, at the same time, a mode of specific action *and* a 'spirit' present in human life which manifest themselves in a number of ways.

There are a number of currents of revolt that arose, as one might expect, in reaction to capitalism. Socialism, Marxism, liberalism, co-operatives, trade unions, and mass political parties are a few obvious examples. The boundaries between them are often blurred, and there were (and still are) many struggles to determine which tendency would organize and control the greatest share of the spirit of revolt. The co-operative movement is both related to those other currents and yet quite separate from them – at least in the early days. The complex historical relations of Christian Socialists, skilled workers, trade unionists, the Labour

Party, and co-operatives has been documented to some extent.[5] The most plausible account of this complex revolt against capitalism finds three reasonably distinct strands emerging from this confusing and fertile period.[6] The first is the 'Jacobin' style, including Marxism and Leninism in their more authoritarian forms. The second strand is the social democratic movement, the one which in the UK has become almost synonymous with the 'labour' movement and the Labour Party. The third is the one most pertinent to this chapter, because it is the one into which anarchism and the more radical co-operatives will be placed. It might be called the libertarian or 'prefigurative' strand. The entire (three-strand) argument will not be made in detail, since this classification should be generally appreciated – remembering always that these partial and small movements of protest have had complex relations with each other and with movements of 'non-revolt'.

The co-operative movement was a *local, community-based* movement. It has a complex beginning, the story depending partly on how much attention we pay to the Owenite (early) phase or the Rochdale (later) phase. But whenever the movement 'began', the co-ops (with the exception of some paternalistic ones) were organized by workers and residents in a particular locality in response to particular needs. They were *spontaneous* responses, that is, they were not part of a general strategy devised by a central group of planners. There are fascinating questions, about exactly why co-ops were organized in specific locations, which do not concern me here. It is noteworthy, however, that both in the recent 'new wave' co-operative movement[7] and in the early days of the Rochdale Pioneers, the provision of 'good food' was the most obvious need they were organized to fulfil. Then, as now, capitalism did not produce cheap and wholesome food for ordinary people to eat. The co-operative movement grew rapidly, as it organized to meet basic community-defined needs, expressed through egalitarian principles and organization. Then, as now, this spontaneous and locally organized movement grew so impressively that most political groups had to develop views about it.[8]

The spirit and structure of the co-ops were a serious attempt to be *democratic and self-managed*. They tried to combat hierarchy as it dominated the economic lives of most people. The co-operative movement has changed over the years, so that this radical democratic tendency has gone the way of most such radical impulses originating in the nineteenth century (until the recent new wave). It is clear that superficial democracy (egalitarian voting/parliaments) and a very marginal emphasis on self-management characterize modern society, including the remnants of the old co-operative movement. Most early co-operators reasoned that *if* all individuals had one vote, and *if* ownership was vested equally in all, and *if* only those who worked in or were actively involved in co-ops participated directly in decision-making, *then* democracy would be ensured. Most analyses of the co-operative movement do recognize this radical democratic spirit,[9] while recognizing too the variety in the actual existing co-ops. We are concerned with emphasizing the radical, directly democratic current in the movement.

In a slightly less obvious way, the co-operative movement was *anti-system*. It quite specifically wanted to *replace* the existing capitalist economic system with one based on the principles and practices of co-operation. The movement was quite conscious of itself as a critique of or an opposition to the existing system.[10] The early Owenites, of course, wanted to create whole communities based on co-operation,[11] as did numerous communal experimenters of the time.[12] What was missing from the early co-operative movement was a very clear vision, a future-oriented theory, linking the small-scale initiatives into federated units that might gradually (or suddenly) blossom into anti-systemic revolution. We must not be very harsh on them, though, because we only have to look about us to see that none of the other currents of protest managed to create a genuine revolution.

Given these general characteristics of early co-ops, it would be remiss not to make a few comments on the 'failures' of the early movement, although that is not a central point of this chapter. The 'reasons' for failure or de-radicalization have been outlined by many commentators. The first mentioned is often the *financial problem*. The background is complex, but basically the unusual structure and aims of co-operatives have always caused problems for the dominant sources of capital. In general, the financial environment has been hostile to the emergence of the co-operative spirit. This is to be expected, because co-ops have always been critical of the existing system, either implicitly or explicitly. Second, the early co-ops were unable to devise structures to *maintain a boundary* between those who work and those who own or control. In short, some claim that the identity between owners and controllers (which meant that all workers must be members and all members must be workers, i.e. no absentee non-participants would have controlling power) should have been maintained more strictly as the early movement matured. It is understood that when outside investors were allowed to have power within the co-op structure, co-ops lost their distinctive qualities and became 'another high-street shop'. Third, some commentators claim that co-ops have *never attracted or developed sufficient managerial skills*,[13] from inside or outside the organization. Therefore they suffered, as would any ordinary organization, from the lack of competent management.

The old co-ops also had the specific problem of both *giving credit* and failing to use the mechanisms of the state to collect the debts (being reluctant to do so). There were also problems in the co-op movement of *competition with price-cutting capitalist firms*, highlighting the inadequate reserves of the under-financed co-ops. Another problem worth mentioning is the attempt by many co-ops to maintain *political neutrality*. A case can be made that co-ops (or any oppositional group) can find themselves swept up in political currents beyond their control, if they do not understand that neutrality usually means support for the existing regime. I shall not attempt to rank in importance the above factors as causes for the decline of the co-operative movement as a radical force for social change.

The anarchist perspective on co-ops has been reasonably consistent. Without commenting on issues such as the importance and role of consumer versus manufacturing co-ops, we can still make some distinction between more and less radical organizations. Bakunin, who was clearly less concerned with 'positive' anarchism than, say, Kropotkin or Landauer, still understood their role:

> What should be the nature of the economic agitation and development of the workers of the International, and what will be the means of these, before the social revolution, which alone can emancipate them fully and definitively, does so? The experience of recent years recommends two paths to us, one negative, and the other positive: *resistance funds and co-operation*.
>
> By the term 'co-operation', we mean all known systems of *consumption*, of *mutual credit* or *labour credit*, and of *production*. In the application of all these systems, and even in the theory on which they are based, we should distinguish two opposing currents: the bourgeois current and the purely socialist current.[14]

One of the purposes of this chapter is to join Bakunin and contemporary anarchists in making distinctions between more and less radical aspects of the co-operative movement.

There are a number of questions that still remain before one could confidently claim that co-ops are an essentially anarchist experiment. Were co-ops more successful in terms of longevity or job security than ordinary firms of comparable size during this era? Were the co-ops organized *from below* more 'successful' than the ones organized from above (by such as the Christian Socialists)? Must we compare the role of professional support (parliamentary, legal, and financial) in the nineteenth century with similar support in the present, recognizing the crucial role of the intellectuals in the growth of the new and old movements? Were the working conditions much better in co-ops than in ordinary factories or shops, and how do we measure 'better'? Did co-ops have a significant and lasting impact? Answers to these and a few other questions would take us further towards elaborating the connection between anarchism and co-operatives. Nevertheless, the early co-op movement can be said to be anti-system, democratic/self-managed, spontaneous, and local. These are, clearly, characteristics with which any anarchist would feel comfortable.

The present economic context

There is, of course, a general economic context within which anarchism develops its theory or its economic concerns. To make the argument easier, let us suggest that there is an anarchist consensus. This general agreement is a way of looking at the world, a set of factors which strike an anarchist as he or she looks at the world-as-it-is. It is, of course, no more solid or clear a consensus than the 'socialist' or the 'liberal' view of economics.

There are two fascinating and important strands of anarchist thinking about economics that will be mentioned only in passing. Anarcho-syndicalism is one, and the 'gift economy'[15] is the other. The first is a tradition which actually fits quite well within the general scope of this chapter, but is usually restricted to the (mostly male) workplace, and has some quite close relations to (largely reformist) trade-union organizing. As such, anarcho-syndicalism is a partial view of the larger context. The gift economy (related to the larger question of the 'informal' economy or 'black' economy) is that part of the anarchist vision which deals with extra-legal (but important) transactions which are removed from the money economy. It is, perhaps, a way of conducting social and economic relationships as if communism and the abolition of money were here today.[16] Since we are restricted to co-operatives (a legal and open option), we will leave aside this important aspect of a complete anarchist picture.

First, the anarchist looks about him or her and sees *protest and resistance* against the dominant economic system. This resistance, however sophisticated the theory behind it, is against the system which is *failing* to provide what it so obviously *can* provide. For almost every individual, the economy fails to live up to the visions it creates. These protests can be against the hierarchical structure of organizations, wage labour, the money economy, the sexual division of labour, or perhaps work itself. Amongst anarchists, there is often disagreement as to whether this incredibly varied protest is increasing or decreasing, or even as to its significance. Some of the forms of this protest are *unemployment*, both as a voluntary and involuntary way of life; *absenteeism*, although its exact meaning and distribution do not always fit easy patterns; *sabotage* at the workplace and elsewhere; non-authorized or *wildcat strikes*; *organized shoplifting*; *looting*; *the black economy*, and notions of the gift and no-money economies. This is not to say that all activities in the black economy or all looting *are* anarchism, or even the work of anarchists. It is simply that, as anarchists look about the world, vast amounts of anti-economic protest spring to their attention. Socialists, liberals, or Tories have other concerns.

Anarchists are also concerned about the problem of *de-industrialization*.[17] In many areas of the rich world, large corporate entities are making decisions to 'relocate plant', to abandon 'declining plant', to 'structurally disinvest' in traditional manufacturing communities. Our concern is not the decision-making process, or the exact location of the new investment, although a good anarchist economics must analyse these matters. We may be witnessing the emergence of a labour force which has vast numbers of permanently 'unemployed' and 'unskilled' people. Unskilled people will be working at boring and alienating jobs, with a very few members of the labour force controlling such work, using networks of information processors of various sorts.[18] It seems that this problem is more than merely 'unemployment', more than de-skilling, more than techno-control. Small[19] new-wave co-ops are quite practical and effective methods of creating meaningful work (although the next twenty years will be the true test of such an assertion). These locally based workplaces may be the only realistic hope for entire communities ruptured by the 'rational' acts of large economic organizations.

Some aspects of the anarchist view of the economic world are obvious enough that they need only be mentioned. The anarchist sees the economic world as dominated by *large, centralized bureaucracies* of various types. The debate continues as to whether it is the state, the multinationals, men, the mega-designers, or the western way of life that is responsible for the most powerful of these organizations. The debate is interesting only to the academic, since there can be no doubt that these various hierarchical forms of economic and social control are the dominant forces today. What is noteworthy about these organizations is that they shift control, utterly and completely, from the local community to a national, regional, or global hierarchy. These styles of organization are best suited for making the same product for people who are defined as the same.[20] It will be argued later that the anarchist form of organization is actually more suited to meet emerging market needs,[21] and even more so truly radical needs based in local communities.

There are some theories of economics which focus on the ownership of the means of production. There are other theories which focus on the actual control of the means of production. The anarchist theory, if it is true to the principles which are often espoused, must do both. It is fair to say that anarchists claim that *both ownership and control* are necessary aspects of a critique of the system, and necessary focal points for the construction of an anarchist economic organization.

A *deep concern for the environment* has re-emerged in anarchist theory.[22] Part of this concern comes from a critique of the economic system (although it should be clear that a wider cultural and social critique is part of the anarchist analysis). According to more and more anarchists, a necessary side-effect of the growth-oriented, money economy dominated by large hierarchical organizations is, essentially, the rape of the earth. There is some disagreement as to *exactly* when the earth will become barren or dead, but there is agreement that it is being damaged. The economics that sees the earth as a 'resource' which demands to be 'exploited' for the benefit of a few (or even for the many) is seen by the anarchist as the economy of death. The variety of theory and practice that is emerging is rich with concepts like 'deep ecology',[23] Green politics, social ecology, and so forth. The process of developing a positive alternative to this environmentally destructive 'economics' has begun.[24] There is no need to discuss the details of this emerging movement, my point being that the 'ecological concern' is an intimate and inseparable part of the anarchist critique of current economic context.

Some aspects of an anarchist economy

There must be some requirements of an anarchist economy, giving it an identity, in theory and practice, different from other economic systems. *All* of those requirements will not be suggested, only those considered most important. The anarchist style or tendency which concerns us is social anarchism (sometimes called communist anarchism).

The need for *immediate beginnings* in the construction of the anarchist economy has been clearly expressed on a number of occasions by anarchists, such as Howard Ehrlich:

> If there are any priorities in my scheme, anything to be called a 'first step', I would say it was the building of *alternative institutions*. The reason for this is that I see such institutions as the building blocks of a transfer culture. They are the institutions of the new society as closely as we can approximate them within the old society. Moreover, in the process of building alternative institutions, we will invariably confront almost all of the problems of fashioning a transfer culture.[25]

Even academic commentators such as Michael Taylor note that anarchists must begin to construct the world as anarchists want it to be, but do it in the world-as-it-is:

> But there is another line of development . . . the development of what might be called 'partial community', covering a wide variety of co-operatives, collectives, neighbourhood associations and other practices and projects of direct action, mutual aid and self-management. All of these . . . further the building of community and directly or indirectly of anarchy too, by (1) fostering of deepening reciprocity; (2) diminishing mediation and political specialization by short-cutting the offices of the state and widening political participation; and (3) in some cases stimulating or even necessitating less specialized relations between people.[26]

Whether it is called a 'transfer culture' or a 'partial community', it is quite clear that there is a stream in contemporary anarchism (the mainstream) which claims that the immediate construction of anarchist economic situations is crucial. As Bakunin said:

> Let us enlarge our association. But at the same time, let us not forget to consolidate and reinforce it so that our solidarity, which is our whole power, grows stronger from day to day. Let us have more of this solidarity in study, in our work, in civic action, in life itself. Let us co-operate in our common enterprise to make our lives a little more supportable and less difficult. Let us, wherever possible, establish producer-consumer co-operatives and mutual credit societies which, though under the present economic conditions they cannot in any real or adequate way free us, are nevertheless important inasmuch as they train the workers in the practice of managing the economy and plant the precious seeds for the organization of the future.[27]

I would claim that anarchist economic organizations would have five common qualities. The economics of anarchism must be (1) decentralized, (2) egalitarian, (3) self-managing and empowering, (4) based on local needs, and (5) supported by other autonomous units in a non-hierarchical fashion. These characteristics, it should be clear, are similar to those ascribed to the earlier co-operative movement. Co-operatives are just such a spontaneous organizational attempt to meet those needs, in the sense that no specific co-operative or anarchist group planned the general developments in precisely this way.

Anarchist economic structures must be *decentralized*. This notion often hides or includes other important characteristics – the notion of *small size*, or that all organizations must be *autonomous*.[28] To complicate things further, there is a distinct emphasis on *community-based or local needs* in the anarchist requirement for an appropriate organization. This is the easiest notion to understand, that local people should control local enterprises, under every possible circumstance. Implicit in this complex concept of decentralization is the notion that those who *live* in a locality are best suited to understand the complex impact an organization has on the local environment. There is a need here for important and fascinating debates about the practicality of small units of production, or the methods by which communication might take place between such units (new technology?).

Equality is another crucial organizational characteristic for the anarchist, in economics as in other spheres of life. The anarchist thinks that, without equality of ownership, there can never be equality of control. But it is also clear that people will not leap instantly into a new anarchist consciousness merely because they have an equal stake in an enterprise. It *almost* goes without saying that in a proper anarchist organization there would be acute attention to the *practical details of the process of deep self-management*.[29] This is why there is such an emphasis on *education* both within and outside any co-operative, as well as in anarchist organizations. The equality of ownership and control for the anarchist is only the *basis* upon which the deep self-management of every organization can take place. Whatever organizations may evolve in the future, it is clearly a part of the anarchist requirement that such organizations have extremely egalitarian decision-making and ownership structures.

Anarchist economics requires some practical organization that can be used now, is consciously concerned with the process of deep self-management, is egalitarian in ownership and control, and is decentralized and community-based. Perhaps it should be added that a critical concern with the actual products would be a part of the anarchist economic theory. There is another important strain of anarchism which would claim that the concern for legal structures and the direct connection to the money economy would remove co-operatives from the sphere of truly anarchist activity. The proponents of this view may be correct, but this is not the understanding of anarchism used here.

What is there to suggest that co-ops as they exist now are part of the anarchist economic alternative? My strongest evidence is a hunch (since comprehensive survey research has not yet been funded), an intuition shared by most of the co-operators and co-operative developers to whom I have spoken. This intuition is presented in its simple form, as it is the *foremost* motivation for my interpretations. During a recent interview with a long-time co-operator, he mentioned that, of the eighteen members of the co-op, one was Labour, another Communist, and the rest more or less uninterested in party politics. They were, however, quite active in various campaigns and groups which are labelled 'new social movements',[30] or what some have called 'fragments'.[31] My informant was the only self-styled anarchist. We agreed that there was a strong 'libertarian streak' in the co-op, and in others of which he had direct experience. Other co-operators (housing and producer) agreed that co-ops were not socialist, liberal, communist, fascist, pacifist, or conservative, so they were obviously anarchist, if they belonged in any category. We agreed there could be no structure that was utterly devoid of 'political implications'; and, upon close examination, anarchism was the only theory which fitted comfortably. Anarchism, they suggested, was a bit more 'radical' than were some actual members of co-ops. In other words, were one to conduct systematic survey research it could be expected that a fair number of co-operators would say that there was most certainly a strong libertarian atmosphere in their co-ops and that the structure and process of the co-ops reflected the anarchist goals outlined. However, this is a matter for detailed empirical research, and it is presented here as an impression shared by many co-operators at the grass-roots level.

It is through the visible structure of the co-operatives and their support organizations that the 'spirit' of anarchism can best express itself. Co-ops, together with the 'informal economy',[32] allow contemporary anarchist economic activity to be expressed. During the 1970s, the libertarian spirit became visible in the lives of a small, but significant, sector of the population. It expressed itself in sexual, ecological, communal, psychological, and other specific forms. After suitable formal approval was gained, that spirit was also expressed economically, in work and housing. The politically non-aligned people, who Jenny Thornley finds so distressing in her pioneering book on workers' co-ops,[33] had finally found a way to express their needs in a practical economic structure.

Co-ops are that facet of anarchism which is positive and practical, and yet attempts to construct a future in the present (prefiguration). Anarchism (unlike nation-state political strategies of the right and left) has tendencies to encourage immediately the spontaneous direct actions of revolutionaries and radicals. The co-op movement is (and was) a spontaneous and local phenomenon, supported by suitably skilled sympathizers.

Anarchists must have clear ideas about how individuals can exist economically, both inside and outside the money economy. Co-ops are the most suitable legal form for working and living in a reasonably anarchist way. Although the relationship, like all emerging and complex human relationships, is not yet totally clear, it is no surprise that parties, governments, trade unions, and other hierarchical organizations have difficulties with co-ops. If co-ops remain in touch with their radical spirit, they will never find a home in such organizations, although co-ops might use them to obtain what they need. Having said this, it is only proper that some of the institutions of the contemporary British co-operative movement be described in some detail.

Contemporary co-operatives

In 1975, the co-operative movement was an inspiring and important memory, a dozen active co-ops, and a few crusty institutions like *the* Co-op. It has exploded in the last decade into a serious social phenomenon (although any aggregate data on the more widely defined Co-operative movement is completely dominated by the old co-operative Wholesale Society and Retail Societies, which have little to do with the concerns of this chapter). At a purely expressive level, it is now the case that all the political parties 'support' co-ops.[34] Where there were a few dozen co-ops in Britain in 1975, there are now (1987) over 1,500.[35] To put this into perspective, the earlier co-op movement never had such a large number, even at its height. It is true that many of these registrations are new ones (seven hundred-plus in 1985–7). The list will also include those that ceased trading or never traded. But whatever the exact figures, they have become worthy of the organizational attention of the state, and the attention of most political parties and large numbers of young jobless people. There are, of course, a number of 'co-operatives' which have not officially registered with the Registrar of Friendly Societies.[36] There is, unfortunately, no way of knowing how many there might be.

What is a co-operative, and how or why did they grow so fast after 1976?

There are simple answers to these questions. It was in 1974 that the Labour government put co-ops into the public eye with its ill-fated experiments with what are now called 'rescue' co-ops. In 1976, under pressure from the Industrial Common Ownership Movement (ICOM), the government passed the Industrial and Common Ownership Act which made common ownership a legal possibility, as well as giving a small amount of money to the Industrial Common Ownership Fund (ICOF) to finance new co-ops. Two years later, the national Co-operative Development Agency (CDA – which also has little to do with the 'new wave' movement) was established and the Inner Urban Areas Act passed, the latter enabling start-up costs for co-ops to be funded from grants. Like the Industrial and Provident Societies Acts of 1852 and 1862, these actions by the state made the explosion of co-ops possible. Before then, the *economic* organization of the libertarian energy generated during the late 1960s and early 1970s was a rather haphazard affair. When ICOM created and publicized its 'model rules' (through lengthy negotiations with the Registrar of Friendly Societies), many groups thought that these legal structures embodied their ideals for the first time in British history.

Although there is no adequate legal or even politically agreed upon definition of a co-operative, some principles have emerged. The most succinct summary of them is in Thornley's recent book:

1 the establishment is autonomous;
2 employees are able to become members of the enterprise by nominal holdings of share capital, usually £5 or less;
3 the principle of 'one person one vote' prevails;
4 formal provision exists for direct employee participation in decision-making at all levels within the enterprise;
5 employees share in profits;
6 return on capital is limited.[37]

There are now a variety of legal frameworks available for those organizations that wish to call themselves co-ops *and* to register with the state in the form of the Registrar of Friendly Societies. Some of these frameworks are beginning to arouse passionate debates as to whether they are 'real' co-ops, with the appropriate radical spirit suffusing the rules and regulations:

The various forms which co-operation may take based on different model rules reflect to some extent the schisms and preoccupations of the movement, although the common ownership form tends to predominate (some 90% of co-operatives register with ICOM). To a large extent divisions are not so much in the base of the movement, within enterprises themselves, but more at the level of sponsoring agencies.[38]

There is some debate as to where the borderline between a 'proper' co-op and a 'normal' organization should be placed. Until now the co-operators have overwhelmingly chosen legal frameworks that are more radical, when they have selected from the off-the-peg options offered by ICOM. This may change, as some of the non-ICOM support groups or national CDA seem committed to 'normalizing' co-ops. The reasons for this de-radicalization are not a mystery, but simply the recuperation of the radical spirit.

Nor, similarly, is the numerical explosion of co-ops a mystery. The social and political energy (of the 1960s and 1970s) had been there all along; it merely needed a legal conduit so it could be formally recognized. This exceedingly rapid increase in the number of co-ops seems to be levelling off slightly, but still increasing.

There is also the support structure that has evolved quietly alongside the co-ops themselves:

> Many of the new promotional bodies grew out of the philosophies which underlay co-operative experiments in the 19th century. Industrial growth and class struggle have affected the structure of industry and the working class and have generated new political campaigns like the peace movement, the ecology movement, the 'alternative life-styles' movements and the women's movement. The pattern of support is not a mirror image of the 19th century but there are enough similarities to make a comparison useful and to raise the question of why this repetition has occurred.[39]

Although there are numerous bodies supporting or encouraging co-operatives, there are only two of importance for this chapter, the *local* Co-operative Development Agencies and the Industrial Common Ownership Movement. It cannot be argued that any of the other co-operative support or enabling organizations have much to do with anarchism.

The ICOM model propagates the 'purest' form of co-operative practice, restricting membership to those who work in co-operatives and limiting individual shareholdings to a nominal

£1, although loan capital is freely used by most common ownership companies. Such restrictions have been widely criticized as too limiting and a disincentive to motivation. However the fact remains that the majority of co-operative ventures in the UK chose this structure in preference to any other.[40]

ICOM has been quite successful over the years in being of some use to the 'new wave' co-operatives, for example, changing the composition of its board drastically under pressure of their tremendous growth. Thornley tells us that the co-operators themselves are more radical than ICOM, which is probably still the case. On the other hand:

> Derrick [during the transformation of ICOM in the late 1970s] criticized ICOM repeatedly for its lack of pragmatism in putting equality before practicality. However the ICOM leaders have been adamant about retaining their ideals. Among ICOM's members and affiliated members there are many co-operatives which support this view . . .[41]

ICOM is now a clearly federal organization, and its long-term support is mostly by member subscription. ICOM offers rules, legal advice, and some possibility of assistance in obtaining funding. Although its future is not at all secure, depending on the growth of the co-ops themselves, it looks exactly the sort of support structure that co-ops need.

During the middle 1980s, ICOM has completed the initial stages of two large new projects. The Women's Link-Up (for women in co-ops) has solidified and promoted the influence of the women's movement within the co-operative structure. There is no doubt that any effort to deal with women in co-operatives in a deep and sensitive way will be a very long-term project, but it has begun. The Pilot Project, with a number of large co-ops in London, has begun systematically to address the problems of retaining a radical (what I am calling anarchist) structure and process as co-ops grow beyond small face-to-face groups. Most co-ops are quite small (less than ten members; few are over fifty), and have only begun to define the problems that result from large size. This is of crucial interest to anarchists developing models of organizational process. Although the ultimate impact of these (and other) new programmes on the development of ICOM and the co-op movement is not certain, there can be little doubt that such initiatives will be crucial to the growth or decay of the 'radical' component in the movement in Britain.

Another example of non-planned (spontaneous) support structures is the CDAs (or sometimes Co-operative Development Groups – CDGs) that have sprung up throughout Britain. It is difficult to describe them succinctly because there is no single model (although they are developing models, much as the co-ops did). Perhaps the best description comes from the excellent Co-operatives Research Unit at the Open University.[42] They claim that CDAs are usually groups of volunteers who decide to go professional. The individuals are local people who are interested in supporting co-ops for a variety of reasons. The individuals are co-op 'hustlers', although each individual may not be a member of a co-op. The groups put together finance packages, the largest part of which comes in one form or another from local councils (many controlled by the Labour Party). The variety of sources tapped by CDAs, of which there are now about seventy, shows that although local government finance is perhaps the easiest source of money, there are other packages that are constructed. The individuals employed by the CDA then attempt to discover people who need some form of support to form a co-op (finance, costings, loan arrangements, group dynamics). They then give that support. In areas where CDAs have been active, the number of co-ops has always increased.[43]

There are a number of varieties of CDA, since there is as yet no national rule which dictates their style. Some of them, according to several sources, are very clearly in the 'radical community development' tradition, or even appear as anarchists to some observers (regretfully, they add).[44] In the main, however, CDAs have come to represent a sort of politically sensitive and supportive influence, and tend to try to reflect very closely the needs of co-ops themselves:

> The CDGs in Hackney, West Yorkshire, Islington and Brent have all approached their work in the radical community development tradition. They have acted as a stimulus in the community so that co-operatives grow up from the grass roots identification of local needs. Nothing is imposed on people, but the CDGs are there to offer opportunities, guide discussion towards co-operatives where they may be appropriate and provide the full range of resources for setting them up.[45]

The recent attempt at a federation of CDAs is not yet a failure, and already has practical spin-offs.

The national CDA does not fit into our story at all, and must be ignored for the moment. The co-op movement itself is divided about the national CDA. Although it may well become a source of funds, at present it does little actual funding of co-ops. Its influence is unlikely to be great in a movement which has been built without much influence from national government.

It is my contention that contemporary co-ops, and the support structure which has grown up around them, are subtly imbued with the anarchist spirit. At the very least they taste like 'local socialism' or 'libertarian socialism', perhaps even Bookchin's 'libertarian municipalism'.[46] Certainly the mainstream of socialism over the last few decades has not been centrally or even peripherally concerned with deep democracy and small, decentralized, worker-owned economic units. Although one might not be able to claim that there are vast numbers of self-proclaimed anarchists in co-ops, objectively the anarchist flavour is present, if elusive.

There are many specific examples of spontaneous federal experiments constructed by the co-operative movement during the past twenty years or so. Here I mention only two, the older Mondragon co-ops and the newly born Co-op America. Each of these examples indicates the possibilities for federation and co-ordination, and each is outside the UK. There are, of course, attempts in Britain to federate and co-ordinate, amongst printers in London and amongst wholefood dealers around the country – as well as other moderate successes and failures. Such British efforts have not gone as far.

Mondragon, begun decades ago in an impoverished Basque area of Spain, has grown to over 18,000 members working in 163 co-operatives, at the last count.[47] They manufacture all manner of heavy and light industrial goods, although not steel or cars or nuclear power-plants. They are a booming success, a group of co-ops supported by and employing the local people, paying wages that have been at the ratio of three (highest paid) to one (lowest) for a long time, and are run in a moderately democratic way. There are several non-anarchist aspects of Mondragon. But what we can say is that some aspects of the structure, and a good deal of experience, might be used by an appropriate anarchist economics.

Co-op America is the offspring of long-time activists in the 'new wave' co-operative movement in the United States, involving some of those responsible for the wonderful magazine *Communities*. They recognized that, in the US climate, if there were some degree of federation, co-operatives could actually begin to offer pension plans, insurance deals, health plans, and all sorts of tangible economic concessions, as well as direct economic co-operation. The latest information is that Co-op America is growing and providing an example of the sort of support that might evolve.[48]

There are numerous other support structures in the USA, and perhaps more legal innovation in land trusts and financing than in the UK.

Another source of inspiration and possibilities comes from recent developments in the high-technology cottage industries of northern Italy. Like Mondragon, Co-op America, and the British 'new wave' co-ops, these developments are quite specifically related to regional as well as global economic changes. As Charles Sabel puts it:

> If you had thought so long about Rousseau's artisan clockmakers at Neuchatel or Marx's idea of labour as joyful, self-creative association that you had begun to doubt their possibility, then you might, watching these craftsmen at work, forgive yourself the sudden conviction that something more utopian is practical after all.[49]

This system consists of industrial production at the most competitive and advanced levels, in units about the same size as the majority of the new co-ops in Britain today.

These industrial organizations are only a possibility, Sabel is careful to add, but they work. Such workplaces encourage vastly increased flexibility of the skilled workforce, often rendering hierarchies virtually non-existent, or at least 'merely formal'. The style of production seems to integrate the manual and intellectual more clearly than in traditional large-scale 'Taylorist' organizations. Sabel claims that the creativity unleashed is extremely impressive. He goes on to claim that the explicit co-ordination and co-operation between the autonomous firms has grown over the recent decades, as the explicitly collective nature of the work emerges. Nevertheless, there is a good deal of autonomy remaining for individual organizations.[50] In short, this example shows that small industrial firms which are federated, either formally or informally, can be competitive in the most advanced sectors of the modern economy.

Although it is reasonably clear that the new co-operative movement has emerged precisely because of the libertarian leanings of the founders and some members of co-ops, as well as the intentions of the members of various support organizations, there are problems ahead. It is the political unity of the co-operators that has got them this far, combined with their obvious practical success (they tend to be longer-lived than ordinary business start-ups).[51] Other publications have detailed their problems.[52] It does seem necessary, however, to list some of the biggest obstacles to be overcome by the movement.

First, finance is still a problem, since co-ops simply are mysterious or suspicious to many conventional money-men. There is some sign of improvement, however (largesse from abolished local authorities?), especially as more skills and expertise are developed within the movement itself.

Second, there need to be more successful efforts at federation both amongst co-ops in the same trade and within particular regions. What form this will take has yet to be decided by the co-operators themselves. This is one area where a detailed study of the anarchist collectives in the Spanish Revolution might be beneficial to the co-operators.[53]

Third, in the early days, wages were for the most part very low and very equal. If co-ops are to succeed, they must, as many have begun to do, pay wages that will attract more than young, single, and healthy people. It is also clear that co-ops may play an important role in creating flexible employment (for part-timers, mothers, and others), acknowledged by many to be an emerging concern.

Fourth, virtually every assessment of co-ops states that both co-operators and developers think that good management practices and good marketing are aspects of business practice that most co-ops lack. It is never clear what the trade-offs are between a deeply egalitarian mode of group process (the key feature of many co-ops) and some sort of bottom-line business efficiency. Debates on these matters enliven the agenda of every co-op. Other than co-ops, it is only the women's movement and perhaps the Greens that pay serious attention to radical democratic ideas involving sensitive and effective meetings and decisions. There is a vast literature and practice evolving to deal with this set of problems.[54]

Fifth and last, contemporary co-ops lack a clear vision of the future. This is becoming more important, especially as various political parties try to jump on the bandwagon and incorporate the radical spirit of co-ops into their hierarchical organizations. I think this is where anarchism has much to add. Any talk of visions within the co-op movement is usually so clearly in the libertarian mode that one can footnote the conversations from episodes in anarchist history. Part of my effort in writing this chapter is to persuade co-operators that the visions exist, and that they must collectively dream up a new reality or they will be doomed to being merely (but not at all trivially) one more marginal choice in an overwhelming capitalist hierarchy.

Conclusion

The anarchist and co-operative movements both have their roots
in the nineteenth century. Although each of these movements has
changed, it is possible to describe each one in general terms, as a
whole. When examining these movements we find they share
numerous characteristics such as a local base, some serious
attention to democratic process, a goal of autonomy and self-
management, voluntary membership, a vision of quite radical
change, anti-system and anti-hierarchy tendencies (while remaining
apolitical in relation to the state), spontaneity, and decentralization,
to name the most important. Because of their day-to-day
economic necessities, co-ops have never been as overtly militant or
confrontational as the anarchists in their opposition to the state,
but many self-proclaimed contemporary anarchists share this 'soft'
tendency. Without mustering detailed survey research, I claim that
the 'new wave' co-operative movement was largely inspired and
organized by anarchists or anarchist sympathizers, and to this day
is personned by such figures to a startling extent. The utterly
crucial place of 'prefiguration' in any anarchist economy requires
us to search for practical and legal alternative employment
structures which fit comfortably with anarchist ideals.

If the argument is accepted thus far, the last part comes easily.
Co-operatives are, in fact, the most viable and acceptable
organizational form for anarchist economics to take. This is not to
say that the black economy, sabotage, the gift economy, and so
forth are not part of the development of anarchism. It is simply
that co-operatives are a legal form, available in more useful
varieties, that allows the practice of anarchism to be conducted
within the larger capitalist economy. In sections of the chapter, I
have described some of the many attempts to adapt the co-
operative structures to meet modern social and economic requirements. In doing so, I hope to initiate a more complex dialogue
amongst co-operators and anarchists, and between the two. Thus
far, the dialogue has not existed. In many cases, the co-operators
have not heard of or taken seriously anarchist theory and practice
(although they may actually be living it at work). In other cases,
anarchists have dismissed the modern co-operative movement
from a position of vast ignorance, or from rigid perspectives which
allow no one to make an ordinary living. It is clear that more
information and more dialogue could promote learning from the
other, so as to strengthen both. There are a growing number of
analysts who see anarchism and co-operation as part of a much
larger social change, sometimes called 'new social movements'. I

agree with this contention, and feel that the growth of the movements as a whole depends on the increasingly complex interaction of the parts of the larger movement. Anarchism and co-operation are not the same: they are necessary and complementary aspects of modern revolution. Oddly enough, this view is not new. The connection struck Bakunin more than a century ago:

> we find them [co-operatives] necessary in many respects. First, and this appears to us even to be their principal benefit at present, they accustom the workers to organize, pursue, and manage their interests themselves, without any interference either by bourgeois capital or by bourgeois control.
>
> It is desirable that when the hour of social liquidation is tolled, it should find many co-operative associations in every country and locality; if they are well organized, and above all founded on the principles of solidarity and collectivity rather than on bourgeois exclusivism, then society will pass from its present situation to one of equality and justice without too many great upheavals.[55]

Notes and references

I would like to thank the following for their exceedingly useful comments on earlier drafts of this paper: David Goodway, Frank Harrison, Robert McKinlay, and Colin Brown, as well as others who commented on specific points. The remaining faults, unfortunately, remain my responsibility.

1 My unpublished paper, 'New social movements and anarchism', carries on the argument in greater detail with reference to the literature on new social movements.
2 H. Ehrlich, 'How to get from here to there – building a revolutionary transfer culture', *Social Anarchism*, 2, 2 (1982), p. 5.
3 P. Kropotkin, *Mutual Aid* (Boston: Porter Sargent, 1973).
4 See G. Landauer, *For Socialism* (St Louis, Mo.: Telos Press, 1979).
5 See, for example, G. D. H. Cole, *A Century of Co-operation*, (Manchester: Co-operative Union, 1944); A. E. Musson, 'The ideology of early co-operation in Lancashire and Cheshire', *Transactions of the Lancashire and Cheshire Antiquarian Society*, 68 (1958), pp. 117–38; and S. Pollard, 'Nineteenth-century co-operation: from community building to shopkeeping', in A. Briggs and J. Saville (eds), *Essays in Labour History* (London: Macmillan 1960), pp. 74–112.
6 C. Boggs, 'Revolutionary process, political strategy and the dilemma of power', *Theory and Society*, Fall 1977.
7 By this I mean the recent growth of the co-operative movement in Britain and the USA, with roots in the radical movements in the 1960s and manifesting itself organizationally in the 1970s.
8 It is ironic that the Labour Party and other socialists of a revolutionary

variety find it difficult to come to grips with the meaning of co-operatives today. Some suggest they are in fact simply slightly modified versions of capitalist enterprises.

9 Musson, 'Ideology', op. cit., p. 121.

10 Ibid., p. 126.

11 Ibid., p. 128.

12 See, for example, H. F. Infield, *Co-operative Communities at Work* (London: Kegan Paul, 1947); and R. G. Garnett, *Co-operation and the Owenite Socialist Communities in Britain, 1825–45* (Manchester: Manchester University Press, 1972).

13 R. Oakeshott, in A. Clayre (ed.), *Political Economy of Co-operation and Participation* (Oxford: Oxford University Press, 1980).

14 'On Co-operation', in R. M. Cutler (ed.), *From Out of the Dustbin: Bakunin's Basic Writings, 1869–1871* (Ann Arbor, Mich.: Ardis, 1985), p. 151.

15 L. Hyde, *The Gift* (New York: Random House, 1983), is a brilliant and suggestive book.

16 For some ideas on these matters, see H. Henderson, *Politics of the Solar Age* (New York: Anchor, 1981); or J. Robertson, *Future Work* (London: Gower/Temple Smith, 1985).

17 See, among others, P. Bernstein, 'Worker ownership and community redevelopment', *Corporate Examiner*, March 1981, pp. 3A–D.

18 *OECD Observer*, May and September 1985.

19 See *OECD Observer*, November 1985, pp. 22–5, for notes on the success of small businesses in job creation.

20 For further detail on the 'end of Taylorism' and other changes in work and production, see C. F. Sabel, *Work and Politics* (Cambridge: Cambridge University Press, 1982).

21 Ibid., chapter 5.

22 M. Bookchin, *The Ecology of Freedom* (Palo Alto, Calif.: Cheshire, 1982), is the most forceful and persuasive outline of this argument.

23 For an anarchist critique of this developing notion, see R. Sylvan, 'A critique of deep ecology', *Radical Philosophy*, 40 (Summer 1985), pp. 2–13 (and the subsequent issue).

24 See, for example, P. Ekins (ed.), *The Living Economy* (London: Routledge & Kegan Paul, 1986). It is not clear that all the suggestions are 'anarchist'.

25 Ehrlich, 'How to get from here to there', op. cit., p. 15.

26 M. Taylor, *Community, Anarchy and Liberty* (Cambridge: Cambridge University Press, 1982), pp. 169–70.

27 In S. Dolgoff (ed.), *Bakunin on Anarchy* (London: Allen & Unwin, 1973), p. 173 (from *Double Strike in Geneva*, 1869).

28 I should make it clear that there is an inherent contradiction here, common to anarchist theories on many subjects. It is obviously impossible for any organization to be utterly autonomous, as it is for any individual to be completely autonomous. The point of anarchist action is to keep this goal at the forefront of organizational theory, while recognizing that the tension will always exist.

29 The practical literature is growing fast. See ICOM North, *ICOM Training Package* (Leeds: ICOM, 1984); M. Jelfs, *Manual for Action* (London: Action Resources Group, 1982); M. Avery *et al.*, *Building United Judgement: A Handbook for Consensus Decision-Making* (Madison, Wis.: Center for Conflict Resolution, 1981); and B. Auvine *et al.*, *A Manual for Group Facilitators* (Madison, Wis.: Center for Conflict Resolution, 1978).

30 See P. Ayrton, 'Moving: politics of new social movements', *Revolutionary Socialism*, 10 (1982), pp. 3–22; F. F. Piven and R. Cloward, *Poor People's Movements* (New York: Vintage, 1979); A. Touraine, *Voice and the Eye* (Cambridge: Cambridge University Press, 1981); C. Boggs, *Social Movements and Political Power* (Philadelphia: Temple University Press, 1987).

31 See S. Rowbotham, L. Segal, and H. Wainwright, *Beyond the Fragments* (London: Merlin, 1979).

32 See, for example, Robertson, *Future Work*, op. cit.; Henderson, *Politics*, op. cit.; and the papers of The Other Economic Summit, which may be obtained each year from TOES, 42 Warriner Gardens, London SW11 4DU.

33 J. Thornley, *Workers' Co-operatives* (London: Heinemann, 1981).

34 Ibid., p. 30.

35 Personal communication from assistant secretary of ICOM. Data verified by details from the national CDA report in *The Times*, 3 August 1987. (The CDA's wildly optimistic estimate of 2,000 by the end of 1987 can be discounted as 'budget politics'.)

36 I know of one nearly ten years old which reassembles every year to do building work, and there are no doubt many others.

37 Thornley, *Co-operatives*, op. cit., pp. 3–4.

38 A. Taylor, 'The expansion of worker co-operatives: the role of local authorities', *Regional Studies* (Policy Review Section), 1983, p. 4.

39 Thornley, *Co-operatives*, op. cit., p. 31.

40 Taylor, 'Expansion', op. cit., p. 5.

41 Thornley, *Co-operatives*, op. cit., p. 43.

42 C. Cornforth and M. Stott, *Co-operative Approach to Local Economic Development* (Milton Keynes: Open University, Co-operative Research Unit, 1984).

43 Ibid.

44 Thornley, *Co-operatives*, op. cit., p. 51.

45 Ibid., p. 51.

46 See 'Theses on libertarian municipalism', *Our Generation*, 16, 3–4 (Spring/Summer 1985).

47 *New Co-operator*, Autumn 1985.

48 *Communities*, July 1985.

49 Sabel, *Work*, op. cit., p. 220.

50 Ibid., pp. 220–7.

51 See, for example, the discussion in *The New Co-operator*, Winter and Spring 1987, for an outline of the debate. Although there is a

persistent notion that co-ops are 'more successful', much more work
needs to be done to draw a clear conclusion.

52 See R. Paton, *Some Problems of Co-operative Organization* (Milton
Keynes: Open University, 1980), among others.
53 See, for example, S. Dolgoff, *The Anarchist Collectives* (Montréal:
Black Rose Books, 1974).
54 See note 29.
55 Cutler, *From Out of the Dustbin*, op. cit., p. 153.

10

New social movements:
the anarchic dimension

Murray Bookchin

Despite the grim pictures that have been painted of the 1960s, the prevailing pessimism towards their outcome has been grossly overstated. The fervour and the creativity that began in America with the rise of civil-rights struggles and went on to generate the New Left and alternative life-styles in Europe as well did not disappear in the 1970s, nor is it quite clear that they have spent themselves in the 1980s. Blanket criticisms of the past two decades as 'narcissistic' and 'career-oriented' are much too simplistic to characterize what is virtually a whole generation. Indeed, if anything, such criticisms are likely to conceal an ongoing ferment that graded slowly out of the 1960s, a unifying continuum that seems to have produced more sophisticated and more serious movements in the 1970s and 1980s.

Although it is fair to say that much of the counter-culture was co-opted by the fashion industry and the boutique world that panders to the Yuppies of today, there has also been a dialectic of growth – of accretion and differentiation – that is all too easily overlooked as we approach the end of the century. The starry-eyed innocence of the 1960s with its gospel of universal love has been pared away by time together with the strident Maoism with its gospel of universal hate that also marked the decade.

More significantly, many of the problems that gave so much energy to the 1960s – problems, I may add, that were slowly incubating in the 'narcissistic' and 'career-oriented' 1950s, a decade that our own times seem to resemble – are with us in an even more exacerbated form. In America, the black ghettoes are seething with a dissatisfaction that has been brought on by a worsening, not a betterment, of living conditions among the masses. Deserted by their own middle classes, who were the main beneficiaries of civil-rights legislation and facial tokenism, blacks now form a permanent underclass of a new and desperate *sans-culottes*, comparable only to *déclassé* elements of the traditional revolutionary era in their sense of desperation and barely concealed fury. In Europe, particularly in Great Britain, a bitter polarization is developing between the permanently displaced, underprivileged, and ignored masses of poor, such as workers in what might be called the 'rust belt' of the British north and midlands, immigrants on the continent, and elderly and minority groups in all areas, on the one hand, and the various affluent strata which occupy privileged positions in high-tech and professional occupations, on the other. Issues like militarism, not only war and peace, still hang like a pall over society as a whole more than a decade after the end of the Vietnam War. If the New Left has now retreated to the academy and its rambunctious followers of yesterday have become the Marxist professoriat of today, a radical ambience still surrounds much of the politics that occurs even among liberals, where the word 'liberal' often seems like a guilty reproach if it is not dressed in the rhetoric of radicalism.

Nineteen-sixties life-styles, in turn, have sedimented into the established culture itself – harmless, to be sure, while they are dressed in designer jeans but menacing when they surface in youth movements like the German 'autonomists'. An entire segment of 'no-future' youth has torn itself away from its privileged peers, generationally speaking, and shows no signs of coming to terms with the present society. Indeed, it forms a defiant, infuriated, and almost nihilistically alienated part of the seemingly placid young people whose goals have been wedded to the uncertain institutions of the next century's society. It is justifiable to say that the 1960s did not comprise a single whole. Quite to the contrary, the decade was slowly pieced together by many tendencies and sequences of tendencies, each of which added to others before and after it, greatly enlarging the decade's definition of freedom and its social imagination.

These tendencies have not disappeared from our time. They have invaded it profoundly under a variety of different names and, potentially at least, form the bases for still newer developments that may lie ahead. Political insight depends profoundly on the ability to understand – not *dismiss*, if you please – what is happening beneath the surface of the seeming harmless ripples of our times; to recognize the latent potentialities that are concealed by a specious 'reality' of social peace and accommodation; to extend our vision beyond the given facts of compromise and opportunism into the logic of events that may radically challenge the status quo; finally, to give present and future movements as they emerge a sense of coherence that was so painfully lacking in the movements of a decade and a half ago.

The most promising of the new social movements that have emerged since the 1960s centre around environmentalism, feminism, anti-militarism, and municipalism or local control – movements that did not characterize the 1960s as such until the counter-culture and the New Left had already begun to ebb. That these movements, particularly environmentalism and feminism, are often placed in the late 1960s or even earlier clearly suggests they share a common pedigree on the ideological plane. It has become customary, in fact, to date a radical version of environmentalism back to Rachel Carson's *Silent Spring* (1962), a work that was actually very moderate politically and largely confined to pesticides rather than broad environmental issues. By the same token, feminism has been dated back to conflicts around the status of women in the New Left generally, a pedigree that, although true, was still highly marginal in the 1960s. Even present-day anti-militarism, which challenges the militaristic mentality as such and social regimentation, not only the adventures of the military in Central America and elsewhere, has been rooted in the domestic conflicts generated by the Vietnam War.

While it is important to recognize the antecedents of the new social movements in older ones, it is no less important to recognize how time has added and enriched the new as distinguished from the old. Environmentalism, tepid as it was at its inception, did not emerge with the publication of Carson's book in 1962 or, for that matter, with an earlier, more comprehensive book of my own a half-year before the publication of *Silent Spring*.[1] The 1960s had not grown up to a mature view of the issues that were to confront radicals in the 1970s.

In retrospect, the innocence of the New Left and the counter-culture in dealing with – indeed, in raising – such problems as environmental deterioration and the development of a comprehensive ideology to embrace the issues that lay on the decade's horizon was little short of laughable. Initially, its fixation on activism was purchased at the cost of any theoretical insight and of the ability to relate parallel issues into a coherent theoretical and political form. When theory finally came to the foreground of the left as an issue, the New Left, guided largely by a narrow, seemingly anti-imperialist fixation on the Third World, simply recycled the worn ideologies of the Old Left, often in their most vulgar neo-Stalinist forms. Trips to Hanoi, Havana, and Peking were to become not only symbols of international solidarity but means for a self-identification that was utterly alien to the American scene and its own unique radical heritage. The New Left thus failed completely to generalize such problems as environmentalism, feminism, local control, and anti-militarism. It took years, for example, to bring civil rights into a common framework with the Vietnam War, which largely remained a 'white issue', despite the fact that a disproportionately large number of American soldiers were blacks. That the war was a tragedy for the American people as well as the Vietnamese and claimed American lives was largely ignored under self-styled 'anti-imperialist' slogans that derided American soldiers as victimizers, not also as victims. By the end of the 1960s, the New Left had migrated like the Old Left before it from the United States to abroad. It even saw itself as the 'enemy' of 'Amerika', not as a voice of the American people against a shared oppressor of domestic as well as international victims.

The counter-culture, in turn, was largely the victim of its own innocence. It suffered from a kindergarten hostility to reason and an infantile vulnerability to exploitation by the media, fashion-mongers, rock impresarios, gurus – either self-anointed or imported from India – and a lumpenproletariat of the Charles Manson type that huckstered its women in the alleys of the Haight-Ashbury district of San Francisco. In short, it died of child abuse. Whatever promising development that could emerge from a synthesis of the best in the New Left and the best in the counter-culture was subverted by a total loss of creativity. Cannibalized by neo-Stalinism and by the conversion of a childlike counter-culture into a sleazy commodity culture, both movements were left unfinished. The immense project of relating a credible and pragmatic domestic radicalism to an imaginative and sensuous utopianism never became a reality – which is to say that this project *still* haunts us and hovers over us, not that it was chimerical from the start as the current, largely reactionary literature on the 1960s would have us believe.

Temporally, however, the environmental, feminist, municipalist, and anti-militarist movements really emerged in the 1970s, often tail-ended by Marxist 'vanguards' that designated them as 'petty bourgeois', 'personalistic', 'individualistic', and other such choice terms from the vocabulary of sectarianism. 'Earth Day' in 1970, although a media-staged event, brought millions to city streets, river banks, and empty lots, and, of course, before the grandstands of effusive politicians to participate in a vast 'clean-up' campaign. That the event was a product of political hucksterism does not alter the fact that it spoke to a growing popular consciousness that the environment was deteriorating at an appalling rate. Kate Millett's *Sexual Politics* (1970), the most controversial single work on the oppression of women at the beginning of the decade, overlaps the clean-up campaign. Taken together, 'Earth Day' and Millett's book turned environmentalism and feminism into focal issues for public discussion.

What is fascinating, indeed unique, about these two social movements is that they were to grow over time, not exhaust themselves and disappear. And not only did they grow but they remained close to their domestic roots. They did not migrate ideologically or physically into the Second and Third Worlds as had the radicals of the 1960s. No less important is the fact they differentiated themselves. Rather than shrivel up and become self-enclosed, they sent out tendrils in all directions that have essentially become an interlacing network of movements and tendencies – gay, lesbian, ethnic, localist (based on citizens' initiative groups and notions of decentralization), anti-militarist as well as anti-war, indeed even new visions of medicine, psychotherapy, nutrition, education, and ethics, and, broadly speaking, new lifeways.

Continuous as these new social movements may be with the 1960s, they preserve much of the social imagination of the decade while steering a healthy course between sectarian militancy and a starry-eyed innocence. That they can be merchandised in part by swarms of profiteers who specialize in innovative products is not surprising. Even the Rothschilds offered to finance the Paris Commune in May 1871, and arms merchants will still sell to anyone they can, even terrorist groups. What is striking about these new social movements is that they have grown well beyond their relatively simple origins, not retreated back to the collective social womb that has absorbed so many 1960s groups. It is important to emphasize that, more often than not, they have increasingly elevated their level of discourse, the quality of their literature, and the intellectual demands they place on their supporters. In so far as the environmental and feminist movements have advanced beyond the elemental level of their origins, the 'gut' intuitions that so fragilely sustained the counter-culture, anti-war activists, and even many adherents of the New Left who turned to simple-minded sectarian formulas, no longer suffice to keep the new social movements intact, much less provide them with viable nourishment.

This process of self-education and intellectual growth can be demonstrated by a few examples. In the United States and Germany – the two areas which I can discuss with a measure of personal familiarity – there is simply no 'Left' in any meaningful sense of the term. The gap in these countries between the rhetoric

of social radicalism and a genuinely anti-capitalist movement is so
wide that what could possibly pass as a left-wing ambience is
almost odiously liberal. In America, even the residual Old Left
operates within the framework of the existing society. Periodicals
with a quasi-communist background like the *Guardian* and
Monthly Review are at best nostalgically radical and, for all
practical purposes, reformist in their domestic politics. Aside from
a ghastly proliferation of academic Marxist journals and books (a
largely campus phenomenon that is being lampooned widely in the
United States), the more popular 'radical' literature of the 1980s
has mobilized almost exclusively around figures like Jesse Jackson
and political hucksters who relate to his largely contrived
'Rainbow Coalition'. The notion that a movement can be built that
validly challenges the social order on grounds that call for
fundamental social change is simply alien to the belief system of
most self-designated 'leftists' in the United States and, to a great
degree, in Germany. Individuals who once earned reputations as
voices for revolutionary change such as Irving Howe, a former
Trotskyist journalist, or Danny Cohn-Bendit, the nearest thing to
a spokesperson for the French student movement of May and June
1968, move entirely within the orbit of the very reformism they
denounced in their younger days. Like the radical movement to
which they belonged and the journals they once edited, they have
followed a trajectory from left positions to the political centre.

The very opposite has happened in the environmental and
feminist movements of the past two decades. In the United States,
environmentalism is simply no longer fashionable as an ideology
among activists who either participated in or followed upon the
'Earth Day' of 1970 and subsequent years. The real debate in the
less institutionalized environmental movements of the 1980s
centres around the source from which an assumed radicalism will
draw its nourishment: whether it will be 'deep ecology' with its
emphasis on spiritual and religious renewal or 'social ecology' with
its emphasis on the social causes of ecological problems and the
need for basic social reconstruction. Nevertheless both tendencies
– 'deep' and 'social' ecology – are explicitly anti-reformist. The
two decades that separate 'Earth Day' from today have traced a
trajectory from a naïve and tepid outlook that was satisfied with
symbolic actions and small legislative reforms to a movement of
many thousands that is largely anti-capitalist, strongly committed
to direct action, and localist, indeed consciously decentralist, in its
image of a new politics based on the neighbourhood and
municipality as the basic arena for political activity. It remains an
astonishing fact, today, that American movements that officially

designate themselves as 'socialist' (one thinks, for example, of the Democratic Socialists of America) or even have a Maoist pedigree have been bypassed by the new social movements in the political night of the late 1980s. The socialists and former Maoists and the radical environmental groups and feminists have moved apart in entirely opposite directions. That the word 'environmental' has now become obsolete and has been replaced by 'ecological', a term that denotes a radically critical and reconstructive outlook, is indicative of the advances that have been scored since the naïve 'Earth Day' movements of the early 1970s, this in contrast to their often patronizing socialist and Maoist critics, who have moved toward liberalism.

These remarkable counter-currents in which the ecological movement in the United States stands in such radical contrast to the Old and New Left backwash of past decades is perhaps best symbolized by the National Green Gathering in early July 1987, at Amherst, Massachusetts. Between 1,500 and 2,000 people convened to hold six days of plenary sessions and workshops devoted to such issues as electoral politics and direct action, national and municipal politics, spiritual and social sources of ecological problems, various forms of feminism, ecological economics, and, in terms of sheer variety, issues that ranged from ecological philosophy, ethics, and the interrelationship between social and spiritual concerns to racism, imperialism, militarism, and libertarian forms of organization.

Apart from academic exotica like the Socialist Scholars' Conference, held a few months earlier in New York City, which often centred around the 'excremental' culture of the French post-structuralists, no such radical gathering like that of the Greens in Amherst has been seen in the United States in recent memory. What is even more striking, no gathering in recent memory of *activists* had been seen for years in the United States which fervently discussed so wide a range of issues and so relevant an agenda of political concerns. That the National Green Conference was often sharply divided on many of these issues and concerns attests not to the uncertainty of new social movements in America but to their passionate level of interest and their creativity. If recent socialist gatherings in America have been relatively untroubled affairs, it is not because they exemplify a clear focus towards deeply held principles but rather because they are marked by a sense of resignation towards a tasteless diet of compromises.

The Green conferences I have attended in Germany, while equal to or larger than the American, have been no less stormy. In contrast to the almost ceremonial nature of German Social

Democratic congresses, the German Greens are notable for their spontaneity and fervour, the sparkling brilliance of their speakers, and, above all, the wide range of social, political, and moral issues with which they deal. No Green conference in Germany is entirely predictable; indeed, the soul of the movement hangs excitingly – as it did at Amherst – on the *extent* to which it will move to the left, not on the certainty of the compromises it will make with liberalism and the establishment.

This leftward trajectory can be found not only among the Greens in the United States and Germany but also among feminists in various parts of the world. Again, I must restrict myself to my more direct knowledge of this movement in the United States and a glancing familiarity with it in Great Britain. But viewed over a span of some twenty years, the development of feminism from the days when Kate Millett's rather limited *Sexual Politics* was the most impressive work in the newly born feminist movement to the present time, when the movement has assumed a highly variegated and often very radical character, is nothing less than extraordinary. The resurgence of women from the torpor of patricentric society has produced a landscape of ideas that ranges from a radical feminism that advocates separatism to eco-feminism that sees woman as the bearer and nurturer of life itself, indeed as the custodian of the biosphere as a whole. The tendencies that make up this landscape often overlap and intermingle. Indeed, the logic of the more insurgent elements of the feminist movement has carried women into the forefront of anti-militarist as well as ecological activities. Gatherings of women have attracted participants in the thousands, many of whom have engaged in sustained work around new social and moral issues, including the right of sexually marginal groups to partake freely of their own life-styles, new approaches to education and health, symbolic and real occupations of military sites, and fervent efforts to give women complete control over their bodies and their lives. What strongly marks the most advanced women in the feminist movement has been their expansive demands for freedom, including freedom from hierarchy and domination of any kind.

What is no less impressive, feminism has nourished a critical form of scholarship in fields like anthropology and social theory that has eclipsed centuries-long traditions in these fields that were notable for their intellectual aridity and their patricentric use of data. The work of Dorothy Lee in anthropology and Mary Beard in history – women pioneers in male-dominated fields – has been taken up by such outstanding workers and thinkers as Yolanda Murphy and particularly Janet Biehl, a searching eco-feminist, whose writings and lectures exhibit a remarkable synthesis of ecological with feminist ideas.

A third significant aspect of the new social movements is perhaps the most episodic and yet one of the most significant in this constellation of new social alignments – the proliferation of grass-roots municipalist organizations that, despite flows and ebbs, have generally persisted when viewed as a whole in America and Britain, and broad citizens' initiative confederations in Germany. The mistrust by the New Left in its early days of all institutions and its demands for a participatory democracy have been translated in the 1980s into demands for grass-roots institutions and a radical expansion of those local institutions closest to the people, institutions that can be used to foster an active citizenry. Admittedly these 'neo-populist' tendencies – using the word 'populism' to denote 'back-to-the-people' movements in their broadest sense – are very mixed and tentative in character. But they differ from the Saul Alinsky movements of the 1950s and early 1960s that swept across the United States in certain important respects. The Alinsky movements were defensive in character; they tried to resist the encroachment of the rights of minorities and the poor. They did not try to restructure the institutions and power bases of a community significantly. Nor did they try to create a truly radical consciousness among their support groups and the population at large. By contrast, the radical tendencies in the new municipalist movements raise demands for neighbourhood- and town-based popular institutions that are *counter* to those of a growing centralized state. They tend to carve out a *dual* level of public power and local democracy in opposition to the authority exercised by the state on a national level. Carried to their logical conclusion, they are really directed against the all-encompassing sovereignty of the nation state.

History has seen such counter-movements to the nation state during the era of nationalism from the sixteenth to the nineteenth centuries. Having dealt with this subject elsewhere, I will limit myself to movements for municipal power in the United States, Canada, and Great Britain.[2] The 1980s witnessed the success by American radicals and left-liberals in several communities that showed some potential for a municipal regroupment of local power against centralized power in several Californian cities; in Burlington, Vermont; in Montréal, Quebec; and, more explosively, in London and certain English northern cities. Californian cities such as Santa Monica and Santa Cruz essentially 'opened City Hall' to the people. City government was taken over by left-liberals, including self-proclaimed socialists. Municipal reforms like rent control and housing improvements were more a matter of responding to the needs of the elderly and the needy. The vision of the socialists in the coalitions that gained control of these communities did not reach beyond administrative and pragmatic goals. There was neither the theory nor the intention of using civic power to raise more challenging issues than material civic improvements. Beyond purely practical considerations, socialism and municipalism do not form a particularly inspiring interaction. The socialists apparently do not gauge their politics by anything more than the services they can deliver, which is hardly more than what a decent liberalism has to offer.

In Montréal, the Montréal Citizens' Movement, the product of a long development in which anarchists managed to introduce extraordinary demands into the Movement's programme for neighbourhood control while the social democrats and even Communists steadily tried to undercut their influence, is the story of an increasing descent from exemplary radical stands on a wide variety of civic issues to a crass social-democratic pragmatism. In Britain, there was much talk of local socialism as a political perspective and challenging situations in which radicals in local Labour Party organizations entered into conflict with the central government and the moderate leadership of the Labour Party itself – alas, not as an expression of a municipalist *policy* but mainly to achieve local reforms in a militant fashion. In Burlington, Vermont, radicals, influenced initially by anarchists, helped establish neighbourhood assemblies in the six wards of the city. The intention of the anarchists, many of whom have entered the local Green organization, was to develop these popular institutions into a countervailing force to the city council (which has a sizeable, highly centralistic socialist contingent that often collaborates with Republicans and local developers!) and, hopefully, to establish an example for other large communities in Vermont. These efforts are inconclusive at the time of writing. They should be of special interest to American radicals because they are occurring in the New England region, where centuries-old town meetings still exist as a viable tradition of local self-government as distinguished from the so-called 'federal' tradition – a euphemism for a highly centralized government – that was established after the founding of the American republic.

The shift from a traditional radicalism based on controlling the centralized state to one that focuses on regions, cities, towns, and even neighbourhoods marks a basic change in orientation and political thinking. This shift is not an isolated phenomenon. Although partly the result of expediency – the United States,

Canada, and Great Britain do not have the systems of proportional representation one finds in Germany and other European countries – municipalism also draws its inspiration from social ecology with its emphases on human scale, regionalism, decentralization, and localism. The two are ideologically congruent. Similarly, there is a congruence of the anti-hierarchical mentality of left-wing feminists and eco-feminists with the notion of anti-hierarchical civic movements based on neighbourhood councils and assemblies. It would require an incredible degree of political myopia not to see that the ecological vision of decentralized human communities, sensitively tailored in their technologies, civic institutions, and use of resources to the ecosystems in which they are located, forms the radical matrix for a humanly scaled political municipalism as well. Feminism, in turn, adds the all-important demand of freedom from domination and from hierarchy which is embodied not only by patriarchy but by the nation state. Viewed against the background of a Marxian orthodoxy which worked with the concept of a centralized state, large-scale planning, traditional party structures, the nationalization of the economy, the primacy of economic over cultural factors in shaping historic events, and the hegemony of the industrial proletariat in achieving social change, we are witnessing a shift to decentralization, local self-management, confederal political structures, and the importance of ethics and culture in changing society.

Although this shift already marked the emergence of the New Left in the 1960s, it is more deeply sedimented into radical thinking than it was twenty years ago – and more all-encompassing as well. As a movement, the New Left emerged from a small student stratum like Students for a Democratic Society and gained a fragile following from the highly diffuse counter-culture of young people generally. It had no theory from which to build and no sizeable following apart from militants mobilized around disarmament and anti-war sentiments. 'Ecology' was simply unknown as a word, and feminism was seen as a protest by a few irascible women whose demands for 'equality' were viewed in a patronizing way by radical men. The New Left and counter-culture were not deeply involved in local affairs, despite episodic projects in a few urban centres. Taken over by Marxist elements in the late 1960s, the movement lost its *élan* and ebbed rapidly into sectarian oblivion.

The new social movements of the 1970s and 1980s represent at their best an absorption of New Left ideas and counter-cultural values without the frivolity and indifference to organization that marked the 1960s. Nor are they movements of young people alone. They are seasoned by greater experience and are developing a certain amount of theoretical coherence. That ecology, feminism, and municipalism have more than a decade and a half of development behind them is testimony to a stability that is in marked contrast to the eight or so years that saw the birth, fragmentation, and sectarian degeneration of the New Left.

The question that faces the new social movements of the 1980s is the development of greater ideological insight and the steps that must be taken to fulfil their promise. Whether consciously or not, these movements are more anarchic than socialistic. Indeed, in America and continental Europe, socialism is in such disarray and its practice is so liberal that it can no longer be regarded as anti-capitalist, much less revolutionary, despite its academic calisthenics and its following among the professoriat. The conversion of the Communist Workers' Party in the United States into a liberal 'New Democratic Movement', the shift of Trotskyism to social democracy, the retreat of the Democratic Socialists of America into the Democratic Party, and the tendency of the Democratic Party to echo neo-conservative ideas advanced by the Republican Party are evidence of a terminal condition in the Marxist Left.

By contrast, the new social movements share a libertarian ambience and, for the most part, adhere to certain libertarian principles that render it impossible for institutionalized Marxist groups to speak to them. If anything, the anarchic dimension of the new social movements today risks the danger of being flawed by exaggeration. Exaggeration takes the form of a commitment to consensus, for example, that is so unswerving at times that a single individual can paralyse the activity of a group for hours and even demoralize it. Exaggeration in the form of a hypersensitivity to hierarchy can also result in a woeful lack of structure, indeed, a 'tyranny of structurelessness', in which a cohesive minority can control the activities of an unstructured majority which lacks clearly formulated means for making decisions.

Here, the seemingly 'anarchic' dimension of new social movements can become a caricature of anarchism, a body of ideas that never denied the need for clearly articulated grass-roots and confederal forms of organization. Similarly, the Spanish anarchist 'affinity group' form of organization which exists so widely in the United States tends to become ingrown groups of friends rather than action and educational groups that have a vigorous public life. That decision-making by voting was the rule in large anarchist movements like the Spanish and that these movements formed clearly defined structures is largely unknown to adherents and opponents of American anarchism.

In its best form, the anarchic dimension of the new social movements is revealed in several fundamental ways. Whether knowingly or not, the textual literature of these movements is more akin to Kropotkin's muscular notion of a radically decentralized society and its complete rejection of capitalism than to Schumacher's 'Buddhist economics', which includes vague compromises with a market-oriented society in which, presumably, 'new forms of partnership between management and men' can emerge.[3] Bakunin's observation that anarchists can participate in local politics because 'municipal elections always best reflect the real attitude and will of the people' (an exaggeration, to be sure, but at least evidence of a certain flexibility in thinking that often does not exist among very orthodox anarchists) is far closer as an idea to new municipalist movements than the statecraft that dominates present-day socialist activists.[4] The best of Proudhon's writings on confederation speak more directly to the needs of the new social movements than the loose groupings that tend to delimit the range of their work to narrow local issues.

Above all, the anti-hierarchicalism that is associated with anarchism, particularly its most recently developed eco-anarchist forms, and its broader appeals to dominated people – women, ethnic groups, the elderly, and the dispossessed – rather than strictly to the proletariat, form the theoretical premises that cohere various tendencies, groups, and regionally based movements into a broad category that can be called 'new social movements'. The all-important conviction that freedom can be attained not merely if classes are abolished but if hierarchy in all its forms disappears brings ecology into accord with feminism and feminism into accord with the community conceived as a new *ethical* as well as functional dispensation of social life. The principle that unites these seemingly independent movements is the notion of participation and mutual aid – not only between municipalities but in the biosphere and between men and women. That this focus is no longer socialist but anarchist; that it is completely removed from notions of liberal adaptations to a society based on domination in the home as well as exploitation in the workplace; that it excludes socialist compromises with the pragmatics of a male-oriented, propertied, and, above all, statist social order – this omnipresent outlook is both the haunting conscience as well as the cohering ideal of the majority of people who enter into the new social movements of our day. Feminist movements would have no reason to relate to social ecology movements and social ecology movements would have no reason to relate to municipalist movements if an essentially anarchic view of a humanity freed of all hierarchy and domination were not translatable into ecological, feminist, and municipalist visions of a harmonized world in the future as well as the need to heal a totally divided world today.

These visions, to be sure, stem partly from the power of anarchist notions to persist throughout history in one form or another – indeed, under one name or another – in humanity's striving to reclaim freedoms that were lost in the distant past. But they also stem from changes in the modern social order. Capitalism has developed technology to a point where the superfluity of human needs in the western world and the capacity to satisfy them has given well-to-do people the opportunity, indeed, the historic luxury, of bringing many of their needs and technics into question on ecological and social grounds. It is not accidental that in a newly emerging era of cybernation and robotization, millions of people can afford to address themselves to such questions as the 'limits of growth', 'harmony with nature', notions that call for restrictions on humanity's intervention into nature, a non-hierarchical sensibility and the like. Arguments for 'simple living', 'animal rights', 'labour-intensive technologies', and 'respect for nature' would have gained very few supporters during those long centuries when the promise of the good life in simple material terms was regarded as chimerical and hopelessly unattainable for all but elite minorities.

Moreover, the radical ideals of the last century, structured around economic interests and a hegemonic working class, have been undermined by the realities of the present century. It is no longer a doctrinal certainty that technological advances yield the subjective as well as objective 'preconditions' for a harmonious classless society. It has become increasingly evident that cultural factors play a more profound role in inhibiting radical social change than economic factors. Materially, all the 'preconditions' for Marx's vision of socialism are ripe, indeed, more than ripe, and they have been so for decades. But even on Marx's own terms, the subjective conditions for the overthrow of capitalism have woefully regressed – at least within an orthodox Marxian political framework. It is no longer possible to ignore the fact that the proletariat is not only less susceptible to revolutionary ideas than it was in the past; worse, the proletariat itself is dwindling in numbers and in economic power – that is, unless one wants to recast all the actors in the Marxist drama and make professionals, managers, technicians, and white-collar employees into a 'new working class'.

Nothing happens automatically in history. This is true not only of the relation of technological advances to social change; it is also true of the relationship of an anarchic dimension to the new social movements. I cannot emphasize too strongly that, without a self-conscious and thoroughly schooled libertarian left in their midst, the new social movements on the present ideological horizon will not remain libertarian on their own. Their anarchic dimension is largely the result of the New Left's legacy from the early 1960s, the exhaustion of traditional socialism as a viable ideology, and technological and structural changes that have occurred in capitalism even in the past two decades – notably, the almost insensate growth that threatens the integrity of the entire biosphere and the accelerating centralization of economic and state power that renders thinking people to feel increasingly powerless.

These factors alone, however, are not guarantees that the new social movements will develop in a consistently libertarian direction. The German Greens are already sharply divided between a so-called '*radec*' or radical ecology tendency and the so-called '*realos*' or realists who are trying to turn their movement into a completely reformist parliamentary party. In America, the rapidly forming Green movement is beset by a macho cowboy tendency that has adopted Malthusianism with its racist implications as a dogma, an anti-humanism that among some of the wilderness-oriented 'campfire' boys has become a brutalized form of misanthropy, and a 'spiritualist' tendency that tends to extol irrationalism and view ecology more as a religion than a form of healthy naturalism. It has become primarily the task of American eco-anarchists to develop a sustained resistance to these primitivistic, misanthropic, and quasi-religious tendencies.

But this project cannot be achieved without a rigorous and conscious re-examination of anarchism itself. To the extent that anarchists feed nostalgically on once-vigorous anarchic ideas that were appropriate in their own era – the era of the Industrial Revolution, of an insurgent workers' movement, and of direct action to the exclusion of grass-roots politics on the municipal level – the new social movements will still seem alien, all their anarchic dimensions aside. If it is true that one cannot refurbish socialism by attaching to it libertarian titbits like 'workers' control', 'human scale', and 'confederalism' and still call it Marxist, so anarchism cannot be sealed off from the changes that have been brought about by history and retain its viability.

Anarchists can celebrate the fact that their non-hierarchical ideals have taken different forms over the course of history because they voiced the demands of genuine social movements, not fossilized ideologies. The populist anarchism of the French Revolution and the Commune articulated the most deep-felt desires of the *sans-culottes* and the Parisian craft workers; the Makhnovite movement in the Ukraine articulated the poignant desires of the peasantry; Spanish anarcho-syndicalism articulated the hopes, even the temperament, of the oppressed workers and peasants of Spain. Hence in its greatest moments, anarchism was always a *people's* movement as well as a body of ideas and visions.

New people's movements are arising today – new in terms of the modern era, influenced by the facts of gender, ecological breakdown, powerlessness, corporate growth and state centralization, and the terrifying nightmare created by modern weaponry. Anarchism will either live or die to the extent that it can fully express these issues in terms that are intelligible to people of the present era, notably, ecology, feminism, municipalism, and anti-militarism. Whether the anarchic dimension of the new social movements can be rendered fully self-conscious by the participation of conscious anarchists may well determine the fate of both movements – anarchism no less than social ecology, eco-feminism, and a radical civic politics. In America and in continental Europe, this much is clear: the traditional Left is dead, indeed, in ideological and organizational decay. If there is to be *any* Left today or in the future, it will have to come from various forms of eco-anarchism in conjunction with the new social movements on both continents.

Notes and references

1 See my book, *Our Synthetic Environment* (New York: Knopf, 1962) (published under the pseudonymn 'Lewis Herber').
2 See Murray Bookchin, *The Rise of Urbanization and the Decline of Citizenship* (San Francisco: Sierra Club, 1987).
3 E. F. Schumacher, *Small Is Beautiful* (London: Blond & Briggs, 1973), p. 18.
4 Sam Dolgoff (ed.), *Bakunin on Anarchy* (New York: Knopf, 1972), p. 223.

Index